Soul and Native Americans

*(Originally Published as: Conceptions
of the Soul Among North American Indians)*

by
Åke Hultkrantz

edited with a foreword by
Robert Holland

Published by Spring Publications, Inc.;
299 East Quassett Road; Woodstock, CT 06281
http://www.neca.com/~spring

Printed in the Province of Quebec, Canada
Text printed on acid free paper
Cover designed by Leila Heald

Contents

Foreword

Professor Åke Hultkrantz wrote this book as a Ph.D. thesis, and it was later published in Stockholm, Sweden in 1953. The style was necessarily academic and the prose, in places, simply denied access to the information. It was also marred by a translation which frequently used Swedish word order instead of English and words which were incorrect.

Despite that, the importance of the book and its originality came through to anyone dedicated enough to spend the time. This is without doubt as complete a text as you can find on this subject, even given the fact that it was published forty-three years ago.

The research is meticulous, and it is substantially aided by the fact that Hultkrantz spent a good deal of time in the field so he was equipped not only to understand what other researchers had uncovered, but to interpret that information in light of his own experience. Even more importantly, Hultkrantz did not simply report, for this after all was a thesis and was intended to illuminate by presenting ideas which were not only fresh, but had been weighed with particular care.

Easily said, but when you choose to investigate soul-beliefs, you come to the subject carrying the baggage of your own soul beliefs and those of the culture in which you were fledged. It seems remarkable that Professor Hultkrantz was able to set aside the Christian belief in a single soul and avoid wallowing in value judgments when he turned to evaluating Native American beliefs.

He did not entirely escape, but in my correspondence with him, he had yet another opportunity to look at the work and at his suggestion, I excised the word "primitive" and used words which do not denigrate Native American beliefs by implying that they are somehow inferior to Christian concepts of the soul. I chose, however, to leave the word "Indian" in the text, simply because it seemed better suited to a work written in the early fifties.

All works which depend upon interviews leave the researcher at the mercy of the person being interviewed. There are language subtilties which may not have been understood. There are cultural non-sequiters which lie hidden like snares in the detritus of time. There is suspicion about motives, and finally, as any journalist can *tell you, people lie, either to mislead and protect what they know, or simply to tell you what you want to hear so you will go away.*

To overcome that Professor Hultkrantz used as many sources as he could uncover and screened them carefully to find both consensus and disagreement. What seems astonishing is the volume of information which had been collected, when you consider how little of it has surfaced outside of academic sources. The amount of material is particularly important here because Hultkrantz's steadfast and meticulous use of his sources makes the work entirely creditable.

My job was not only to make the work accessible, but to reduce it in size by nearly half. A good deal of the trimming came simply from removing footnotes and inserting references into the text. But by far the largest cuts were simply that: cuts. I left out the material which did not directly descend from the title of the work. That was hard. The material is interesting and informative, but there is hope that it can be assembled in a later work.

As a writer first and secondarily an editor, I tried to find the writer's voice and to be as true to it as I could. Plainly, that was difficult, if only because I was working with a translation, but also because this was a thesis and such documents are written to satisfy academia. Sadly, fluid prose style does not fall high on the list of salient considerations in the academy.

Yet for readers interested in learning more about this subject; readers not steeped in the juices of academe, the way a work is written becomes critical. If the prose is not accessible, the book does not get read. To that end I have taken some license, while taking particular care not to alter meaning. Rest assured that Hultkrantz was aware of what I was doing and was provided with copies of the work in progress. His comments and suggestions were taken to heart, as well they should have been, because this is, after all, his work. The hope is that I have made this work available to a wider audience, and have contributed to a better and clearer understanding of Native American beliefs. Perhaps then we can begin to understand the people from whom we gained a continent and come finally to understand as well the value of an ancient culture.

Robert Holland
Woodstock, Connecticut
1997

Introductory Remarks

Boas, who acquired a thorough and detailed knowledge of the ethnography of the Kwakiutl Indians, says that among these Indians "the soul of man is rarely mentioned." And though their silence in this case was not a function of the Indians' usual reserve towards strangers, in as much as Boas's assistant, George Hunt was a Kwakiutl, the fact is that Indians simply don't talk spontaneously about such things.

Perhaps the concept was self-evident or perhaps it was too abstruse. But even when the Indians do talk, what they offer is often confusing and contradictory. Jette discovered that among the Coyukon concepts of soul "do not form a body of doctrine taught in schools, nor even a coherent system orally transmitted, but are preserved in loose shreds, scattered here and there in the superstitious customs of which they form the substratum."

But that should come as no surprise, for people even now find it difficult to define what they mean by soul, and their attempts are often surprisingly primitive. Among the Indians such vagueness of religious conception springs from the nature of tradition itself, a tradition which allows them to abandon older notions. Sometimes different lines of tradition run side by side and sometimes individuals have carried on separate traditions. But more often the discrepancies come from the inability or unwillingness to codify the more subtle notions, either because these notions are not susceptible to such a process, or because the person supplying the information has no interest in casting such notions in stone. Olbrechts observes that the soul-concepts of the Cherokee are now hard to grasp because they have in large part been forgotten.

An example of that occurred when the Bear River shaman, Nora Coonskin, told Nomland that all souls, ghosts, and spirits were called by a single name, but then she contradicted herself when she used different Bear River words for each. It is also equally important to consider the ways in which tradition has been fragmented. Professor Linton, an expert in the way soul concepts develop through cultural and traditional contacts, says that soul pluralism may occur when varying legends about the soul are gradually merged to create a uniform doctrine. There can be no doubt, as well, that the forms in which the free-soul appears have often been stimulated by cultural contact. The Sinkaietk, for instance, have a newly formed free-soul as a result of a collision between their native religion and Christianity.

Even as separate lines of tradition merge, they may be carried on by individuals within the same community. The Wind River Shoshone, for example, have beliefs for both the more conservative idea of two alternating souls and for the newer, Christian belief in one soul. The synthesis occurs among those who believe in a single soul with two designations.

It seems to me that the tendency to uniformity always operates after contact with an outside culture splits the old tradition. That can also occur when the shamans isolate themselves from the majority of the people and the shaman tradition becomes a secret doctrine, opening a gulf between the popular religion and the shamanistic religion. The effects of internal or external changes in tradition can also prejudice the view of Indian conceptions of the soul held by an outsider. But the deeper causes which obscure our understanding of these conceptions lie in the difficulty native peoples find in selecting words to shape their beliefs.

Psychological soul pluralism also causes confusion between early concepts of the soul. As Boas points out, different patterns of life give rise to different soul-concepts, and when a consistent system of belief is lacking, various conceptions overlap. And when it comes to their practical immediate beliefs, such peoples do not see the difficulties implicit in trying to define their soul-concepts until they try to explain them.

"In our ordinary everyday life we do not think much about all these things," an Iglulik Eskimo told Knud Rasmussen, "and it is only now you ask that so many thoughts arise in my head of long known things; old thoughts, but as it were, becoming altogether new when one has to put them into words." Such contradictions draw attention to patterns in Indian thinking. It is inevitable that the idea of the soul should have assumed a much sharper definition in the minds of a few philosophically and religiously gifted individuals than in the minds of the great mass of believers, but all, the speculatively inclined and the less speculatively disposed alike, have been limited in their thinking by the narrow lines fixed by cultural tradition.

That the Indians conception of the soul was incomplete, at least according to European standards, was pointed out by the Jesuits. Brebeuf writes of the Hurons: "to put them in great perplexity it is only necessary to ask them by what exit the soul departs at death, if it be really corporeal, and has a body as large as that which it animates; for to that they have no reply." Le Jeune and other modern field-anthropologists made similar discoveries. Lowie investigated the Crow. "The metaphysical tendency," he says, "is moderately well developed among the Crow. There are no profound theories as to the soul and such reflections as may occasionally be garnered on this and related topics are not infrequently mutually contradictory."

"With rare exceptions," Hewitt says in his discussion of the Iroquois, "no one person possesses a definite and persistent conception of the soul and the future life." But if these "rare exceptions" are the shamans, in what way do their soul-conceptions differ from those of the common man, either in knowledge, or in the method of considering the problem?

The shaman is not always a "psychologist" of greater insight than his fellow tribesmen, especially when there is no organized, esoteric shamanistic doctrine. For example all Mohave according to Devereux, "exhibit much interest in matters relating to the soul and its fate. This is only natural, since dreams are believed to be real adventures of the soul." What's more, almost identical information came from two shaman as well as two ordinary tribesmen which suggests that in these cases ordinary dreaming by ordinary people has limited the power of the shaman to delineate specific soul concepts. In other cases, according to McIlwraith, medicine-men and other philosophically gifted people possess a deeper knowledge of the mysteries pertaining to the life of the soul.

Often enough the medicine-man owes his authority to an extraordinary capacity for vision. And though among many North

American peoples only the shaman can see the soul when awake, it does not follow that he alone has knowledge of the soul, however much he may remain a better authority, based upon the secret knowledge handed down by tradition.

It is, of course, important to understand at the outset that Indian conceptions of the soul are based more in experience than speculation, and that alone best describes the gulf between their concepts and our own philosophically based ideas. Our soul is not a self-evident concept for the Indians. The Wind River Shoshone when confronted with occidental concepts of the soul cannot do without *navujieip*, the dream-soul. The divergence between our notion of the soul and that of the Indians may indeed be quite radical.

It takes very careful study to discover the soul among the mass of terms and concepts which the Indian uses to explain the individual and individuality. When in the summer of 1948 my excellent Arapaho informant wished to give me the Arapaho Indian equivalent of what we call the soul, he included the heart, the brain, and the breath, as well as the peculiar term *betanayaha*, "the mysterious force of human structure," literally, "your body molded as a living man." It is not easy to get a precise idea of what constitutes the soul among the Arapaho using that sort of information.

There are also occasional reports from widely separated parts of North America of Indian tribes which do not believe in the soul. Cooper, who worked among the Cree at James Bay says that even among the older Cree the old, traditional belief is a thing of the past. "There was no belief in a soul; there was no thought of one having a soul or spirit," declared one of the older Cree. It would of course be over-hasty to draw any conclusions concerning an earlier absence of a belief in the soul from such material, especially since my own field-studies among the Shoshone and the Arapaho showed that Indians who had been converted to Christianity or the Peyote religion very often denied that their former religion had contained even elementary eschatological concepts. In the case of the Cree, however, Richardson mentions at least one designation for the soul, *atchak* or *akhchak*. Quite likely this term stands for the free-soul, or the shadow soul.

Additionally, a number of reports from the Plateau-peoples give rise to the false notion that no concept of the soul existed before the introduction of the Christian soul-concept. Brinton says that the Lower Pend d'Oreilles (Kalispel) had, according to a report from the Commissioner of Indian Affairs in 1854, "no word for soul, spiritual existence, or vital principle." The missionaries are said to have made the Christian idea of the soul understandable by comparing it with "a gut which never rotted." Such statements should be regarded with circumspection. For example, the soul-concept of the Pend d'Oreilles was so different from the Christian notion that it was not understood for what it was.

According to Curtis, the missionaries coined the Kootenay term for the soul. But the very significance of the term—roughly: "two-fold human flesh"—sounds like the free-soul. Curtis also says that before the missionaries arrived the Kootenay had a vague soul-belief. Chamberlain's notes from the Kootenay indicate that the structure of their soul-belief was dualistic, and therefore original. Other instances from the Plateau Indians and others show that Christianity has transformed rather than ousted the native conceptions of the soul. Cline's list of the five souls of the Sinkaietk, includes an "immortal soul derived from Christianity." From his report it seems that the Catholic priests adopted old notions of the free-soul and transferred them to a new, Christianized soul concept. Among the Delaware Indians Lowie found the process reversed. There, the indigenous term for the soul was given a new content by the mission.

Yet among the Shoshone and Arapaho Lowie has shown that statements about a foreign origin for their soul concept cannot be correct. "Though this idea was said to have been derived from Mormon teaching, the concept and term were obtained among the Lemhi, and its occurrence among the Paviotso in practically the same form establishes its antiquity." On the other hand, it seems inescapable that the significance of the term has been changed by Christian influence, so that what was originally a body-soul now approaches Christian notions of soul.

The Christian influence has been responsible for the development of a unitary concept of the soul and in most cases the native soul-belief has been given both names. Sometimes missionaries coined their own terms, as they did for the Navajo, whose rather amorphous set of souls did not appeal to the Catholic Fathers. Consequently, Richard says, they introduced a new concept of the soul. They made up a word meaning "that which stands within" to explain the "spiritual, undying part of man. It refers to a belief that in the chest of man there is an image, a symbol of turquoise, which will make him strong, as long as it remains upright. It belongs only to those who have undergone certain ceremonies and therefore is not inherent or immortal, but rather something ritualistically added to defend body and spirit."

At best, reports about Indian tribes which have no belief in the soul, are sketchy and ill-conceived. Belief in the soul is probably universal, with people everywhere believing in souls in human beings, though that does not necessarily imply that all human beings are conceived of as having souls. It may happen, for instance, that certain categories of individuals, especially members of a social out-group, are denied any form of soul by those in control, as is the case in Africa and Polynesia for women and low caste people.

That occurs in another way in North America. Chapman relates one such instance from the Ingalik. "The Tinneh freely admits that his medicine has no power over the white man. His explanation of this is that white men have no souls." Viewed in the light of his belief that white men are deceased Indians, this is not, perhaps, so irrational.

Like the dead person, a still-born infant also has no soul. The Menomini, according to information gathered by Skinner, say that a still-born child lacks a soul because it has no life in this world and therefore has no life after death.

Sometimes, however, there is said to be a special soul which the still-born infant lacks. Among the Wind River Shoshone it is believed that a still born child has possessed, but has lost, its body-soul. Presumably a child has no other soul. The Payne manuscript says that Cherokee children are without souls. Ray reports that among the Tenino, embryos and babies have no souls, whereas among other Plateau peoples, adults, children and embryos have souls. In both cases the child lacked a free soul because it was far too young to have developed a free-soul. The Eskimo at the MacKenzie River assume the existence of a provisional vital principle in the child before it has been named, which seems to be identical with the spirit of a deceased ancestor.

In such cases you can only guess at the nature of the absent soul. When a soul is lost, the information is more satisfactory, and often it is possible to determine from the context of the explanation which soul is being discussed. If, for example, an Indian says he has lost his soul because an artist has made a portrait of him, it is of course the free-soul (the image-soul) he is talking about.

A soul cannot only disappear, it may also return to its owner, making it possible for an individual to have a differing number of souls on different occasions. Hewitt says that Iroquois belief provided people with one or more reasonable or intelligent souls or psychic entities, with some people at times having four or five souls. At other times the same people may not have had one such soul.

Despite an inclination to deny that some living individuals possess souls, as a general rule every person, according to the current soul-ideology, has one or more souls. In addition, belief in the soul has been extended to include other living beings, indeed, even inanimate objects.

In the end only careful examination of the patterns of Indian conceptions of the soul can help define the nature of the soul-belief in question. Any such discussion must begin by considering the general features of soul-belief among different Indian tribes and groups.

The Dualistic Schema in North America

The soul concept among less philosophically sophisticated people is characterized first by soul finds, which have their modern counterparts in the alter ego, experienced in states of trance, and in the memory image of the living individual; and second, in those conceptions which arise from observations and inner sensations and give expression to psychic and vital physical activity.

Many of the forms which both the free-soul and body-soul assume have been forged into dogma by generations of shamans. A hundred years ago Schoolcraft could write after studying the Ojibway, "The Indians of the United States believe in the duality of the soul." But their beliefs were in "a sensual and local soul, as distinguished from an ambient and absent spirit."

Since then various instances of dualistic soul-belief among North American Indians have appeared in the literature, leaving little doubt that genuine dualism between souls exists in North America. Schoolcraft provides an example drawn from Ojibway

Indian burial customs. "Over the top of the grave a roof-shaped covering of cedar-bark is built, to shed the rain. A small aperture is cut through the bark at the head of the grave. When asked why this was done, a Chippewa replied, 'To allow the soul to pass out and in.' 'I thought', I replied, 'that you believed that the soul went up from the body at the time of death, to a land of happiness. How then can it remain in the body?' 'There are two souls,' replied the Indian philosopher. 'How can this be?' I responded. 'It is easily explained,' he said. 'You know that in dreams we pass over wide countries, and see hills and lakes and mountains, and many scenes, which pass before our eyes and affect us. Yet, at the same time, our bodies do not stir; and there is a soul left with the body, else it would be dead. So, you see, it must be another soul that accompanies us'."

Boas offers an example taken from the Kwakiutl. Lebid, a Kwakiutl, had been sick for a long time and on the midwinter day when he died, his corpse, wrapped in blankets, was left on a rock just outside the village. Toward nightfall there was a snow-storm, and many wolves began howling around the spot where the dead man lay. At daybreak Lebid was heard to sing a sacred song among the howling wolves, and the Indians understood that he had become a shaman. Soon, with the wolves, he disappeared into the forest. His corpse was gone, but his footsteps were visible in the snow. Two days later he appeared again, singing his sacred song. He was "really naked, only hemlock was wound around his head and hemlock was wound around his neck."

Following a number of ceremonies to mark his return as a shaman, Lebid described his experience. He had been very ill when a man came up to him and asked him to get up and follow him. Lebid did as he was asked, but at the same time he made a strange observation. "I saw that my body was still lying here groaning." Lebid followed the stranger into a house in the forest. Here, among others, lived a man named Naualakume who declared that he intended to make Lebid a great shaman and to give him his own name. Whereupon Naualakume departed. "It was not long before he came back and said, 'Now his body is dead on the ground, for I am holding his breath, which is the owner of the soul of our friend. Now I shall give him my shamanistic power,' he said and then vomited a quartz crystal. All the men beat fast time on boards and Naualakume sang his sacred song as he threw the quartz crystal into the lower part of my sternum, and then I had become a shaman."

Toward evening the wolves assembled once more in the mysterious house. They donned their wolf masks and Lebid walked back with them to where his lifeless body lay. Naualakume came with Lebid's body-breath, "for only his soul had been taken by the wolves." When they reached the corpse, they removed the shroud. Then Naualakume called Lebid, told him to sit by his side, and blew the breath into Lebid's body. The wolves were then instructed to lick the body. "Now my soul was sitting on the ground and was just watching the wolves as they were licking the body. They had not been licking it long when it began to breathe."

Naualakume pressed both hands over the head of the soul, and the soul shrank until it was finally no bigger than a large fly. Naualakume then seized it, placed it on the crown of Lebid's head and blew it into him. After this Lebid stood up immediately and sang his sacred song.

It is important to note here that the individual, the ego, is represented by the free-soul as long as the body is without consciousness. Whether the breath (the body-soul) is present in the body is of less importance.

The legend of Lebid offers an extraordinarily clear account of the Kwakiutl Indians' belief about the soul, including reference to the free soul (the ego of the individual in the state of absence), the breath or the body-soul (which gives the body life), the body (which has life when it contains the breath-soul, and consciousness when the free soul stops wandering about on its own outside the body), and finally, to *mana*, the supernatural power which is separated from both the body-soul and the free-soul and which invests the individual with shamanistic power. The picture is not always so clear.

Chapter One
Soul Dualism

Eskimo conceptions of the soul present a confusing picture if you try to apply them to all Eskimos, but if you reduce them to a lowest common denominator, the Eskimo, like adjacent circumpolar peoples on the Asiatic continent, hold a clearly dualistic view of the soul. Lantis writes: "This much can be said of Eskimos generally, they believe in: 1. A soul-being that can become a soul-spirit like other supernatural beings. Occasionally the shadow is identified with it. In different places it takes other forms; a ball of fire or a light, steam, a skeleton. 2. The name has personal qualities but has no form, no lasting existence as a separate entity. It does not go to the afterworld. 3. The life essence, warmth, breath."

Boas suggests that by eliminating the name, which is less soul than a mystical individual extension typical of Eskimos, there remain two basic conceptions: the free-soul and the life-soul. Some of the oldest examples come from Greenland where Holm's work with the East Greenlanders has provided the basis for understanding their soul beliefs. "The Angmagsaliks believe," he says, "that man consists of three parts; body, soul, and name." This combination of elements is also characteristic of people from West Greenland and among the Polar Eskimo according to Birket-Smith.

It is possible to penetrate deeper, into the real soul belief if you understand that the word soul covers a much more complex pattern of beliefs. In both East and West Greenland people believe in more than one soul. Holm quotes the catechist Joh. Hansen, who wrote in his diary: "A man has many souls. The biggest of them lives in the larynx and in man's left side, and are manikins the size of sparrows. The other souls live in all other members of the body and are about the size of a finger-joint. Now, when an Angakok removes one of them, that part of the man which has lost its soul falls ill. If another Angakok on examination finds the soul removed and then fetches it back and replaces it, the man becomes well again, but if it is found impossible to get the soul back, the man dies and the soul wanders about to the dismay and terror of all around."

It is impossible to say exactly which souls these are, though the majority of them appear to have been specialized body-souls. Hansen's report agrees with the information imparted to Rasmussen by an East Greenlander, who admitted, however, his inability to correctly interpret the beliefs of the older generation. But his explanation of how the many small souls "concentrate the whole life force of a man, which is radiated through the mouth," is of great value. His focus, for example, on the cessation of breathing at death, makes it clear that he was talking about life-souls. And his description of a fragmented soul, a soul which inhabits each part of the body, likens the soul to an independent human being. There was mention of the free-soul.

Kroeber, in his work among the polar Eskimos, also found evidence of the life-soul, as breath-soul, connected to the body. This soul leaves the body during illness. The same Eskimo group, according to reports from Rasmussen, regarded the soul as immortal, following man the same way his shadow follows him in the sunlight. But if the soul leaves a person for a longer period he falls ill and dies.

Still that information does not provide absolute evidence of a dualistic soul scheme. Not until you connect Thalbitzer's work among various eastern Eskimo peoples and examine the philological and psychological nature of those people does that come clear. Thalbitzer has shown that the most common Greenland word for soul is *tarnik,* which includes the many organically functioning souls common to East Greenlanders. But in addition to this there is another word, *tarrak,* which stands for image, shadow, and the free-soul. It is presumably this *tarrak* which Cranz refers to as the shadow-soul.

Of greater importance is the *tarnik* reported by Birket-Smith from large parts of the central and eastern area. *Tarnik* refers chiefly to the body-soul, but in all likelihood once referred primarily to the free-soul as appears evident from shamanistic practice and the etymology of the language.

There is a close link between the *tarnick* connected with the body and the souls connected with the breath in West Greenland, among the Angmagsalik and among the Polar Eskimo. In West Greenland, as well as among the Polar Eskimo, the word for breach refers to the life-soul. But where, then, is the free-soul? In West Greenland it was probably the *tarrak*, the shadow.

In East Greenland the matter is more complicated. According to Hanserak, the Eskimo there believe that our bodies contain several localized life-souls as well as two chief-souls. Thalbitzer says that it is the loss of the larger soul situated in the larynx that causes death.

Here, I think, you can see a remainder of the free-soul concept, for among the Polar Eskimo, the life-soul and the free-soul seem to have merged. The explanation for the dying out of the free-soul among the Eskimo in Greenland probably lies in the way the body souls have acquired a marked independence of the body, and as Thalbitzer points out, man's chief *tarnik* has become identical with the name-soul.

On the American continent, Eskimo conceptions of the soul show the same principal features, even if in certain quarters the dualism appears to take a more definite shape. The Eskimos of Labrador, according to Hawkes, "distinguish between a man's body and his spirit. There is also another soul which corresponds to the vitality of the body, as exemplified by breath and warmth. This soul leaves a man at death, but the spirit lingers around the village for three days before taking his final departure to the other world." Here the dualism is pronounced.

From Baffin Land and Hudson Bay, Boas reports that the Eskimo believe man possesses two souls, one which remains with the body and which may temporarily reside in a child that has been given the dead person's name, and another which goes to one of the spirit-lands. It would appear that here, too, dualism exists.

Rasmussen says that the Iglulik have two words for soul, *tarnina* (*tarnik*) and *inu sia*. The *tarnina* soul is conceived of as an image of man on a diminished scale, while *inu sia* signifies "appearance as a human being," and lives in an air-bubble in the groin. "From it," Rasmussen says, "proceed thoughts, appearance, strength, and life." It seems clear that the Iglulik believed in a dualism between free-soul and life-soul, although Rasmussen has tried to merge them into one conception.

Rasmussen, in his descriptions of soul-belief among some more westerly Central Eskimo groups, found the same tendency toward belief in a unitary soul. Among the Netsilik, he says, "the soul is that which gives man life; it has its place somewhere or other in the body, streams through the whole of man's body and being, will, and faculties, as long as he breathes." This is of course a body-soul. But in addition to this he says that "the soul is the being and appearance of the living, and that it appears as an alter ego outside the body." He also says that it has two names, *tarneq* and *ino'seq*. It appears probable that here, too, Rasmussen has merged two separate ideas.

The Eskimo at Point Hope distinguish two "qualities" in men and animals, *inyusaq* and *ilitkosaq*. The former means soul or life, the latter, spirit or character. But Rainey writes, "it is probable that at least forty years of Christian teaching and much discussion have confused even the old peoples' ideas to its original meaning. I believe the native idea is that *inyusaq* was the life quality which disappeared at death (or actually four days after death for a man, five days for a woman); that *ilitkosaq* was the character, personality, individuality, or spirit of a person or animal which could be transferred from one individual to another and which could remain at the grave, the village, or the place of death." This is clearly a dualism between life-soul and free-soul.

Another group of Eskimo, living in Alaska at the Bering Strait, believe, according to Nelson, in two or three separate souls. The one, the invisible shade, "is formed exactly in the shape of the body, is sentient, and destined for a future life." The other "has a form exactly like that of the body and is the life-giving warmth. It is without sense and takes flight into the air when a person dies." The third shade remains with the dead body and possesses certain evil powers and is possibly the grave-ghost. Quite likely the animal guardian, *inua*, is equated with the free-soul, but this does not alter the dualistic soul belief of the Alaskan Eskimo.

Chapter Two
Soul Dualism in Northwest North America

The Athapascans of the Mackenzie River Basin in Alaska, the tribes along the extensive coastline, the scattered groups of Salish and other linguistic stocks in the Interior Plateau country, the Eyak, Tlingit, and Haida all believed in a dual soul.

Birket-Smith, in his work with the Eyak, says they believed man had two souls, but the statements of the natives are vague, and the only certainty is that they recognized a free-soul. The North Athapascans, on the other hand, as Hill-Tout reports, believe in a dual soul. Osgood found that the Tanaina distinguish between man's breath and his shadow-spirit which leaves him some time before he dies. Chapman too found evidence of a distinction between body-soul and free-soul among the Ingalik.

Osgood found several soul terms in the Ingalik vocabulary for body-soul and shadow-soul, but a closer study shows that the terms for shadow and spirit-soul are identical and reoccur in the word *yega* as the designation for free-soul among the Coyukon, the northern neighbors of the Ingalik. The free-soul, *yega*, was seen as an emancipated guardian spirit, a notion which occurred frequently in North America. Osgood also says that the Crow River Kutchin believed that the shadow possessed "a spiritual existence of its own," which offers evidence of a free-soul belief.

From the Chipewyan, comes a complicated body-soul concept that turns up in the writings of an earlier investigator, Petitot. He says that among the Chipewyan only the soul may be emancipated from the body. But he also offers the terms *souffle*, *haleine*, and *vent*, which raise the question of whether a special life-soul lies concealed in those terms. Morice also says that the Eastern Denes have many words for the soul animating the body; words which, though they vary by dialect, are all counterparts for the Latin word *spiritus*.

One of the names cited by Petitot for the free-soul, *ettsine*, seems to designate the shadow, and in its linguistic form is similar to the term for free-soul among the western Athapascans, *ne-tsen*. Those Athapascans, chiefly the Tahltan, Kaska, Sekani, Carrier, and Chilcotin had, according to Morice, once believed in a dualistic concept of the soul. The free-soul, *ne-tsen*, was invisible and dwelt in the body when the individual was in good health, but it was sometimes heard and seen as a wandering shape outside the body when its owner lay sick or dying. They also had a body soul, *nezael*, which means roughly human heat. This soul gave warmth and vitality to the body.

Goldman, who did his field work among the Carrier, says that dualism existed between the soul and the ghost. But the name Goldman offers is a dialectal variant of the designation for the free-soul Morice recorded. There the ghost is the deceased person, and the free-soul after death has a new designation, *nezul*, meaning after death.

Morice also says that the Carrier have one word for the mind and three words for the soul and this agrees with Jenness's findings among the Carrier at Bulkley, "that beyond his actual body every human being possessed a mind or intelligence, warmth, and a third part, called his shadow, (while he was living, it was his shadow cast by the sun or moon, or by the ghost or apparition of a living person, or by his reflection in water) and after death it was called his shade. In other words, these people possessed a free-soul, an ego-soul, and a life-soul.

The real Northwest Coast tribes, the Tlingit and Haida, besides the Eyak, belong to the Nadene family. Though the soul beliefs of these peoples has not yet been fully defined, Swanton reports that the Tlingit have two words for the soul of the living and three for the dead. The words for the first mean what feels, because "when a person's feeling is gone he is dead." This is an ego-soul. One of the words for the soul after death is shadow, and coincides with the word for image which seems clearly to describe the free-soul.

Such notions also occur in the folklore of the Tlingit, and Boas tells the story of a Tlingit who was brought back to earth from the realm of the dead. He "heard a child crying that had just been born. He himself was the child." Here the man's ego represents the extra-physical soul or the individual himself outside his body. The Haida Indians described by Swanton also had three words for soul or spirit. Two of these refer to the soul in the living body and one to the soul after its separation."

The first two seem to express the vitality or the life-soul and are more or less synonymous, but "the Haida denied that there are two souls." They said that the body-soul departs at death to be reincarnated later, perhaps in another human being. Now the question is whether the soul which continues the existence of the individual after death, *giet*, is also the free soul of the living person. The body-souls have shown an existence of their own after death and cannot be represented by *giet*, which goes to the realm of the dead. Moreover, a special word exists for the ghost, so it is natural to assume that *giet* refers to the free-soul or the disembodied soul, which exits whether its owner is alive or dead.

A third Northwest coast people, the Tsimshian, do not share the linguistic connection of the two previously mentioned tribes but are culturally close. The Tsimshian probably had, like the Tlingit and Haida, a dualistic soul-belief, at least based on a legend of the Niska clan, a Tsimshian group. Collected by Boas, the legend tells of a young man who fell ill after a meeting with a ghost. The ghost carried off his soul, meaning the young man himself, to the realm of the dead. There he felt ill again, and the shamans of the dead tried to cure him by taking out his heart. That failed, however, because he was wearing a protective talisman, and the dead were forced to send the youth back to the land of the living. This would appear to be an example of soul dualism where the soul is the free-soul, and the heart is the life-soul whose continued activity keeps the sick man from being incorporated into the circle of the dead.

Among the northwestern peoples (who for linguistic reasons Sapir has placed under the name Mosan: the Wakashan (Kwakiutl and Nootka), Salishan and Chemakuan) there appears a well-developed soul dualism, first between the free-soul and the ego-soul, and second between the free soul and the life-soul. "The soul or living essence of a human being is conceived of as a manikin, a shadowy doublet, which can be held in the palm of a shaman's hand. It may leave the body through the crown of the head but may either return of its own accord or be brought back through the ministrations of a shaman. Distinct from the soul is the *hlimaksti*, often translated as heart. This is not the anatomical heart, but the mind or soul in its psychological, not theological, sense. It is the seat or principle of intelligence characteristic of human beings alone, and is generally localized in the heart or breast."

Drucker declares that the life-principle, *tititcu*, is distinct from the free-soul, that it resides in the heart and acts through the heart. These accounts contrast sharply with Sproat's description of a unitary soul principle among the Nootka. This soul, according to Sproat, has the freedom of the free-soul. A similar view of the Nootka's soul-belief is represented by Boas in his second report on the Indians in British Columbia.

The sources for soul conceptions among the numerous Salish tribes, especially inland, are very unequal. Teit's scanty reports from the more well-known Plateau Salish tribes, for example, contrast sharply with the detailed descriptions from a less well-known group, the Sinkaietk. And though Teit's information does not shed much light on the soul beliefs of the Salish, he does say that the Shuswap, Lillooet, Thompson River Indians, and Oka-nagon believed in a unitary soul.

What he describes, however, is a dualism of souls. "Each soul has a shadow; and when a person dies, it remains behind in this world. It is the ghost of the departed." A careful examination of Teit's interpretations shows that he blithely equates the soul of the living person with the forms assumed by the dead. He uses the terms soul and ghost, the former referring to the soul of the living person and to the deceased in the realm of the dead, while the latter refers only to the wandering ghost.

The soul has the character of a free-soul during the individual's lifetime, especially among the Shuswap. The ghost seems not to appear while the person is alive, making its association with the shadow metaphorical. "Ghosts are the shadows of souls," Teit says of the Lillooet. "Every soul has its ghost, as every body has its shadow." In other words, the grave-ghost appears as an earth-bound reflex of the deceased in the realm of the dead. What Teit has really described is the tension between these post-mortal forms of existence, not between the souls of the living person.

The problem is trying to decide what value Teit's observations

have when trying to determine whether a unitary soul-belief existed among several Plateau Salish groups. The fact that among the
Sanpoil and Nespelem, Ray found a strictly unitary soul concept
speaks in their favor, but this does not exclude the possibility that
both tribes may originally have known a soul-dualism which
gradually disappeared. As a matter of fact, Teit's comments on
the soul-beliefs of the Thompson River Indians leaves no doubt
that this people believed in dual souls. He says: "The soul may
leave the body a long time before death. Life and breath are necessary to this life. The soul does not need them, and has no real
connection with them." This seems to be pronounced dualism,
and since the soul-belief of the Shuswap, Lillooet, and Okanagon
are described variously as similar to that found among the
Thompson River Indians, it is hard to avoid concluding that these
groups also had a dualistic soul-belief.

It is striking that Teit's notes on the unitary soul among the
northern Okanagon are in conflict with reports of a richly differentiated soul belief among the southern Okanagon, the Sinkaietk.
Cline says that "The spiritual parts of the individual hardly lend
themselves to rigid definition. Apparently there were five: the
mind, the shadow soul, the breath soul, the immortal soul derived
from Christianity, and the ghost."

But behind this pluralism there is a dualism between the free-
soul and the ego-soul or life-soul. This is apparent less from
Cline's interpretations than from his overall account. In fact the
soul-belief of the Salish Indians was more complicated than Teit
has led us to believe and deserves a closer analysis.

Among the Sinkaietk the traits of the body-soul are represented
by the mind and the breath, and though the likely conclusion is
that the shadow-soul plays the role of the free-soul, this is not the
case. The shadow-soul is not a real soul but an extension of the
individual's essence. Cline says that it stands for "the vital principle," but this is not to say that the shadow is the life-soul. The
shadow-soul is, after all, an extension of the individual which is
supported by Cline's observations, for he says that the shadow
"seems to have been closely connected with the sweat, spittle,
hair, underwear, and other materials intimately in contact with the
individual, for these, as well as the shadow, should not be allowed
to fall into an open grave."

The real free-soul among the Sinkaietk is the *sinkakius*, a term borrowed from the Spokan through Christian mediation, but the concept Spier says, is much older. Cline assumes that the concept is an extension of the shadow-soul, but his report disagrees with that. "You have a shadow when you walk," one of his informants told him, "and there is another little shadow, the *sinkakius*."

Clearly, two different concepts are at work here, the shadow and the shadow-soul, or the free-soul. "Each individual" Cline says, "had only one *sinkakius*. It looked like him, but it could go fast without walking, like thought, and could fly. It was the part of him which dreamed. It left the body during sleep and fainting. Its failure to return to the body meant death." It is, finally, this soul that after death becomes the ghost.

Memories of more than one soul have also lingered on among two other Salish groups on the Plateau, the Coeur d'Alene and the Flathead. Teit says of the Coeur d'Alene, "Besides the body, people knew of nothing else belonging to a person except a shade, which they believed survived after death. Some thought there were two of these, one of which remained near the body, the other going off to some place, they knew not where, to a land where all shades finally lived together. Many, however, believed only in the one shade, which became a ghost after death."

Turney-High notes that "even the oldest Flathead can remember but little of the former doctrine of the soul. There is the slightest indication of a former belief in a plurality of souls, but informants are by no means in agreement on this point." It would of course be over-hasty to conclude that in the two last cases a regular dualistic soul belief existed. There is, however, some evidence of the existence of dualistic soul-conceptions in earlier times. Tylor noted the dualism between two souls in the beliefs of the Salish Indians on the coast and the groups related to them. Recent information from these peoples emphasizes the role which soul dualism has played in their beliefs. This is the more remarkable as the notes were made at a time when the native culture had for the most part become but a pale memory.

The soul concepts among the isolated Salish in the north, the Bella Coola, have been given varying interpretations. Boas for instance, describes a unitary soul of predominantly free-soul character (though without the dream-soul aspect), while the shadow is described as a mystical extension of the individual.

McIlwraith offers a different account of the soul beliefs of the

Bella Coola, describing a pluralism of souls which forms a fundamental dualism. First among the soul elements is the spirit, a small but immortal soul of supernatural origin, equipped with the functions of a protective spirit. It appears as a dream-soul, either by itself giving rise to the dreams or by figuring in them. As a protective spirit it also organizes the individual's daily thoughts, meaning it appears in the guise of an ultimate authority over the mind, which is "somewhat vaguely regarded as a separate entity." The spirit is also vital to the life of the individual, for without it the person dies.

In contrast to this free-soul of guardian spirit type is the life-soul, which is as independent of the great guardian soul as is the mind. That the life-soul may be temporarily absent from the body is, according to McIlwraith, the result of the disintegration and confusion of the original, clearer soul concepts. At death, the life-soul (according to some, the shadow) goes to the underworld, while the free-soul goes to heaven. For the Salish, Barnett says "there were two souls; one in the head, the other in the heart. They could wander off in sleep, be abducted by shamans and ghosts, or be displaced by a sudden fright."

The reports from the coastal Salish and the groups related to them on the northwest coast of the United States, provide much greater detail. The Quileute, says Frachtenberg, believe that every human being possesses several souls which "look exactly like the living being and may be taken off or put on in exactly the same manner as a snake sheds its skin." There is an inner soul, called the main, strong soul, an outer soul, called the outside shadow, a life-soul, referred to as the being whereby one lives, and the ghost of the living person, or the thing whereby one grows. The Quileute believe that none of these four souls is identical with the physical shadow. The outside soul seems to be the free-soul.

In contrast to the free-soul are the life-soul and the ghost, which should, according to native linguistic usage, be designated as the growth soul because like the life-soul it animates life. The quality of the inner soul is harder to define because the only thing we know is that it leaves the individual a couple of days before death. Logically the main soul represents the ego-soul.

Nor do the Indians at South Puget Sound seem to have been unfamiliar with soul dualism. At least this is the impression left by Marian Smith's excellent monograph on these Salish groups.

She does, to be sure, describe the soul as being undivided. "The presence of this soul in the body meant life and its permanent removal meant death." But in her description of the activity of this soul outside the body, the free-soul appears. Smith also describes a diffuse soul aspect best explained in terms of personality. The point here is that the personality was so connected to the individual that its loss resulted in loss of the soul. The dualism between free-soul and life-soul, among these Salish, is a less common dualism between free-soul and ego-soul.

Finally, of the Chinook, who do not belong to the Salish but share the latter's coastal culture, Boas says that each person has a large and a small soul. "When a person falls sick the lesser soul leaves his body." The smaller soul, we presume, is identical with the free-soul. When both the souls have departed, the person dies.

Of the numerous coastal groups in the south (in Oregon), we know from Barnett only that the soul had the nature of breath or was associated with the heart.

The Kootenay live in the vicinity of the Salish groups of the interior, on the borders of the Plains country, and according to Chamberlain, they believed in at least two souls, one connected with the body "its psychic correlate," and one free and not bound by the body. The first-mentioned is the seat of emotions, will, thought, intellect, and is the heart. The other soul is the free-soul, for which Chamberlain has two separate names. He says that the free-soul has the shape of a bird, land-animal, or flower. According to Curtis, it dwells in the body in the shape of a human. It is important to note here the Protean character of the free-soul in order to explain its polymorphous appearance among the Kootenay.

Chapter Three
Soul Dualism in Eastern North America

Schoolcraft confirmed the belief in dual souls among the Algonquin peoples, though the earliest report of this dualism came from Le Jeune, a French Jesuit missionary in New France in the 1630's. An Algonquin Indian told him that his soul had left him more than two years before, going off to his relatives in the realm of the dead, and that he now had only "his body's soul" which would in time descend into the grave.

Soul dualism does sometimes occur disguised as a functional, but not as a nominal reality, which is the case among the Naskapi and Montagnais groups in Labrador. However, in his preliminary survey in 1924, Speck said that they know of only one soul, commonly called the Great Man, which has three names and the same number of functions. It is frequently represented as a shadow-soul, but it is much more. "It seems indeed to represent the ego," Speck says, while pointing out that the soul serves as a protective spirit, whose "communications are conveyed chiefly through dream visitations."

In his monograph on the Naskapi, Speck offers still another name for the soul, noting that "it is at first rather confusing to encounter several synonyms for soul in discussions as well as in the texts." What he is saying, of course, is that the soul is a unitary concept, identified by more than one word. The problem, however, is that unity seems to have been acquired late, either through speculation or through influence from Christian thought.

That seems especially true when you consider that each name for the soul covers different functions. For example, a term like *atca'kw* is used with soul or shadow, and according to Speck, it is the name of a diminutive soul. This soul is the person himself, as he appears, for example in his reflected image, and it is the free-soul or the image-soul. Another term, *nictu'tsem*, signifies mind (including intellect and comprehension), and plays the role of ego-soul. The opposition between these two souls is bridged by the Great Man, *mista'peo*, a peculiar soul concept which combines several soul conceptions with the idea of the supernatural helper. This superior soul concept shows, in my opinion, clear traces of being a product of shamanistic speculation.

My sources for the soul concepts of the coastal Algonquin are often of older date, which would be an advantage if the majority of cases were complete. Even so some sources seem to indicate a possible soul dualism among a few coastal Algonquin groups. You can see glimpses of that in Speck's notes on the Penobscot Indians in New England. The free-soul there is also the soul of the dead person and is distinct from the shadow, which should probably be understood as the shadow in its ordinary, physical sense. In addition, the free-soul is likewise distinct from the breath, which perhaps can also be seen as a soul.

The Micmac, according to Maillard and Rand, seem to have differentiated between a free-soul, called the shadow, and the life-soul, or seat of life, according to the way they were treated in stories about the external soul. This was probably a life-soul. Although other research from New England seems to offer proof of the existence of a dual concept of the soul, I have omitted that here as the basis for a judgment is unreliable.

Our knowledge of the soul concepts of the Delaware Indians (Lenni-Lenape), on the other hand, is far more certain. Conrad has developed a soul terminology for these Indians based on the research of three different authorities, Zeisberger, Brainerd, and Brinton. This new contribution is surprising, for Harrington's notes from the modern Delaware serve to show how the old beliefs faded and were transformed and began to disintegrate after the introduction of the Christian idea of the soul.

Zeisberger, Brainerd, Brinton, and Speck all designate the soul with one name, *tsitschank, tsítsan*, which signifies shadow or image. This is an old name for the soul, reoccurring among several coastal Algonquin groups, including the Abnaki, Naskapi, Mohegan, Pequot, Natick, and Narragansett. In addition Zeisberger says, "they formerly used the word *Wtellenapewoagan*, meaning the substance of a human being, to describe the soul, a word they use to the present day. They also use the word *Wtschitschank*, meaning Spirit.

According to Zeisberger, the change in soul terminology is the result of contradictions between Christians and non-Christians within the tribe. Speck agrees, saying that the old term for the soul, *tsítsan*, was adopted by Christianity, and the unconverted then constructed a new concept, *lennape-ekkan* or human being. Both soul concepts are undoubtedly free-soul in character.

A term introduced into the debate by Brinton, *tschipey*, seems to refer to a supernatural entity separate from the individual. The name is used for the dead, and it has nothing to do with the souls of the living individual. Of more importance are the statements by Brinton and Speck that the heart and the blood are the seats of soul qualities, which indicate a differentiated body-soul concept. According to Brinton, life and the feelings are concentrated in the heart, while according to Speck, the life-soul is associated with the blood. Speck also says that after death this life-soul remains on earth as a ghost. Evidently the Lenape, too, believed in dual souls.

Our best accounts of the ideas of the soul held by the Algonquin peoples come from the Central Algonquin in the region around the most westerly of the Great Lakes. We know less about the soul beliefs of the more southerly groups. Volney says, for instance, that among the Miami the soul, or one of the souls, has been represented as a flying phantom. According to Jones, the Kickapoo believed in a shadow-soul and have preserved the name, while the Shawnee believed in a breath-soul.

The soul beliefs of the more northerly Central Algonquin are clearer. It was typical of these groups, William Jones writes, to believe in more than one soul, one of which was thought to live on with the individual after death.

Despite being scattered in autonomous groups over a wide area, the Ojibway shared common beliefs about the soul and its function, though some accounts challenge credulity. Kinietz for example, was told by John Pete, his chief informant in the village of Katikitegon, that man had a large number of souls. Pete said that "he was sure that every person had more than one soul, perhaps six or seven different souls." One of them, "the real soul," goes to the realm of the dead, another is reincarnated in the womb of a pregnant woman, while other souls may transmigrate and take the shape of deer. Kinietz attributed that ability to the myth of *Manabozhu* (the culture hero) who constantly changed his shape.

If Pete is right, this Ojibway group had, like the Malays, a belief in seven souls. But Pete appears to have lost touch with old Ojibway beliefs about the soul. His seven souls come from adding forms of the free-soul to the changes in shape and function attributed to the dead person. But what is at issue here is only the number of souls, for clearly Pete was convinced that a human has more than one soul. What he offers here is a faded memory of the dualism between two souls that once characterized the soul belief of the majority of Ojibway.

A typical example of such dualism between free-soul and life-soul, described so realistically by Schoolcraft, is replaced among several Ojibway groups by a dualism between the free-soul (the shadow-soul) and the ego-soul. According to Jenness, the Ojibway on Parry Island believed that man consists of three parts: the body (*wiyo*), which decays after death, the soul (*udjitchog*), which at death departs for the realm of the dead in the West, and the shadow (*udjitchbom*), which after death becomes a grave ghost. The so-called soul is "the intelligent part of man's being, the agency that enables him to perceive things, to reason them out, and remember them." This is what we have called an ego-soul; the soul which is lost during drunkenness or insanity. But both in its independence from the individual (especially as will-soul) and in its ability to differentiate the ego-soul from the individual, it is close to the free-soul and therefore also close to the shadow which is its manifestation.

"The shadow," Jenness says, "is slightly more indefinite than the soul, and the Indians themselves often confuse them attributing certain activities or phenomena now to one, now to the other." Of note here is that the shadow is seated in the brain, and that it is the brain which the guard removes at the entrance to the realm of the dead, forcing the dead person to forget earthly existence. Even as the shadow plays the role of the ego-soul, it remains a free-soul, active outside the body even when the individual is awake, presumably because it is conceived as the shadow in the physical sense. And as a shadow it is a warning that arouses the individual to perception and knowledge.

The soul beliefs held among these Ojibway show how easily the oppositions in the dualistic formation of the soul can be resolved. This is especially true where the ego-soul and the free-soul are in opposition. For the living individual, the loss of the free-soul generally implies the loss of consciousness, since the free-soul in its wanderings carries the conscious ego of the individual. As the free-soul is associated with the consciousness of the ego, so the loss of the ego soul is associated with that of the free-soul.

Among the Ojibway on Parry Island, the two souls are less distinctly separate, but their outer integrity is untouched. All the elements required to bring a person back to life are here; body, soul, and shadow. The heroine in the legend of Orpheus recalled by Jenness, "built a sweathouse, placed inside it her husband's body with the two boxes containing his soul and his brains (shadow), poured water over the hot stones and waited outside. Within a few minutes her husband rose up alive and well."

The soul beliefs of the Menomini, Sauk, and Fox are characterized by a life-soul associated with the heart being the surviving soul, while the shadow-soul emerges as a complementary soul, presumably a free-soul whose functions have faded with time. At the same time that the life-soul represents the continuity between the living and the dead, it is to a certain extent also the bearer of the attributes of the free-soul. The Menomini, says Skinner, believed in two souls in every human being. The one which is called "a shade across," resides in the head and is the intellect. After death it becomes a grave ghost. The other is the real soul, *tcebai*, which has its seat in the heart and at death travels to the realm of the dead.

The soul in the heart is probably the life-soul, while the so-called intellect-soul is both ego-soul and free-soul, and therefore stands for the person. Skinner and Satterlee also reported a tradition which describes how to recall someone who has been massacred back to life. First, his numerous bones are fitted together, then his "scattered shade" is restored. This dualism between the souls appears in a so-called true story about how a dead woman returned to life. First her shade appeared, "like a shadow on the wall," and much later "she really came to life." Another story describes a man suddenly falling down dead after returning from the wilderness. "His heart had been taken out of him in the night by the powerful god, Owl, and it was only his shade that arrived home." The intellect-soul remained when the life-soul had been taken away, but it was unable to sustain the individual for more than a short time. What makes it clear that the life-soul has been taken is the way, in cases of illness, that the shaman, in order to effect a cure, first catches the life-soul and then forces the fugitive to return to its place in the breast.

The soul concepts of the Sauk Indians were first reported by the members of Long's celebrated research expedition in 1823. Keating reports that one Sauk Indian, Wennebea, described "a difference between the soul and the spirit; the former being probably, in his opinion, nothing else but the principle of vitality; with its seat in the heart." The dualism noted here was probably of the same sort as that among the Menomini.

The soul beliefs of the Fox, closely connected with the Sauk Indians, have been noted by Jones and Michelson. "There are two kinds of souls," Michelson was told, "one is like a shadow in the daytime and also at night. When this soul leaves you, you die. When the same soul inside leaves, we stop breathing and die." The outer soul (the soul that stays outside) is the large soul, the culture hero's gift to man while the inner soul is the small soul, a gift of the Great Spirit. "The small soul is the same as life. The large soul simply watches over the other. When a child is still unborn, the small soul is already within it, and the large soul is close to the unborn child." The dualism here is between the free-soul and the life-soul. The supervising function of the free-soul brings it closer to the guardian spirit. Michelson says that the large soul exercises an evil influence over us, while the small soul a exerts a good influence. Quite likely this value dualism in soul belief originated in the same ethical contrasts that created the distance between the Supreme Being and his powerful offspring, Wisaka.

Skinner says that the Plains Algonquin, specifically the Plains Cree in Saskatchewan exhibit a soul dualism resembling the Menomini. "There are two kinds of souls," Skinner says, one, the *tcipai*, which stays behind with the corpse in the grave, and another, the *niukaneo*, which goes to the hereafter." Now it seems probable that *tcipai*, at least here, is not a soul so much as a ghost. Mandelbaum tells us that the dead who have not been given a proper funeral feast linger in the vicinity and haunt the dwellings of the living, and "are called *tcipayak*, or ghosts." At the same time the deceased in the realm of the dead seem also to have been called *tcipai*, at least, according to Richardson. Among the more easterly Cree the soul was called *atchak*. This soul appears to have had a predominantly free-soul character.

Tcipai is evidently the designation for the dead person, but Mandelbaum introduces in its stead the word *ahtca'k*, which he defines as an undifferentiated life force. "The soul," he says, "entered the body at birth and left at death. It resided along the nape of the neck. Only when danger threatened did a man feel the presence of his soul along the back of his neck. During a vision the soul could leave the body and travel about with the spirit helper. This was the soul that experienced all contacts with the supernatural visitor." To judge from this quotation, *ahtca'k* is rather more free-soul than life-soul. It is harder to define the character of *niukaneo*...perhaps it was life-soul or ego-soul, but whichever it may be, the Plains Cree certainly believed man had two souls.

Among the Atsina, Curtis says, "there are three souls, or perhaps it should be said that the soul has three forms," the black shadow, which follows one during the day, the light-black shadow, which is "the ghost that goes about doing mischief," and the invisible shadow, which is "the spirit that goes to the Big Sand," the realm of the dead. Probably none of these conceptions deserves the name soul and might be best interpreted as the natural shadow, understood as a mystical extension of the individual, the ghost, and the deceased individual in the realm of the dead. Possibly the latter is the free-soul during the person's life-time, and the spook-ghost an inner soul, or vice-versa.

The information about the Cheyenne is both sparse and obscure, giving rise to the question of whether it is possible to establish a belief in dual souls. Grinnell, the chief authority on the Cheyenne, says: "A man's spirit or living principle is called his shade or shadow, his *tasoom*, which is the soul, mind, or spiritual part; the immortal part of a dying person who has lost consciousness and merely breathes. Of him they may say his *tasoom* has been gone a long time; he is only just breathing." What is more a man can see his shadow-soul when in a fully conscious and active state, though this generally forebodes his death. A woman, however, may often see her shadow-soul without coming to any harm. The shadow-soul is evidently the free-soul. Grinnell tells us nothing about the life-soul, which exists here only by implication.

There is, however, a tradition among the Cheyenne in which life is seen as a special entity in man, and it is probably by no means out of the question that Grinnell is talking about the life-soul.

Chapter Four
The Mound Builder Peoples

Of the non-Algonquin peoples in eastern North America (inspired by the mound builder culture of the deeper South), the Iroquoian, Muskhogean, Siouan, and Caddoan believed in dual souls.

The Iroquois, according to Hewitt, carefully discriminated between the soul which animates the body and the soul which resides in the skeleton after death; the reasonable and intelligent soul. Where people believed in multiple souls, only those endowed with reason and intelligence could be divided. The animating soul is never split into multiple souls. In addition Hewitt recognized that not all individuals had the same number of souls. While that makes it difficult to draw up a complete and systematic soul-schema, it is still possible using Hewitt's results to reconstruct the soul beliefs held by the Iroquois

The dualism Hewitt found between life-soul and intellect-soul occurs in the older source material (work such as Jean de Quens did with the Iroquois Onondaga). "These people," he said, "believe that sadness, anger, and all violent passions expel the rational soul from the body, which meanwhile is animated only by the sensitive-soul, which we have in common with animals."

What that seems to show is a life-soul identical to an ego-soul governing the passions, and that the intellect-soul was associated with the concept of free-soul. The ego-soul was a fairly plastic entity among the Iroquois. It was split, according to de Quens, into two intellect-souls and a wish-soul. The wish-soul, "the mind considered as the seat of sentiment," may very well have functioned as an assistant to the life-soul. Its essence is the opposite of the intellect-soul, and it was like the free-soul in its opposition to the emotive-soul. Hewitt, too, points out that the reasoning-soul can leave and return to the body at will, especially in dreams and visions, which would seem to indicate a kind of fusion between the ego-soul and the free-soul. The dualism between the intellect-soul and the emotive-soul is much like the dualism between free-soul and life-soul.

The Cayuga, Speck says, believed in two souls, one which they called the real or main soul. It is eternal and goes to the Great Spirit. The other was called the ghost spirit, which unless satisfied was apt to gad about on earth disturbing people and causing illness.

Boyle, who investigated the soul beliefs of the "civilized" Iroquois in Ontario, says that the Iroquois were slaves to their dreams, regarding them as the experiences of the first of their three souls. The second soul always remained with the body, and the third became visible as the shadow. What is also surprising is how little the soul beliefs of the Iroquois changed following the invasion of the Jesuits and Christianity. Even the Iroquois reformer, Handsome Lake, did not purge dualistic soul beliefs from his doctrine.

Brebeuf says that the Huron believed in a single soul, but they gave it different names according to its condition or function. Brebeuf gives one name to the soul which animates the body and gives it life, and he then offers three other names for the soul, "in so far as it is possessed of reason, in so far as it thinks and deliberates on anything, and in so far as it bears affection to any object." What he is talking about are three different ego-souls, including two intellect-souls and one wish-soul. Finally, he notes that once the soul is separated from the body the Huron called it *esken*, and they even had a name for the bones of the dead, *atisken*. Such notions were entirely foreign to Brebeuf: "...they think of the soul as divisible, and you would have all the difficulty in the world to make them believe that our soul is entire in all parts of the body."

The soul dualism of the Huron emerges more distinctly in other notes from Brebeuf and in Ragueneau's account. The many souls are quickly reduced to two souls in the following explanation by a Huron chief. "Many think we have two souls, both of them being divisible and material, and yet both reasonable; the one separates itself from the body at death...the other is bound to the body and informs the corpse." Further light is thrown upon this dualism by Ragueneau's observation that one soul was a reasoning soul, the other a sensitive soul, and that in dreams the reasoning soul acted outside the body.

Because both free-soul and life-soul were connected with ego-soul conceptions, the effect is to supplement the dualism between free-soul and life-soul with a dualism between the ego-souls. The Orpheus-like legend of the Huron offers an example of how this all operated. In this story the hero brings his dead sister back to life by fetching two pumpkins from the realm of the dead. In one of them he has the sister in miniature, in the other he has her brain. By the rules of native psychology, the sister represented the free-soul and the brain the ego-soul. What appears is a life-soul, with the sensitive ego-soul as complement, and on the other hand, a free-soul, whose functions have been completely identified with the activity of the ego-soul, or at least one of the ego-souls. This fusion might signify a move toward a unitary soul concept but for the cleavage of the ego-soul which counteracts it.

This also applies to the soul beliefs of the Creek. Of the Southeastern folk groups, at least the Creek and the Choctaw believed in dual souls. Bartram has shown that the Creek believed in a life-soul residing in the intestines, a soul which did not leave until after death, and an extra-physical soul as well. His information on this subject is valuable, as it throws light upon Hewitt's discussion of *inu'tska.* According to Hewitt this soul (the name signifies talent and genius) gives rise, to "thought, planning, and devising," and is therefore an intellect-soul; an ego-soul on a higher plane. But Hewitt goes on to say that "man's *inu'tska* is also the spirit which goes with him through life and talks to him in his dreams and is called the good spirit."

If you compare that with Bartram's report, you might get the impression that this soul constituted a semi-independent potency outside the body; a free-soul that has developed into a being or spirit wielding actual power. But in truth this soul is what Hewitt calls life spirit, a life-soul, which is a sensitive-soul, meaning that the dualism of Creek soul structure is close to the Iroquois.

The Seminole, who are for the most part descendants of Creek Indians who had fled to Florida, believed that at death both souls go, after a few days, to the realm of the dead. The soul which departs first, according to both Hewitt and Swanton, is a free-soul with a distinct dream-soul character. We may assume that the other soul is a body-soul.

Wright says the Choctaw thought that man had two souls. They believed that "every man had *shilombish*, the outside shadow, which always followed him, and *shilup*, the inside shadow or ghost, which at death goes to the land of ghosts. The *shilombish* was supposed to remain upon the earth. The dualism between external free-soul and internal body-soul seems clear. Time and Christian influence have combined to efface the former dualism among the modern Choctaw, and now the soul appears both as dream-soul and as a soul which dies with the body. Bushnell writes: "They seem to have had a vague idea of a spirit in the body, but when the spirit died, then man, or rather the body, ceases to move." That leads to what seems a reasonable conclusion, that the Choctaw once believed in an external free-soul, which was also a dream-soul; an interior soul, probably of ego-soul type, which took its name and appearance from the fact that it represented the individual after death; and finally, a life-soul that died with the body.

Among the Siouan peoples of the Southeast there are no definite instances of soul dualism. But the more westerly groups, linguistically related to them have for the most part, believed in several souls in every individual, and some of them have believed in dual souls as do the Winnebago at Lake Michigan. Significantly, this tribe was surrounded by the Central Algonquin, who had a well-developed soul dualism.

In the origin myth of the Thunder Bird clan, we are told by Radin that the Creator, Earthmaker, gave man a mind or thinking soul, a tongue, soul, and breath. If you eliminate the tongue, (which was most likely added to reach the sacred number four), you are left with an ego-soul and a breath-soul, or two body-souls, and a soul which is probably the free-soul.

Using Winnebago religious terms, Radin distinguishes between "the soul which inheres in living man and which dies when he dies," and "the soul that leaves man upon death, the soul which is eternal and which returns to spirit-land, in other words, to the universe at large." The first-mentioned soul is evidently the body-soul, the last-mentioned, the free-soul. In discussing the free-soul, Radin adds that "this concept is not clearly developed as a separable entity among the Winnebago because of their strong belief in reincarnation. Their notion of the soul is merged into that of the non-corporeal ghost who eventually comes to earth again." The idea of the free-soul is thus subordinate to the concept of the deceased who bears its name (*wananxirak*).

The Sioux on the Plains are in general known for their belief that man has four souls. This may mean, of course, that in many cases the fourfold soul is a theoretical construction, a superstructure erected on an original soul dualism, which seems natural if you accept the psychological viewpoints applied here. As a matter of fact, a closer analysis of the four soul concept of several Sioux groups shows that the dualism between two souls should be understood as fundamental. It should be pointed out that the distinction between *Wanare* and *Wahkan* among the Dakota, reported by Keating, refers to the difference between soul and power, and not between two souls, as Brinton thought.

The Eastern Dakota, Skinner writes, believed "like the Cree and Menomini that each person had two spirits (some say four), one of which, the soul, went to the other world." It is useful here to add what J. O. Dorsey has to say about the soul beliefs of the Sioux with special reference to the Teton Dakota. "Among the tribes of the Siouan Family," he writes, "the word *wanaghi*, rendered here as 'ghost,' means more than apparition. The living man is supposed to have one, two, or more *wanaghi*, one of which after death remains at the grave and another goes to the place of the departed." Despite the presence of four souls, the functions of only two souls are mentioned and in a way which leaves the impression that it is a matter of body-soul and free-soul.

The more detailed reports of the soul beliefs of the Dakota tribes by Lynd and Walker do not invalidate the view advanced here, but appear, on the contrary, to confirm it. Of the four (or five) souls which according to Lynd belong to every individual, the first is "supposed to be a spirit of the body, and dies with the body," and the third "accounts for the deeds of the body, and is supposed by some to go to the south (by others, to the west) after the death of the body." This is functional soul dualism behind an outer facade formed by the four soul system.

Walker worked with an important branch of the Teton Dakota, the Oglala, whose soul terminology is obscured by ingenious religious speculation, though not enough to prevent a glimpse of the underlying original belief. The free-cum-ego-soul here is *nagi*, which "abides with its recipient until death, controlling the disposition and actions of the person." When the owner dies it goes to the spirit land and becomes the spirit. Another soul *niya*, "abides with the person like a shadow until death," and functions "to cause vitality, to forewarn of good and evil, and to give the power to influence others. When it departs from the body, this is death."

In the words of the Oglala Indian, One Star, the dualism between the notion of power (*sicun*) and the soul concept, and between free-soul and life-soul, appears clearly: "A *sicun* is a man's spirit. A man's real spirit is different from his *sicun* spirit. *Ni* is also like a spirit. It is a man's breath." Clearly the Oglala have among their many souls a free-soul and a life-soul.

Dualism is also concealed behind the multifaceted soul beliefs of the village groups belonging to the Sioux in North Dakota. Curtis mentions three souls for the Hidatsa (four souls according to Matthews). The first is the physical shadow ("the shadow that follows the body in the day"), the second, obviously the free-soul ("the spirit that is active in dreams and visions, leaving and acting independently of the body"), and the third, just as obviously, the ego-soul ("the mentality, always present with the body"). The dualism is complete if one sees in the shadow an extension of the individual, which certainly seems reasonable.

Soul dualism is less distinct among the Mandan, but now and then you can catch a glimpse of it in discussions of the lighter of human shadows, and how it goes, after death, to the realm of the dead, while the other, darker shadows remain with the body.

The third village tribe in North Dakota, the Arikara, hold a less complicated soul belief than their Sioux neighbors. By all appearances, they believed in a unitary soul. Their linguistic kin in Nebraska, the Pawnee, are renowned for their well-developed ceremonies, their secret societies, and their powerful mythology. Here, if anywhere, you might expect to find a concept of the soul shaped by philosophical speculation.

But the Pawnee are a conservative people, and the dualism between free-soul/ego-soul on the one hand and life-soul/or better, life-stuff, on the other hand, can be seen in a medley of ritual and symbol. Fletcher says the initiated priest proclaims that the winds from the four corners of the world, not the ordinary winds, have proceeded from the breath of the Heavenly Father, and "bring to man the breath by which he lives." Here the life-soul is embedded in a pantheistic context typical of the religious imagination of the Pawnee. The pendant of the breath is *chixu,* "the spirit or mind of a person or thing." This soul is first and foremost a free-soul. Fletcher says the Pawnee "regard the spirit of man, animals, and all other things as able to travel about independent of the body. But it is also *chixu* to whom the priest refers in the Hako rite when he says 'we must fix our minds (*chixu ti uchitika*)' on the object of our activity." In the final analysis the Pawnee have a life-soul combined with a free-cum-ego-soul, a permutation which may have been driven by mystical meditation.

Chapter Five
Soul Dualism in the West and Northern Mexico

This last area includes the Pueblo culture, the Great Basin, Southern California, North Mexico, and the peoples in the peripheral Plains regions and Northern California. The Shoshone groups that populated an extensive area from the Plains in the east to the Pacific Ocean in the west in a great many cases believed man had dual souls, and that is certainly true of the Plains Shoshone of Wyoming, some Paviotso and Paiute groups, the Tubatulabal, and some southern Shoshone groups in Southern California.

The Wind River Shoshone in Wyoming possess two dominating soul aspects, *mugua* and *navujieip*. The former originally represented vitality, life, while the latter was the individual as he appeared in dreams and in other psychic absences. More precisely, *mugua* was the corporeal soul, *navujieip,* the separable soul. Over time *mugua* absorbed elements which originally belonged to the free-soul, while *navujieip* approached the notion of tutelary spirit. They also had a third soul concept, an ego-soul which was associated with the breath.

While among these Plains Shoshone soul dualism seems clear, it is difficult to penetrate among their linguistic kin in the Great Basin. In some quarters people even seem to have developed a belief in a single soul. Another difficulty arises in trying to compare different concepts among the numerous Paviotso groups. There can, however, scarcely be any doubt that a belief in dualism existed, with one soul identified as *mugua* and the other the breath or mind, though later, as Natches pointed out, they became identical.

The interplay between the souls is splendidly illustrated in a shaman song about bringing back the soul, in which the expressions for the soul vary frequently. First the person's spirit emerges, then the person's soul leaves, and finally the shamans bring the person back. The spirit is the breath-soul, the soul is *mugua*, and the person combines the two souls with the living individual. Based on observations by Park, Natches, and Stewart, the breath-soul or mind (the soul contrasted with *mugua*) is at the same time the free-soul. The Shoshone term, *mugua*, is not clearly defined as a life-soul, but tends to play the role of free-soul, as it does with the Wind River Shoshone.

The life-soul of the Paviotso is clearly similar both to the Shoshone and the Eastern Mono. J. H. Steward recorded the soul concepts of this group. "One has a soul, *mugua*, and a ghost, *takawahuva*. The soul is like a shadow, in no special part of the body, it 'makes life,' and goes to the land of the dead. The ghost remains in the country of the living after death, visiting people and serving witches." The ghost is perhaps a rudimentary free soul, but *mugua* is both life-soul and surviving soul, and in addition it is an ego-soul which certainly represents the individual's own ego-consciousness.

According to Stewart, the Ute believe in two souls. The loss of one causes sickness, and if both souls depart the owner dies. Among the Ute in the Wasatch Mountains, one of the souls appears to have resided in the head, the other in the heart. The Colorado Ute believed the souls resided in the heart and the stomach, but whatever dualistic relationship once existed between those souls, is now difficult to reconstruct.

Sometimes it is hard to avoid the impression that in more modern times dualism has fallen into oblivion, or at the very least, ambiguity. Consider the following quote from Kelly about the Las Vegas Paiute in South Nevada. "After the mind leaves the body it turns into the soul, which has wings and goes into the air." Two different names stand for mind and soul. The soul described here seems to refer to the dead person for the souls of the living do not merge, either terminologically or conceptually. Such a union of souls may take place after death as it does among a couple of Sioux tribes and among another Shoshone people, the Tubatulabal.

The soul beliefs of the Tubatulabal have been analyzed by

Voegelin. What she refers to as the soul is a free-soul concept. The free-soul temporarily leaves the body during sleep. "When you dream it is your soul that goes out and does the things you dream." But there is also a breath-soul. "When a person dies, his breath, which stays in the heart during life, goes out, together with soul, and the latter becomes breath, but looks like a human being, and is referred to as a devil or ghost." Here the dualistic concept is undeniable.

Finally, among the Shoshone groups in the deserts of Southern California, in particular the Juaneno and Luiseno, people exhibit a clear soul dualism. Kroeber writes: "Of immaterial essences, the *piuch* (*piuts*) or breath was distinguished from the *shun* (*pu-suni*) or heart. The former corresponded somewhat to our idea of life, the latter rather to the soul." The life-soul here is contrasted with the free-soul.

Among the Luiseno Kroeber found that *shun* was "the part of the person believed to go to the stars." It is probably this soul Sparkman described in the following passage: "When a person dies people blow three times, with the idea of assisting his soul or spirit (heart) to rise to the sky." The counterpart of the Juaneno's breath-soul should be *piwish*, a term for the Milky Way, which leads to the notion that the Milky Way and the breath of life are connected. When you consider that the Milky Way is called "the Spirit to whom our spirits go when they die," according to DuBois, and is symbolized by a special figure, *wanawut*, which represents the spirit of man, it seems likely that *piwish* has alternated with *kwinamish*. This word signifies root or origin, and Kroeber says it "is much used to designate the spirit." This being is called "our spirit," says DuBois, and in the symbolism it is compared with *wanawut*. The life-soul, whether it has been called *piwish* or *kwinamish*, corresponds to a free-soul, the heart or *shun*, which after death became *towish*, the deceased, the ghost.

The source material does not make it possible to say definitely just how widespread soul dualism may have been among the peoples of northern California. The soul beliefs of the Modoc come to us through Curtin's collection of legends, one of which describes a visionary experience. It tells of a young man's calling to the office of shaman. The youth fainted when he met a female ghost (*Skoks*) who took out his heart. "The boy lay on the ground as if dead, but his spirit heard the *Skoks* talk to his heart as she sat on the air and held the heart in her hand. After a while she opened her hand and let go of the heart. Then the little boy thought he saw a bird coming from the west. It came to him and lighted on his breast. That moment he jumped up."

It is probably not going too far to see in this a soul dualism of the ordinary kind; a free soul which operates while the individual is unconscious, and a life-soul connected with the heart. From information gathered by Powers, it appears that the life of the individual was identified with the breath.

The Shasta constitute an uncertain case, reminiscent of the Plains Cheyenne. According to Dixon, the terms for soul and life were identical among the Shasta, but that depends, of course, upon what is meant by life. Holt describes how the body of a sick man "lay breathing quietly...when in fact the life had already departed." It is natural to assume that life is the actual life-motor, whose absence would, of course, cause death. But it is also possible that life is nothing other than the free-soul, which may depart while its owner is still healthy. This seems likely when you compare Dixon's information with de Angulo's notes on the Achomawi, one of the more easterly branches of the Shasta at Pit River. They have a shadow-soul, *delamdzi*, which is identical with the soul that leaves the body in dreams, and with the deceased himself...clearly a free-soul.

The Atsugewi, the linguistic kin of the Achomawi and their nearest neighbors in the south (based on the work of Voegelin) describe a free-soul which left the body during sickness and in dreams. Definite instances of dualism are known from two other northern Californian peoples. The Karuk in northwestern California distinguish between *pikship* the shadow-soul, the free-soul, and *imya*, breath and life. Loeb says that one of his informants among the Eastern Pomo "believed in two souls. He had discussed the matter with a female sucking doctor and found her ideas much the same. One of these souls went out in times of dreams to return to the body upon awakening, while the other soul left the body at death." The last was by all appearances an ego-soul.

It is likely that the Penutian peoples held corresponding beliefs, but it is difficult to produce any binding proof in the face of modern reports from the Nomlaki and Yokuts which seem to afford evidence of a belief in a single soul. The ethnographical notes have, however, shown that a memory of a real dualism existed among at least one of these peoples, the Northern Wintun, or Wintu, who used the word, *les*, to refer to the souls of both the living and the spirits of the dead. "It is what a person has with him. Maybe it is somewhere in the back of the head," one Wintu Indian explained. "When a person is alive his *les* is always around the house. If you travel your *les* follows you, but doesn't get there until evening. Your *les* is always about a day or half-a-day behind you." DuBois says that the soul is not believed to wander about when a person dreams.

From the pronouncement of another Wintu it appears that *les* is thought of as a shadow, which allows it to fulfill the function of a free-soul. The life-maintaining soul is called *winesxuyat*, and its features are preserved only in the mythology. DuBois, however, recognizes it as "the vital principle." From her description it appears to be a combination of ego-soul and life-soul, and therefore, a body-soul in the wider sense of the term.

The soul beliefs of the Central Wintun, the Nomlaki, seem in modern times to have been concentrated around the free-soul. We know little about the soul conceptions of the South Wintun or Patwin, and though a number of designations for the soul from the River Patwin have been preserved by Kroeber, the notions covered by these terms have not been recorded. For the Maidu, our sources are a good deal more scanty, though Dixon and Kroeber seem to say they believed in a single soul. Dixon writes, "All human beings, and all animals as well, are supposed to have souls. These are generally spoken of as 'hearts,' and often, in speaking of the death of a person, it will be said that 'his heart has gone away.' This 'heart' seems to be regarded as identical with the ghost seen occasionally by shamans and other persons." Kroeber says "what we call the soul, the Maidu called heart. In a swoon or in a dream a person's heart leaves his body."

The free-soul concept that Dixon and Kroeber identify with the heart fits *hon*, or soul-heart, among the Yuba River Maidu. But the question is whether it represents the only soul among these Maidu. In his account of their religious terminology, Loeb also offers the designation for breath. Among the Northwest Hill Maidu, *honi* is heart-soul, but it is not the only soul, as *wono* is used for the soul that leaves the body when a person faints or dies. Both the Maidu groups also had designations for the ghost and the shadow, both of which belong to the sphere of religion, but it is uncertain whether they had anything to do with the soul concepts proper. However, the question is not important because what we know about the soul concepts of the Maidu establish their belief in more than one soul, which quite likely shared a du-alistic relationship.

The Yuman peoples, which include the Kamia, lived in the Southwest proper, which begins, ethnographically, in southern California. At first glance their beliefs seem confusing, but upon examination a fundamental dualism comes clear. Gifford says these people believed in *matahaau*, the apparition of a living person, and *isasli*, the invisible spirit or ghost, which is probably identical with the heart, or *yuuspum*. After the cremation of the corpse, the heart is transformed into an owl. The shadow seems to be without religious or magical significance, and the dualism lies in the relationship between man's spirit and his soul, which after death are united to restore his individuality. By all appearances the spirit is nothing other than the body-soul, which gives expression at the same time to life and consciousness. At death *isaslich* carries on the consciousness of the individual. The soul, on the other hand, is the free-soul which "as an apparition" leaves a man during dreams, in sickness and at death. Curiously enough it was possible to possess several such souls, sometimes as many as four.

The Cocopa distinguish between a dream-soul or spirit and a soul localized in the body, which is also a surviving soul. Gifford reports that dreams are caused by the dream-soul, *matkwisa* or *mitha'au*, leaving the body and experiencing dream events. This spirit is distinct from the soul or ghost which left the body at death. The last-mentioned soul, the *loxachak*, also resides in the body, but leaves it temporarily when a person falls into a faint or a trance, and it leaves permanently at death in order to carry on the person's life in the realm of the dead. The surviving soul among the Yuma is a body-soul, *metr'ao*, which "dwells within the body and is associated with the heart." Besides this soul there are a number of smaller body-souls. "The pulses which can be felt at various parts of the body are considered as small independent souls, and their loss may cause sickness." Finally, Ford says, the shadow, *metkwica*, has a soul-like quality, and its loss (through witchcraft) means sickness for its owner. The shadow, which on the death of the individual disappears into space, is obviously the free-soul.

The soul-beliefs of the Maricopa are similar to the Yuma according to Spier. The free-soul of dreams is the shadow, which after the death of the individual appears as a ghost in the whirlwind and "the ghost is just the shadow of the dead person." Kutox, Spier's chief informant among the Maricopa, offered this description of dreaming. "If I am asleep here, there is my shadow. If the spirits wanted to talk to me, they would take me out, that is, that part of me something like my shadow. A dreamer's shadow (*matkwlca*) has the experience with the spirit birds, not his soul (*wipai*)." Spier finds this pronouncement vague and unsatisfactory, but against the background of what we know of the way in which soul dualism functions and of the nature of the soul beliefs held by other Yuman tribes, there is nothing vague or strange in the account of the Maricopa Indian. It speaks, on the contrary, quite clearly. The *wipai*, of the soul proper, the vital principle, seems to be the chief life-soul, which in cases of sickness leaves the body and which after death carries on the life of the individual in the realm of the dead. Other life-souls are the souls of the heart and the pulses, which do not leave the body until it is cremated.

Spier has compared these soul-concepts with the soul beliefs held by the Havasupai, a closely related tribe living in the vicinity, who exhibit a similar dualism between heart-soul and free-soul. "Each human has a soul in his heart," Spier writes and "the word, *yuwativ*, refers to both soul and heart. It leaves his body at death, but not when he dreams or lies unconscious. More explicitly, when a man dreams that he is in a foreign land, he sees (or feels) his fleshly self as actor, not his soul. To be sure when he wakes he is lying where he fell asleep, he is fully aware that he has been dreaming, yet he offers no explanation why others saw his slumbering form when he thought himself in another place."

Among the Northeast Yavapai the soul dualism is distinct. Here, *yapei* is life, alive, spirit, soul. It leaves the body during dreams and experiences the events of the dream, afterwards returning to the body. At death it departs, never to return. Alongside this free-soul there is *chilkomal* or "soul of living person," which also disappears at death. This is a life-soul, and it is closely associated with the breath and the mind.

An account of the soul beliefs of the Walapai is given in the

"Walapai Ethnography" published by Kroeber, in collaboration with many others. The picture which emerges shows that during the life of the individual, one soul is attached to the body, and after death goes on living. It is called heart, soul, spirit. Another soul, spirit-in-heart, can leave the body even during the lifetime of the individual, creating a condition known as empty body. Presumably only the body-soul goes on living.

The beliefs of the Piman tribes fit well with these groups, and a dualism arises in the soul beliefs of the Papago Indians. The Kikimai Papago assumed the existence of two souls, one of which left the body immediately after the person died, while the other, probably the body-soul, remained in the corpse until eight days after burial. Gifford says it then became an owl.

Dualism appears also to have existed among some very southerly Piman tribes in Mexico, among the already mentioned Cora, and among the close neighbors of the Cora, the Huichol, who believed in a rather comprehensive body-soul (ego-soul and life-soul) and a free-soul identified with the individual.

The relatively late arriving South Athapascans, the Apache, and Navajo, may well have believed in dual souls, but the available reports do not allow such a conclusion without further evidence. In a couple of cases Goodwin says that the White Mountain Apache held the notion of a single soul. "Life and breath are one and the same," he writes, "and no other element in man is separately comparable to a soul." This may be the case, but it is strange that when someone dies there is mention of still another soul component, the shadow. "On the fourth day after death, the life or breath and shadow starts to the land of the dead."

The Jicarilla Apache, according to Opler, assume a distinction between the breath or spirit, and the ghost. At death, the breath goes to the realm of the dead, while the ghost remains with the corpse for four days and is then transformed into an animal, as a rule a coyote. "Even though you are still living, your ghost is around you. Sometimes the ghost goes into a bird or animal before you die." But as long as the breath is there you are alive. Is the ghost here a free-soul?

Further confusion comes from Goodwin. "If a person marries a Pueblo Indian first and then a Ute, when he dies one part of his body becomes owl and the other prairie dog." Even having intercourse once produces that effect, and as Goodwin's source says, "it is just as bad." Opler has shown how this belief in metamorphosis functions as a brake on undesirable tribal exogamy. By illegally marrying a woman of another tribe you become at death the animal represented by the other tribe and forfeit the right to fellowship with your original group. Is, then, the ghost's division after death simply a consequence of this social attitude, or does it afford evidence of an experienced participation mystique? In the case of the Apache, a free-soul seems possible, but with the Pueblo it seems to have been more a matter of social control.

The soul concepts of the Navajo are confusing. There is no agreement between investigators, and moreover, there is no comprehensible summary of Navajo soul beliefs. Much better information is available about the body-souls of the Navajo. The myth tells us how the two first human beings created by Talking God received life. *Niltshi,* the wind, blew the breath of life into them, Rock Crystal Boy gave them senses, and Grasshopper Girl gave them voices. Of these souls the breath is the most important or so it would appear from work done by Wyman, Hill, and Osanai. "It is the breath or wind which leaves the body and goes to the afterworld. Breath is a manifestation of life. Those winds are localized in all the fingers, a Navajo Indian explained, "these Winds stay in the body directing its movements until death and then emerge." Alongside these life-souls there is a Great Wind which streams through the body. This Wind controls our speech and is the good part of a man."

This soul, a light-element emanating from the Sun and at death returning to the Sun, has two names, which are translated as, "by means of which there is life," and, "by means of which one breathes." This is the actual life principle, the breath as a spiritual potency, a superior life-soul. Reichard's work outlines a new soul entity; mind, will power, volition, reason, awareness, an ego-soul, which "keeps body and spirit in adjustment."

The Navajo quoted by Wyman also described a symbol or guiding principle of evil thoughts and actions with its seat in the back of the head, "where you see the depression." This evil soul is a second ego-soul. It is also a forerunner of *tcindi*, the ghost, and it can be separated from the individual before his decline if he reaches an advanced age.

It becomes increasingly difficult to establish beliefs in a dual soul as you study people with more developed cultures, especially those tribes adjacent to the central ethnic groups of the Southwest culture, the Pueblo peoples, who tend to merge their soul concepts. The direct influence on other tribes by the remarkable Pueblo culture was considerable, and among the Pueblo a belief in a single soul is firmly anchored in their history.

Only among one Pueblo tribe, the Zuni, is it possible to trace the remains of an older, possibly dualistic, soul concept. "According to Zuni belief," Bunzel says, "man has a spiritual substance, a soul. This is associated with the head, the heart, and the breath." This is the modern belief, and it seems possible through this to arrive at the older concepts behind the single concept.

The soul signifies thoughts and refers, to judge by the name, to the psychic qualities constituting an ego-soul. In this case it should be associated with the head and the heart. The head is the seat of skill and intelligence, but the heart is the seat of the emotions and of profound thought. "I shall take it to my heart" means "I shall ponder it carefully, and remember it long." Bunzel also uses the word for life, which translated literally means light of day, with the breath as its symbol.

This makes it possible to distinguish between ego-soul and life-soul, but where is the free-soul? "In rare instances," according to Bunzel, "the soul can leave the body and return to it again. This occurs during sickness and is a serious matter." Soul loss is generally equated with the free-soul but by no means always. The probability is that the notion of the free-soul has paled and fallen into oblivion, and that, as Hagar points out, its functions have been assumed by the ego-soul which can be projected outside the body, even when the individual is not ill.

In so far as I can apply statistical viewpoints, and here I am exercising great caution, the dualism between free-soul and life-soul is the most common form of soul dualism. This is certainly not an accident. By emphasizing those functions in man connected with the life process, the life-soul appears in sharp relief to the unbound free-soul, and this operates to make the dualism between free-soul and life-soul the most pronounced and typical form of soul dualism.

The dualism between free-soul and ego-soul contains the seed of its own dissolution in as much as the ego-soul, because of its inadequate physical anchor, easily changes places in the dual relation or ends up at both ends of the equation. The dynamic structure of soul dualism is easiest to understand if you look at the way it functions. But without more detailed knowledge of how soul elements function (a knowledge not provided in the literature), using such an approach cannot be justified.

From the research it is possible to reconstruct, on broad lines, the distribution of soul dualism, though because the information does not completely cover the areas in which soul dualism has actually existed, the information cannot be used to develop a statistical base. Even so, it is clear that dualism in soul beliefs has existed in a rather even distribution over the whole of native North America with the exception of the Pueblo region, which must instead be considered as a part of the area where belief in a single soul belief held sway. The center of this area was probably in Mexico and the countries to the south of Mexico in the American high-culture.

I have, from other points of departure, tried to establish the origin of belief in the dualism of the soul, and in this connection soul dualism constitutes a psychological phenomenon which has probably occurred among all peoples. What decides the priority of the dualistic concept of the soul is, it seems to me, the fact that it has a directness and an inner self-evidence that belief in a single soul lacks. Functionally and psychologically, the single soul represents a younger soul than the concept of two souls. Ehnmark has quite rightly pointed out that in the study of early religion, historical and psychological arguments have been mixed, and both have been used to throw light on the problems of origin.

The picture of the age of soul dualism in North America that develops by using historical methods agrees well with the notion that dualism preceded belief in a single soul, a concept which has also been reached using psychological methods. The nearer you get to high-culture, the more the single soul predominates, and this helps in establishing a chronology. The single soul in the Pueblo culture, based on its uniformity, arose at around the same time, which justifies the assumption that the belief came from the same late cultures that produced the Mexican high culture. Soul dualism, on the other hand, reflects earlier cultures.

The geographical distribution of soul dualism is in itself enough to give the impression that it dominated soul belief in North America. That impression is strengthened by the fact that about eighty cases of soul dualism were recorded as against some forty cases of belief in a single soul, many of which are uncertain. What is certain is that in its most typical form, soul-dualism demonstrates reciprocity between free-soul and life-soul, represents the oldest form of soul-belief in North America up to the Christian mission period (and frequently enough even up to our own days), and was the most general form of soul belief in North America.

Chapter Six
The Life-soul

The life-soul is the body motor which controls respiration, heartbeat, pulse, circulation, and muscle movements. This vital principle can also be subdivided among several lesser life-souls whose existence does not, however, exclude the presence of a life-soul holding all the parts together. Behind this belief lies the everyday experience of being alive, completely independent of conscious power.

Older writers maintain that the life-soul is identical with the organ it instructs. It is, however, not possible to show that such a soul belief ever existed among the native peoples of North America. Instead the breath is an expression for the life-soul itself and is not understood as a physical substratum (as it is for us). It is simply the soul which gives the individual or certain of his organs life and vitality.

In many cases there is a distinct difference between the life-soul and its organs. The general life-soul among the Netsilik Eskimo and the Western Dene seems to flow through the entire body as uniform energy, free from association with any definite organ. It is such a detachment which characterizes breath-soul belief among many peoples. Sometimes the temporary absence of the life-soul causes illness, but this does not imply that the organ associated with the soul has also departed. Michelson says, for example, that among the Fox the life-souls of husband and wife are always together during their lifetimes. That would be impossible if the souls could not free themselves from the bodies they animate.

It is clear that despite its vital importance for existence, the life-soul need not be completely bound to the body. The detached character of the life-soul is possible because it is not identical to particular organs but is a source of strength which imbues these organs, or the individual, with life and activity. The Wind River Shoshone describe the life-soul as a potency, a driving force which steers the entire organism: *"Mugua* makes you live, it makes you breathe, move, and see," Reichard says.

Even movements in a dead body may be ascribed to spiritual activity. DuPratz once saw a dead kingfisher that a Natchez had hung on a thread from the ceiling of a house, fly up in a draft as if it were alive, causing an Indian to remark that its soul must still be controlling the body. The power of movement is clearly an independent "motor-potency." Fletcher says that "the ability to move is to the Omaha mind synonymous with life."

It seems equally likely that in the consciousness of the Indians, the idea of the free-soul as a personal being might have been applied to a separable body-soul. In the shamanistic theology of the Oglala, according to Walker, *niya* is "an immaterial god whose substance is visible when it so wills." It is called to bear witness against the free-soul after death. "Its functions during the life of the person are to cause vitality, to forewarn of good and evil, and to give the power to influence others." From the Iroquois, Wolf reports that the "sensitive soul was usually malevolent, being fond of human flesh, which it hunted." The White Knife Shoshone have taken the process of detachment a step further, identifying their life-soul with a supernatural power, *buha*. Harris says that "Merely in order to live every person must possess the bird-like *Buha*, the life-principle." In the last instance the life-soul has assumed the role previously played by a now vanished concept of the free-soul. Its appearance as a bird makes that clear because such a symbol only suits a life-soul which is also a free-soul.

The life-soul assumes many forms. Among the Wind River Shoshone, the life-soul also functions as a free-soul and is conceived of as a hair or a thin thread. The Wintu, DuBois reports, say that "no one knows what it looks like." The Havasupai saw the heart-soul as a sphere. The life-soul of the Bella Coola "is an ethereal substance, having the form of the body which it animates." The Eskimo at Bering Strait conceive the life-soul as shaped in the image of man, while the "growth-soul" among the

Quileute "is a trifle longer than the rest of the body, extending somewhat beyond the toes and above the head," a notion which would seem to fit the concept of a growth-soul.

In general the life-soul is often seen as concrete, and in this connection borrows its external features from the free-soul. But it is impossible to say with any certainty how often this is so, because in a number of cases appearance has been determined less by a former conception of the free-soul than from the manifestation of the life-soul as an extra-physical soul.

In some cases the life-soul appears as a hybrid conception of both free-soul and guardian spirit. But this does not mean the life-soul was emancipated from the body it administered. Even in cases when it occurred, the emancipation always remained incomplete as long as the individual was aware that the soul was fulfilling its vital functions.

The relationship of the life-soul to the organism itself is vital for the latter's existence, which means that the life-soul can never compete with the free-soul in detaching itself from the body. The Athapascan Indian soul beliefs afford solid examples of life-souls closely connected to the organism. The Coyukon call the life-soul "our soul which is from (or next to) our body," in contradistinction to the free-soul, which they refer to as "our outer, or secondary, soul," (Jette,1911).

The Carrier at Bulkley River declare that the life-soul never leaves the body during the lifetime of the individual (Jenness, 1943). The Western Dene have an eloquent expression for the intimate connection between the body and its animating principle, believing "man is vivified by a soul which is nothing other than his natural warmth," (Morice, 1889). "According to the early Denes, man is made up of a perishable body and of a transformable soul which they knew as *nezael*," Morice says.

Curiously enough, this conception also occurs among the South Athapascans, the Lipan Apache in particular, who believe that at birth a human being is penetrated by lightning which becomes "the force that keeps you warm, keeps you alive," (Opler, 1945). Oddly, warmth also appears to have in some way characterized the dislocated free-soul, and the wandering free-soul of a sick person was often caught in his down-lined moccasins. If the down felt warm, then the wearer knew his free-soul had entered them (Morice, 1906; Jenness, 1943). Despite this the life-soul is most commonly connected with vital warmth through the breath and the blood.

Additional evidence of the way the life-soul is bound to the body can be measured in how it dies when the individual dies, while the free-soul goes on. Among the Fox the life-soul appears in the unborn child (Michelson, 1935). If the life-soul is injured, this may affect the state of the body. For example if the life-soul of an Oglala falls into the power of the demon Crazy Buffalo, he becomes paralyzed.

Like the free-soul, the life-soul is sometimes exposed to great dangers. The Oglala mention the water spirits which may chase the life-soul out of the body (Walker). Among the Cowichan, the soul may literally fall into several pieces and the individual dies (Boas, 1894). As a rule, the loss of the life-soul means death, because in the absence of the life principle, the body cannot function. Yet among the Oglala, the free-soul may assume the life preserving and life maintaining activity of the life-soul when it departs (Arbman, 1927). But normally the individual is regarded as dead during the temporary absence of the life-soul.

The bondage of the life-soul to the body is also reflected in its fate after death. Arbman has shown how in most cases the life-soul dies at the same moment as the individual, but some say that the life-soul continues its existence in the dead body, a consequence of the life-soul being bound to the body and its organs.

The interaction of the life-soul with the free-soul in a dualistic soul belief throws further light upon this profound divergence. After all the life-soul is little more than a biological life factor. Sometimes, as among the Fox, the relationship between the souls implies the subjection of the life-soul to the free-soul (Michelson). In a number of cases the life-soul is at the same time the principle of consciousness (ego-soul) as it is among the Huron, Wintu, Havasupai, and other tribes. Such examples illustrate a first stage in the movement toward a unified soul concept.

To better illustrate the ways in which the life-soul differs from the personality-soul, two things need to be understood. First is the way the life-soul can dissolve into several life-souls, and second, the way that the life-soul can have a vital force, however neutral and impersonal it may appear. Life-souls are, however, in no way identical to the organs they animate, and in this respect, what is true about the general life-soul also applies to them. Nor does their existence exclude the simultaneous occurrence of a general life-soul.

According to the Eskimo in Greenland, man has several smaller souls and two large souls, one in the neck and the other in the diaphragm, and the latter is apparently the general life-soul (Thalbitzer, 1930). While the loss of the latter is connected with risk to life, there is no danger in the departure of one of the small souls (McIlwraith). This emerges clearly from Cranz's description of the soul beliefs of the West Greenlanders.

Despite its peculiarly ethereal nature, the life-soul among the Bella Coola has "four intangible elements which unite to form the immaterial whole. One, including the voice, is located in the throat, another in the trunk, a third in the legs, and a fourth in the feet, effectively dividing the body into four quarters." However, connecting "these with one another and with the spirit, the mental director of life, is a matter of advanced Bella Coola theology on which opinions differ." (McIlwraith). Bancroft says that "some Oregon tribes gave a soul to every member of the body."

Among the Wind River Shoshone *mugua* is the general life-soul. Yet it does not stand alone for more specific vital functions (such as the breath or the heart) may not only form the focus for *mugua's* life, but they may also be associated with the activity of life-souls which behave in some ways like free-souls.

According to the Navajo, the movements of the body are due to the wind-people. "In the spirals on the ends of the thumb and fingers are located the Winds which move the legs and feet, black wind on the thumb, blue on the forefinger, yellow on the middle finger, white on the third, spotted on the little finger. These Winds stay in the body directing its movements until death and then emerge through the spirals." In addition there is "one big Wind," which fills the body and constitutes a superior life-soul (Wyman, Hill, and Osanai, 1942).

And even though the eye-design of the Northwest coast Indians does not occur south of British Columbia, according to Boas, it would seem to be based on similar notions. Niblack reports that "in the Haida drawings an eye is placed in the breast, in the ear, paw, tail, etc., of figures, presumably in the belief that each member of the body has the power of looking out for itself or controlling its own movements." What Niblack is talking about here is the occurrence of smaller organ-souls.

Finally some words concerning the two body-souls found among the Quileute which cannot be classified with special souls or organ-souls. These are the life-soul, "the being whereby one lives" and the growth-soul, "the thing whereby one grows." Frachtenberg who reported these beliefs, never did develop a clear idea of the role played by the life-soul, but it seems to have been separate from the body and to have had the appearance of the free-soul, while residing between the free-soul and the growth-soul. If it is lost, it may be restored by a competent shaman. If, on the other hand, the growth-soul should escape, it cannot be restored, and its departure means death.

That produces a pluralism of the life-souls which comes from using life and experience as the basis for belief. Where such a pluralism exists, it guarantees the separation of the life-soul and the personality-soul. Other evidence supports this assumption, and that is the striking tendency among the Indians to associate the life-soul with ideas concerning life-stuff and life-essence.

If the concept of the personality-soul constitutes one pole in the conceptual complex developed around the notion of the life-soul, then the other pole is the idea of the life-soul as an impersonal, fluid essence. Theoretically it seems possible to distinguish between a qualitative conception of life as a sign of existence, a quantitative idea (life as life-stuff), and life as an actively operating cause of all vital manifestations. For most Indians, life-stuff and the life-soul tend to merge, although in certain cases there is a clear distinction between them. The Bella Coola, for example, distinguish between the life-soul which animates the body and is more or less conceived as separate, and the breath, *sininits*. The word signifies more than the act of breathing, denoting instead the physical state of being alive (McIlwraith).

Morice indicates that some West Athapascans distinguish between "the vital principle" and "the outward sign of life, breath, and by extension, life itself." One Oglala shaman drew a subtle distinction between *niya*, the life-soul and the concept *Ni*. "A man's *Ni* is his life. It is the same as his breath and that which gives him his strength. It is *Ni* which keeps the insides clean. If the *Ni* is weak, one cannot function, and if it goes away one dies. *Niya* is the ghost or spirit which is given to a human at birth and is that which causes the *Ni*." (Walker, 1917).

The Navajo also observed the same rough difference between

life and life-soul. They use a special term, *'ajt,* which signifies "manifestation by breath and sound of the life and power of a being; that which keeps one powerful."

The Pima distinguish between the respiration and its motive power, the soul. "The soul is in the center of the breast. It makes us breathe, but it is not the breath." (Russell, 1908). But even if such a distinction occurs, not even the trained thinkers among the speculative Oglala shaman could indefinitely maintain the distinction between the concepts *ni* and *niya* (Walker).

The notions of life-soul and life-stuff originated in two disparate psychic experiences; one the impressions of psychic activity behind the manifestations of life, the other the perception of the variations in the life-force, based on the varying ages and states of health among individuals. In that connection, especially through association with life maintaining breath, life-force takes on its concrete character. But these distinctions cannot be maintained because the quantitative idea of the life-stuff has been transferred to the idea of the soul. Consequently, the life-soul sometimes appears in the light of an impersonal *fluidum* which may be transmitted to another living being, sometimes in a measurable capacity as a sort of graduated life-force.

The best way to understand how the notion of life-stuff developed in North America and how it has been woven into the idea of the soul, is to look at examples. The notion of how the life-soul or how life "flows over" into other beings occurs more often in fairy-tales and legends than in attempts to codify belief. One example comes from the Cheyenne. Some men on a journey found a weak and hungry old wolf and gave him food. Grateful for their benevolence, the wolf said, "I will give you my life. You will live, in this world, your full lives. You will go all over the world and have success in war. You will live free from danger and sickness, until your old age is passed." (Kroeber, 1900).

It is often the breath which is transferred from individual to individual as a vital *fluidum,* as you can see in the following custom of the Ingalik: "Sometimes a dying person will send for one to whom he wishes to pass on his powers. Then the dying one looks to the North, breathes on the other and spits on him."

An Ingalik woman said to the young man who reported this: "I think a great deal of you. I could do almost anything for you and I would like to give you some of my power, but if I did, I would die within the year. I must live for my children, providing the Good One sees fit for me to live." (Parsons, 1921-22).

Parsons recorded such beliefs in the power of breath in the Southwest region right down to the Tehuantepec Isthmus, and especially in the Pueblo region. But there life is conceived of as a quantitative entity, expressed through the breath, and the donor does not jeopardize his life-force by dispersing it. What is more, in the southwest region, ritual breathing sometimes assumes a new significance. The breath is not only the symbol of life among the Zuni, as Bunzel points out, but "it also is the means by which spiritual substances communicate and (it is) the seat of power or mana. Inhaling is an act of ritual blessing. One inhales from all sacred objects to derive benefit from their mana." Breathing on someone to strengthen their life potency, without the donor's life being jeopardized, makes life-stuff transferable. That occurs not only among the Pueblo, but also among other southwestern peoples. (Parsons, 1929).

Outside the Southwest cultures the notion of the breath-soul appears less distinctly, sometimes submerged in other forms. The Winnebago celebrated their victories in battle with a scalp-feast, at which they tried to acquire the life-force of the deceased. "If we trample upon it (the scalp)," said the Winnebago who had issued the invitation to the feast, "all the goods of life that were still coming to him when he was killed will be transferred to us...so all you women and men see to it that you dance with all your strength. Do not take this matter lightly, for we obtain life thereby." (Radin, 1923). He went on to explain, Radin says, that "the dancers and the feasters, indeed, all who had counted coup, tried to obtain some of the dead enemy's residuary life. All tried to add some new life to their own."

What this illustrates is the ease with which the life-soul may be conceived of as a measurable, quantitatively determined entity. The life-soul may be measured by outer behavior, chiefly through physical prowess, though the concept of force is distinct from supernatural power.

To take a closer look at the variations in the potency of life or the life-soul, it is perhaps best to go directly to the source. According to the Polar Eskimo, every person is equipped at birth with a certain amount of "vital force," which ebbs with age (Rasmussen, 1908). The life-soul of the Iroquois develops the whole of its strength in wrath and passion, but only after it drives away "the rational soul." Among the Fox, however, it is the free-soul or the "large soul" which plays that role and when it becomes too large, its owner is seized with a lust to kill. The life-soul of the Oglala provided "the power to influence others." (Walker, 1917).

A Bella Coola is helpless without his vital principle for then "there can be neither strength nor growth." The life-soul grows with the body, and "as a person becomes older, so does this element grow, always taking the exact shape and form of the body." In addition McIlwraith says, "It is the life (soul) that suffers whenever the skin is broken. Any wound may prove dangerous, but particularly one that cuts either of the invisible lines along which vitality flows from the little finger to the little toe. An injury to one of these channels spreads rapidly and is in many cases fatal."

Among the Shoshone of Wyoming the life-soul is sometimes conceived of as a graded life-force. But this life-force is peculiar in the way the manifold quantity of life-stuff in a person is measurable, so that a human being with a great amount of life-force is understood to possess several life-souls. "If *mugua* (the life-soul) was strong, one might shoot at the body as much as one pleased," a Shoshone woman said. But since *mugua* is fragile, the only way a warrior could survive was to have had several *muguas*. "In the old war-like days," she said, "bullets might even pass through strong warriors, without their sustaining any injury, so they must have had several *muguas*." Clearly, the concept of life-force here comes close to supernatural power.

In some shamanistic speculation the idea of soul seems to have been replaced with an elastic life concept, or at least this appears to be the case in the following passage from the mythology of the Medicine dance among the Mascoutens. "When the Great Spirit created mankind, he dipped his finger in water and put it in their mouths. Therefore, water is life. It has perpetual motion; it is the blood in our bodies. It is the life in our hearts. Our hearts are only wind and water moving." (Skinner).

My impression is that the more common soul, the heart, did not fit well into shamanistic cosmic symbolism and was replaced by the blood, a more easily managed phenomena associated with the vital functions. But in popular soul belief the blood is not the life-soul itself, though in several instances blood was believed to contain the life-substance, especially in the legend literature. "The Lenape say," Harrington reports, "that the blood in the dead body draws up into globular form and floats about in the air as a luminous ball, but this is not the real spirit." According to Speck the life-soul connected with the blood becomes a wandering ghost that injures the living by afflicting them with paralysis.

The life-soul or the life-souls may also be associated with the gall bladder, the lungs, and the heart. The Bella Coola, Luiseno, and Navajo believe that the life-soul is in the lungs as the Bella Coola story "The Black Bear" shows. The Bear woman "had taken her heart and lungs from her chest so an arrow shot into her body would not kill her." You can see in this, as well, a glimpse of the connection with the so-called external soul.

It is certain that the breath-soul among the Navajo resides in the lungs, while the Ute place at least one soul—it is uncertain just which—in the stomach. The Creek say the life-soul resides in the intestines. The Hopi point to the region above the navel as "the place where the breath of a man lives." Among the Tepehuano the soul dwells between the stomach and the chest, and the Haida, Arikara, Pima, and some Gosiute locate the life-soul in the chest. In most cases when a life-soul is associated with the chest, it is probably in the heart, if only because the heart is without doubt the most important center for life in the minds of most North American peoples. Very likely the so called life-line on North American rock-drawings, a line connecting heart and mouth in human beings and animals, is intended to symbolize the breath-soul associated with the heart. If that is so, then these drawings constitute the oldest documents concerning Indian soul belief.

The usual explanation for the life-line connects it to hunting magic (Gjessing, 1944). That has come out of comparisons of the life-lines in the rock drawings in America and elsewhere. Hoffman's reports on hunting magic among the Ojibway offer support for that view. When an Ojibway shaman wants to ensure hunting success for his client "he will draw with a sharp-pointed bone or nail, upon a small piece of birch bark, the outline of the animal desired by the applicant. Frequently the heart is indicated by a round or triangular figure, from which a line extends toward the mouth, generally designated the life-line, or the line by which the magic power may reach its heart and influence the life of the designated animal." The most typical (and by far the greatest number of) life-line drawings on rock in the whole of North America occur on the outskirts of the Ojibway region. Interpreting these drawings as part of hunting magic makes sense especially since they show a connection with old circumpolar hunting and gathering cultures. Furthermore, the life-line is a symbol for the life-soul, a notion which turns up in reports of modern Indian belief. That is why the sign for the life-soul (heart and soul) among the Wind River Shoshone resembles the life-line.

The modern Pueblo Indians have also preserved and kept alive the symbolism of the life-line. Franz Boas writes that "the Pueblo Indian paints the form of a deer with a fair degree of perspective accuracy, but adds to it a line running from the mouth to the heart as an essential symbol of life." The Oraibi (Hopi) generally lay a feather-string, *puhtabi,* on the chest above the heart running to the mouth of someone who has recently died; the string is called the "breath-leg" (Stephen, 1936, and Voth, 1903). When anyone is initiated into the Hopi Antelope Society, the master of the ceremony swings a corn-cob fetish toward the initiate with a movement from the head down toward the heart as he pronounces his blessing and offers his wish that the inductee enjoy a long life.

The research on soul belief in North America shows that Indians thought that the heart was the seat of the life-soul, though the belief is certainly more common to some areas than others. There are no such instances at all from interior portions or from eastern Canada. In addition, believers in a heart-soul occurred only sparsely among the Athapascans of the Southwest (the Navajo and Apache). The Eskimo, on the other hand, made such a connection (Thalbitzer, 1930) as have many of the peoples along the Northwest Coast. East of the continental watershed, some Algonquin groups belonging to the coastal and central Algonquin believed the life-soul was seated in the heart, and it may well have been far more widespread, but there is simply not enough information.

It is surprising that on the Plains, where so many tribes have been carefully investigated, more information did not surface. The Wind River Shoshone are one exception. They locate the life-soul in the heart, but as Shoshone they should be grouped with the Basin peoples, several of whom have had the same view.

The tribes in North and Central California also agreed that the life-soul is the heart. That reoccurs among the Yuman peoples, and in at least a couple of the South Athapascan and Piman peoples. Finally, there are many instances from the Pueblo region where the life-soul occurs wrapped in a single soul. "In Pueblo ideology the heart is the life," Parsons says, "and considerable attention is directed both ritually and in stories to the heart: 'heart' is given to ritual objects or persons or 'heart' is renewed, cleansed, or replaced. Witches steal the 'heart.' Medicine may be made from heart." Here the association between life-soul, life-force and supernatural power in the heart, which is so typical of the Pueblo peoples, is clear.

Two things in this stand out. First, the almost one sided Western distribution of the heart-soul, and second, the way Southwestern culture-groups stress the connection between the life-soul and the heart. The concept reaches maximum intensity there with its peak in Pueblo ideology. In "the significance of the heart as the seat of life" Alexander sees one of the links between the Pueblo and Mexican high-culture. The notion of life here is the common denominator for such disparate conceptions as the life-soul, the life-stuff, the life-force, the ego-soul, and the free-soul.

In this way the heart becomes the focal point for widely differing spiritual concepts, and it seems natural that people in their attempts to explain the mystery of life should focus on the heart. In both early North American and Occidental cultures, the heart has symbolized the center of existence. The Cheyenne, for example, even call the center for all directions "the heart of the world." The beating heart is the ultimate evidence of life and is therefore the chief residence of the life-soul. But the movement of the heart is also connected with our psychic reactions as the Huron and the Iroquois understood, associating it with desires and wishes. When the soul is bound to the heart, it becomes the organ of psychic life itself, the ego-soul.

Most often in North America the heart-soul is the vital-soul rather than the ego-soul, but the connection between ego-soul and heart is by no means rare (Arbman). No evidence has been found that the heart-soul *is* the heart, and the Indians recognized the non-spiritual structure of the physical heart. This strict boundary between the material and the spiritual characterizes the connection of the heart with the life-soul but dissolves as soon as the heart is coupled with the notions of life-fluid and life-force. This includes powerful qualities such as courage, endurance, and strength of will, as well as supernatural power.

But the life-soul only acts in the heart as long as the latter is a part of the entire human organism. The other potencies associated with the heart continue to act independently of the heart's connection with the organism. It is as if the heart *contains* them, as if they are material entities. This explains the custom of eating the heart of a dead person in order to acquire his vitality or whatever supernatural power he might possess. The life-soul, which animates the heart, has nothing to do with these customs, although there seems to have been a connection between the heart-soul and cannibalism in Southern California.

Similar notions arise in considerations of the "bone-soul," another of the forms in which the life-soul appears. In North America the bone-soul is best known from the Iroquois when the word for someone who has died, which signifies "bone," has been transferred to the life-soul. What that does is confirm in language what is known from tradition, that the Iroquois regarded the bones of the dead, the skeleton, as the final resting-place of the sensitive or animating soul" (Hewitt, 1895).

From other peoples we have only legend. One story from the Jicarilla Apache tells of the Fox and the man-eating Bear. "Fox not only cut the flesh from the legs of Bear, but also broke the bones with his knife, thus killing the dreaded man eater" (Russell, 1891). The significance of bone-breaking seems to have come from the ideology of a hunting people who had well-established traditions about how to treat the bones of an animal they had killed. Such tribes believe that the retention of the bones (as well as arranging them in anatomical order) will guarantee the resurrection of the game for a future hunt. Still it would seem logical to associate the mystical properties of the bones with life-stuff.

Gatschet connects the belief in the bone-soul with secondary burial, the custom of "cleaning" the bones of the deceased after they have lain in the grave for some time. He says that behind this custom lies "the idea that the real seat of the human soul is in the bones." This can hardly be correct. Secondary burial has nothing to do with the bone-soul but is a case of continuity magic aimed at ensuring resurrection, even though that notion is not among the common beliefs in North America (Riggs, 1883).

Sometimes the life-soul occurred in a person's look, or it may have resided between the brows, or in the nape of the neck, but there is never any mention of its existing in the hair. The hair contains the life-force among the Omaha, and it sometimes represents the individual after death, but it does not become, so far as known, a seat for the life-soul in North America.

Locating the life-soul in the head may also seem odd until you consider how the impulses to vital reactions originate there. The Arikara connected the life-soul to the head in a number of ways: in the spoken word, in a look, in the death-rattle of someone dying, in the movements of the muscles (Curtis, 1909). It also seems natural to locate the seat of the life-soul in the nape of the neck. But it is certainly strange that the Navajo should have located the vital force of the coyote in its nose (Matthews, 1897), though that may well have been the work of the famous trickster of Southwestern cultures. Among the Wintu the life-soul has its abode behind the ear, but probably because it is also an intellectual principle (DuBois, 1935). And the life-soul among the Wind River Shoshone resides between the eyebrows, as it has increasingly come to take over the function of the free-soul.

However it is uncommon for the life-soul to have its seat in the head. Where it occurs it seems to come from a growing belief that the life-soul is identical with the ego-soul or the free soul. It is important here to refer once more to the life-line symbolism discussed earlier, especially among the Pueblo, where the connection between breath and heart appears.

As I said earlier, the breath is not considered a physical substrate. It is the life-soul, though in a number of cases it seems as if the breath functions as a physical "organ" for the life-soul. The Juaneno, for instance, couple the free-soul with the heart and the life-soul with the breath (Krober, 1925).

Examples abound from Greenland to Nicaragua in which the life-soul, as breath, has been connected with the heart. The result is that in a great many cultures, the soul is attached to the heart, but its essence is the breath. Its significance can scarcely be overestimated. But the breath-soul has almost always drifted farther and farther from its original function, and it represents the perfect transition in the movement from a dual soul to a single soul concept.

Chapter Seven
The Breath-soul in Speculative Belief

The breath-soul is difficult to define as a soul entity because it appears as either a general expression for the life-soul or a specialized part of the life-soul. The alternating meaning occurs because this soul is closely associated with life-stuff, but the breath-soul emerges as a dominant soul-type in North America.

It is psychologically a secondary soul formation, originating through the obvious connection between the life-soul and the breath, and it fuses the concepts of the life-soul and life-essence. The breath is the concrete idea of life-stuff, an almost visual, tangible image of life flowing through the body. In addition, the developed breath-soul can be transferred to others without injuring the owner, something the life-soul cannot do.

The linkage between the breath and the life-soul occurred in several ways. First, the breath-soul is a conception of life, ethereal and yet concrete, which made it more acceptable to thought and belief. Second the breath is never identified with any physical organ, allowing the soul and life-stuff to fuse and form the concept of the breath-soul. Finally, as a symptom of life the breath becomes a source of life in the imagination. If the breathing stops, the life-motor stops. The Sinkaietk, Spier says, expressed "dead" with the phrase "can't breathe any more."

In this final connection between life-soul and breath, the breath becomes an undifferentiated entity with both life-stuff and life-soul aspects. That concept has affected Indian religious belief, for the breath-soul has become the central focus in two different thought-systems. Mystically oriented speculation has resulted in an emanational view related to pantheism, while rationally oriented speculation has transformed the breath-soul to a single soul. A prerequisite for mystical belief lies in identifying the breath with the wind or the air. That concept, and a more elevated notion of the deity, appear to be the foundations for emanational speculation. The notion that the breath-soul is a part of the wind sweeping over the world is found in several places in North America. Among the Kaska, Honigmann says the breath-soul is referred to as "the wind." The Haida have drawn a parallel between the breath and the air, identifying the life-breath with the clouds. "When the clouds hang low the Haidas believe that a soul is being snatched away, and expect to see one of their number shortly die" (Hill-Tout, 1899). The Tsimshian believe that the "breath of the twins" control the weather, and therefore (Boas says) they pray to the wind and the rain.

A Sauk chief said that his body was "a substance animated in some way by the air," and he believed that death meant the complete end of existence (Jones, 1939). The Mascouten shamans allude to the identity of the breath with the wind, calling it the breath of the earth goddess (Skinner, 1934). Dorsey says that the four poles in the sun-dance lodge of the Arapaho represent the gods of the four corners of the earth. "They cause the wind to blow, and human life is dependent on them for their breath. In fact, all life is dependent on the 'breath of the air,' which comes from the Four-Old-Men," which is to say, the four poles.

In a myth from the Seneca, the breath of the Wind penetrates a woman and makes her pregnant, and Hewitt says that "is the statement of an early form of anthropic parthenogenesis; its enduring implication is that air (wind), that is, breath, is the source of life." An Omaha Indian said that a dead person goes to the four winds (LaFlesche, 1939). And the Osage say that a dead man is taken to the realm of the dead by the four winds (Walker, 1917). An Oglala shaman told Walker that the life-soul "is like smoke and it goes upward until it arrives at the stars." The life, *ni*, "is a man's breath. It is the spirit of smoke. It is the spirit of steam. It is the spirit of the sweat lodge."

The winds, according to the Pawnee priests, are "from the breath of Tirawa (the sky god) and they give life to man, that is to say, the breath by which he lives" (Dorsey and Murie, 1940). "At death, the soul goes off the way a cloud comes up and disappears, or the way a wind blows up and dies down." The Wind River

Shoshone also use the same word for air and breath, while the Athapascan Kato in northwestern California refer to dying with the terms "wind drop-out" or "wind thrown-out."

The Juaneno in southern California regarded the breath as an emanation of the atmosphere (Bancroft, 1875). A Cahuilla Indian, by his own account, hit upon the notion that the soul must be the breath by itself, but "breath is just like wind, so the winds which we hear at night are the spirits of the dead" (Hooper, 1920). According to the White Mountain Apache "the last breath of the dying person remains on earth in the form of a little wind" (Goodwin, 1938).

Like many other North American peoples, the Navajo have a single word to denote life, breath, and wind. Although a theoretical distinction is drawn between life and life-soul, the breath, as "man's wind," seems *de facto* to correspond to both concepts (Reichard, 1950). From the Navajo myth concerning the genesis of man, it is clear that the breath is the essence of the soul. "It was the wind that gave them life. It is the wind that comes out of our mouths now that gives us life. When this ceases to blow, we die" (Matthews, 1897).

That the Pueblo peoples have seen in the breath an emanation of the cosmic wind is no surprise, because as a conception of life the breath is in accord with their well-developed ritual apparatus (White, 1932). Among the Acoma man's breath is a part of the atmosphere. The Zuni, Parsons says, identify the breath with wind and light. The Hopi, according to Stephan, believe that the universe is filled with the same breath. A Hopi Indian of high cult rank pointed out that, "the universe is endowed with the same breath; rocks, trees, grass, earth, all animals, and men." These people also put great stock in a feather-topped prayer stick. When the feather moves and shifts in the wind it represents the breath of life and is seen as a messenger from the divinity. The connection in the Pueblo culture between human breath and the wind, air, and clouds lies in the notion that after death the individual becomes a cloud-being. It is important to remember that among the Pueblo the breath-soul is a single soul. It represents the individual and his life, and it also becomes his surviving principle.

The Hopi, Parsons says, paint the face of one newly dead with cloud symbols, a sure sign of the connection between the dead and the atmosphere. Reports from the Pueblo in New Mexico indicate that they believe a person's breath merges with winds and clouds when he dies. In some cases the clouds are designated as rain clouds or thunder clouds.

The causes of the dead appearing as clouds or in the clouds has aroused a substantial amount of speculation. The Indians have tried to explain this, but these attempts seem only to show that the original motives have been lost in time. Among the Zuni when the dead appear behind cloud-masks, "the clouds are produced by the breath of the gods and smoke," and the Hopi hold the view that ceremonial smoking among the living hastens the formation of clouds (Stevenson, 1904). The Hopi also say that the dead can easily be changed into clouds because of their spiritual food; "they never eat the food, but only the odor or the soul of the food," so they can float in the air (Voth, 1905). The appearance of the dead person in the shape of a cloud, both when he leaves this life and later, occurs because his breath-soul is identical with his personality, which after death becomes a part of the atmosphere.

The idea of identity between the breath and the wind is the first condition for believing in the identity between human breath and the breath of the deity, the cosmic wind. The second condition is that individuals who have the capacity to speculate about such things, usually, but not always medicine men and priests, have worked out the relationship between soul concepts and the concept of the deity. One of the interesting discoveries in the examples I have shown is that the most remarkable instances of correspondence between the breath and the winds of the universe derive from shamans or from communities with important cults.

The breath occurs as the cosmic element in man and provides the identity between man's life and that of the deity. This must be kept distinct from real pantheistic belief, which did not exist in North America, and from the concept of the deity as the giver of life. Several reports from other Eastern groups show that where the deity has sometimes been characterized as the master of life or breath, people have made a connection between the life of man and the life of the deity. That occurs chiefly among the Lenape and the Creek.

Similar trains of thought occur among the Mascoutens who regard man's breath as the breath of the earth goddess. According to the Creek and the Chickasaw, the souls of the good Indians went after death to a supreme divinity called "Master of Breath" or

"Breathmaker" (Swanton, 1928). In regard to that Spence says he sometimes "appears to be the personification of the wind, the name being onomatopoetic because the sound of the name represents the emission of breath from the mouth. He was the god of wind, and, like other divinities in American mythology, his rule over that element was allied with his power over the breath of life...one of the forms of wind or air."

This explanation also emerges from Hewitt's notes. "The term *hisakita*, 'the breath,' was applied to the agency of the great prophet above, but was also applied to the life spirit." This life-soul does not seem to have represented the person after death. The Seminole name for the supreme God, *Hisakitamisi,* also means "master of breath" (MacCauley, 1887). But whether he is called "master of breath" or "master of life," the Supreme Being by no means manifests his own life in man.

The emanational mode of thought occurs in several of the Sioux peoples. I documented it earlier among the Winnebago where it is an ancient myth concerning the origin of death in which four sacred beings proclaim: "Into your bodies Earth-Maker has placed part of himself. That will return to him if you do the proper things" (Radin, 1909). It is certainly tempting to imagine that the Biblical narrative of the creation was known long ago by the Winnebago, but Radin observes that Christian influence on the notion of the deity has not been very marked.

Among the Omaha Dorsey says, "some of the old people say that their ancestors always believed in a supreme *Wakanda* or Mysterious Power. The principal *Wakanda* is in the upper world, above everything." The older members of the tribe told Fletcher that at the puberty fast "the appeal was to *Wakonda*, the great power. There were other powers...the sun, the stars, the moon, the earth...but these were lesser; the prayer was not to them." Fletcher emphasizes that the thunder, the animal spirit, the mythical monster "may be spoken of as *wakondas*, but they are not regarded as *the Wakonda*." She says "these two uses of the word are never confused in the minds of the thoughtful."

In other words the term *wakonda* has been ascribed to several gods, but as well to one in particular which, judging by all the evidence, is a sky or sun god. He is not mentioned by name since he is an abstract, anthropomorphized deity, a concretion of the divine, and He is most frequently referred to as the Creator, the source of all things. He cannot be imagined, but the people are certain that he exists. As Soderblom and Radin have shown, such vaguely outlined figures originate with philosophical thought. The Osage, who are closely related to the Omaha, still claim to remember how after a long search for the origin of life, their forefathers finally "came to the thought that it issues from an invisible creative power to which they applied the name *Wa-kon-da*" (LaFlesche, 1930).

What appears here, as it did in the case of the four-soul concept, is a belief in a Supreme Deity. This developed as the product of deepened religious speculation. *Wakonda* is abstract, cosmic, part immanent, part personal, a *fons et origo vitae.* It is not a question of a pantheistic divinity, but it is possible that man was conceived as a part of his being, as Fletcher says.

There are signs that shamanistic speculation among the Dakota arrived at a similar view regarding the relationship of the soul to the deity. Charles A. Eastman, a Santi Dakota, writes that his fellow tribesmen believed "that the spirit which the 'Great Mystery' breathed into man returns to Him who gave it, and that after it is freed from the body, it is everywhere and pervades all nature." His statement is reminiscent of such statements from another branch of the Dakota, the Oglala of the Teton Dakota.

In Oglala shamanistic speculation, of which Walker has given a detailed account, *Wakan Tanka* is mentioned as "the Great Mystery," "the Great God." He reveals himself in gods, spirits, and demons of various rank; he is manifold and yet is unity itself. "The shamans know how this is, but the people do not know," the medicine-man, Finger, said. "It is *wakan* (a mystery)." All man's souls are *wakan.* From their connection with the great mystery it is also evident that they are simply included therein. The word *Wakan Tanka* means all of the *wakan* beings because they are all as if one" (Walker, 1917).

Several Dakota groups, the Sisseton, Wahpeton, Oglala and Assiniboin, call this divine being *Wakan Tanka.* Among the Eastern Dakota he appears as a theistic creative deity frequently ranked above other gods (Wallis, 1919). But for the most part he is a *deus otiosus,* who has performed his creative tasks and has now retired from the affairs of the world (Eastman, 1849). At times, however, even the *Wakan Tanka* of the Eastern Dakota becomes vague in outline, and among the Assiniboin and Teton

Dakota this is the rule. *Wah-con-tun-ga* or *Wakonda* is for the Assiniboin the Creator, who seems to dwell in the sun and speak in the thunder (the latter according to De Smet); but at the same time he is the great Mystery.

"They think *Wakonda* pervades all air, earth, and sky; that it is in fact omnipresent and omnipotent" (Denig, 1930). Yet this ubiquity by no means implies that this god is identical with the thunder-god or the sun-god, and in the sacrificial rites all three are separate. The same applies to the religious beliefs of the Teton Dakota. Deloria describes the Supreme Deity here as an immaterial, ubiquitously active power, who is worshipped in various shapes. But she is uncertain concerning the deeper import of the conception.

In her analysis of the *Wakan Tanka* concept Densmore says, "The exact significance of the term in the mind of the Sioux is as difficult to formulate as the exact meaning of the word God in the mind of Christians." The Indian Red Bird characterized *Wakan Tanka* as "a mysterious power greater than all others." The medicine man Brave Buffalo called him "the maker of all."

"We know that all the creatures on the earth were placed here by *Wakan'tanka*," Chased-by-Bears told Densmore. "We talk to *Wakan'tanka* and are sure that he hears us, and yet it is hard to explain what we believe about this. We believe that he is everywhere, yet he is to us as the spirits of our (deceased) friends, whose voices we cannot hear."

Wakan Tanka emerges as an unformalized divinity, slightly anthropomorphous, but weakly individualized. Yet he is an individual which shows in Walker's reproduction of the Oglala shaman Sword's account of his conversion. "When I believed the Oglala *Wakan Tanka* was right I served him with all my powers. In war with the white people I found their *Wakan Tanka* the superior. I then took the name of Sword and have served *Wakan Tanka* according to the white people's manner and with all my power."

Sword found few differences between his concept of *Wakan Tanka* and the Christian God, yet Densmore says that "the unvarying opinion of the old men is that the Sioux have always believed in *Wakan'tanka*." And while the influence of French trappers and *coureurs du bois* cannot be excluded, the uniformity of the concept of the deity among the different Sioux peoples of the Plains seems to support the assumption that it is very old.

The Assiniboin separated from the other Dakota (in particular the Yanktonai) before 1640, when they allied themselves more with the Cree than with their Dakota kinsmen, but their concept of the deity shows the same special features as that of the Teton Dakota. Then there is the striking resemblance between the *Wakan Tanka* of the Teton Dakota and the *Wakonda* of the Omaha. In each case the same word covers both the concept of a vaguely personified supreme divinity that the people believe they recognize in the sun and the thunder, and of independent divinities behind these phenomena.

Here shamanistic speculation is at odds with popular belief. Among the Oglala the shamans have tried to combine manifoldness and unity into a coherent system, which leans toward pantheism, if the deity is understood as a universally essential substance with a partially developed personality.

The general character of *Wakan Tanka*, the Supreme Deity, is a vague and shadowy figure among the Teton. "In old times," Densmore writes, "the term *Wakan'tanka* was not used in ordinary conversation, because it was held too sacred to be spoken except with due reverence and at a proper time."

Both Walker and Deloria mention *Taku Skan-skan*, the sky-god, as the great mystery in one of its most representational forms. This god, "the source of all power and motion," gives everyone their soul at birth and receives them again when they die. One of his names, *Nagi Tanka*, is translated by Walker as "Great Spirit," though he should be called "the great soul." *Nagi,* after all, is the name for the free-soul among the Oglala.

Among another Plains people, the Pawnee, the supreme god is more personal and less diffuse than the Supreme Being of the Dakota (Dangel, 1929). Man's life is understood by the Pawnee priests as a part of the sky-god's breath. The same belief also occurs in Pueblo culture, leaving the impression that religious speculation took different channels in the eastern and western parts of the Pueblo region.

In the East, the conceptions connected with the breath do not seem to play any role. White points out that in San Felipe, maize is identified with the heart and the heart-soul. In another connection an ear of corn is identified with the Mother, the goddess of motherhood, death and fertility, producing a sort of panvitalism proceeding from the goddess. It is not out of the question that a similar belief occurred in other places in the eastern Pueblo area where the earth goddess is conceived as creator, guardian of the crops, and ruler of the dead.

The western Pueblo base their beliefs on the connection between the breath, the wind, and the deity. Among the Acoma, the breath is regarded as part of the wind, and the breath of life is the breath of the mother goddess (White, 1932). The Zuni's androgynous creator, referred to as "He-She," is according to Stevenson, "the symbol and initiator of life, and life itself, pervading all space." The word for life among the Zuni literally means "daylight" (Bunzel, 1932). Further, the life-symbol, the breath, is identified with the wind. What this seems to indicate is that the Zuni may possibly have believed that the soul constituted the divine element in man. The Zuni identification of life and light appears among the Navajo, where the life-soul is also a part of the sun to which it returns at death, and it seems likely that the Navajo took these ideas from the Pueblo, whom they imitated in so many other respects (Stevenson, 1904).

Cosmic speculation concerning the breath soul also appears, unexpectedly, in northern California. In a Modoc myth, Isis, the divine hero, takes his child's life by transferring its breath to himself. "The breath is mine," Isis declares. "I have taken the breath into myself" (Curtin, 1912).

In southern California the Shoshone Luiseno produced a remarkable, grandiose, cosmic speculation, of which only some relics remain. Among other things, the same symbol, a cruciform grass dummy called *Wanawut*, was used to designate the life-soul in man and the Milky Way above. *Wanawut* was used in the initiation rites at puberty and connoted both the breath and the home of souls after death, the Milky Way. "The main *wan-awut* would be in the sky, but we do not see it. We send our spirits to it in breathing, groaning invocation" (DuBois, 1908). The groaning sounds, according to Kroeber, have a ritual significance, seeming always to occur in threes and to constitute a symbolic reference to the soul.

What is this invisible *Wanawut*? Kroeber's study of the impressive Luiseno cosmogony reveals that the male creative element is revealed in the Milky Way, crystallizing out as the Heavenly Father. *Wanawut* refers to "the spirit above," and it must in the final analysis be the Heavenly Father who is so designated.

Kroeber says that in the Luiseno cosmogony there is "a remarkable attempt at abstract conceptualizing, which, though it falls short of success, leaves an impression of boldness and of a rude but vast grandeur of thought." He says that it is more reminiscent of Polynesian creation narratives than of other North American cosmogonies, though he noted that the marked belief in a creating, divine pair is characteristic of Southern Californian peoples, perhaps influenced by the nearby Pueblos and Navajo.

Of course the question arises over whether Christian impulses, particularly influences from the Spanish Missions, lie behind the cosmic symbolism developed by the Luiseno. The initiation procedures are known to have been connected with the so-called Chingichnish religion which derives from the Gabrielino on Santa Catalina and was introduced at a rather late period. Moreover, its main figure, *Chingichnish*, is described as an enthroned, omnipotent Jahve. But it should be observed that *Chingichnish* properly has nothing at all to do with the cosmogony, either among the Juaneno or the Luiseno, and turns up abruptly and without any mediation in the primeval mythology. Further, the *Wanawut* ceremony is supervised not so much by *Chingichnish* as by the Heavenly Father.

However it may be possible to prove that the ritualistic and speculative tendencies in the wider Southwest culture are connected with Mexican high-culture, especially in its earlier phase (Kidder, 1936). Several centers of development share this culture basis, among them the Maya, Nahuatl, and Pueblo peoples. Emanational speculation occurs in three places in this wide culture-belt: the Luiseno, several of the Pueblo peoples (including the Navajo), and the Aztecs. Brinton points out that, "with the Aztecs, *ehecatl* expressed both air, life, and soul, and it was said to have been born of the breath of *Tezcatlipoca*, their highest divinity, who is often called *Yoalliehecatl*, the Wind of Night."

What this demonstrates is that the soul is identified with the breath almost wherever it is a life-soul or a single soul. Only in the reports from the Lenape and Omaha is the identity of the soul uncertain. There is no reliable evidence that any element other than the breath has formed the basis of the speculation. But in some cases the breath is gradually succeeded by a diffuse concept of the individual. Such is the case with the Oglala where all the soul constituents were believed to form a part of the deity.

It is clear that the monistic philosophical trend, which identified the soul of man as an original part of the deity, came in most cases from the identification between life and life-soul, and breath and wind. In a more developed form this belief belongs to cultures with a complicated social structure, where the concept of the deity has attained cosmic dimensions, and where there is a priestly hierarchy. Only in some cases (chiefly among the Lenape, Omaha, and Oglala) is there a glimpse of pantheism arising from this system of thought.

What is certain is that the life-soul played an important role in the development of a single soul concept. Among the Wind River Shoshone and the Canadian Athapascans the process was enabled either by the free-soul losing its actuality or by the transition of the life-soul to states typical for the free-soul including the principle of consciousness, instability, emancipation, relative immateriality, and the tendency to identification with the ego. Such qualities are found in the life-soul when it has been combined with life-stuff and manifests itself as a breath-soul. Among the Pueblo the transition occurred when the dream and trance functions of the free-soul were suppressed.

The breath-soul is the soul of great possibilities. It is at once material and immaterial, bound by matter and yet free. From a psychological viewpoint the concept of the free-soul is identical with the memory image of the dead person projected to supernatural reality. Therefore the surviving soul and the breath-soul have qualities which favor a merging. But the fusion takes place only when speculation has started or dualistic beliefs have weakened.

The breath-soul also shows its intimate association with the free-soul among the Wind River Shoshone where it is the life-soul instead of the free-soul that departs in cases of serious illness, when breathing is only barely perceptible. An example of the transition of the breath-soul from life-soul to free-soul shows in an example from the Kaska. These Athapascans once distinguished between the breath of life and the free-soul. Today it is only the breath-soul, the "wind," that is looked upon as the soul. It appears probable that the life-soul, in its character as a breath-soul, has emancipated itself from its immediate physical functions and because of its airy consistency been absorbed by the concept of the free-soul. That is the only way to explain how it operates as a dream-soul without the respiratory apparatus ceasing to function. The life-soul would never have been able to overcome the well-developed dream-soul if the breath-soul had not been capable of performing the functions of both souls.

An interesting notion of the breath-soul as free-soul in a dualistic soul union occurs among some Shoshonean groups. The breath-soul seems to play the role of the free-soul among the Paviotso and Ute (Honigmann, 1949). Among the Hamilton Shoshone the single soul is identical with the breath and appears frequently as a free-soul. Among the Wind River Shoshone, who probably possessed a well-developed dualistic soul belief, the breath-soul consulted with the body-soul and the free-soul.

This brings us to the problem of the transition of the breath-soul to a principle of consciousness. The ego-soul is in most cases regarded as a body-soul; as a soul connected with the organism and representing certain psychic functions, above all in the spheres of consciousness, understanding, will, and emotion. As the ego-soul and the life-soul frequently merge, so does the breath-soul form a substratum for both of them, even though it is closely connected with the concept of the life-soul. Among the Navajo, for instance, the central life-soul is also half ego-soul, since it controls speech (Wyman, Hill & Osanai, 1942). Whether we count it as ego-soul or life-soul, it is identical with the breath or the wind in man. It is certainly as an ego-soul that the breath functions after death as the surviving principle of the individual. Another Athapascan people, the Chipewyan in Canada, regard the breath-soul and the thought-soul (an aspect of the ego-soul) as one and the same (Birket-Smith, 1930).

It may seem at times as if the breath-soul is nearer to the ego-soul than to the life-soul. Among the Shoshone the linguistic connection between the breath and the ego-soul is close, and at least among the Wind River Shoshone, there is an actual connection between the two concepts. A third reason why the breath-soul can be understood as a principle of consciousness is found in its acquired identity with the free-soul or the surviving soul. Both of these souls represent the consciousness of the individual when the body is insensible or dead.

Finally, the emanational speculation referred to earlier probably exercised a decisive influence upon the development of the breath-soul. As soon as the breath-soul is looked upon as a higher, divine element in man, it becomes the focus of the highest individual values, which explains how it becomes the bearer of the ego-consciousness as it appears to have done among the Oglala. Different thinkers among these peoples have in different ways tried to make sense of the inherited, often confusing traditions concerning humanity's many spiritual potencies, and finally managed to harmonize or simplify them by seeking the central soul in the breath-soul. In this way a good many thinkers recreated the concept of soul. Others have helped displace the meaning in the inherited concepts, and that has gradually resulted in the formation of an entirely new single soul. In several cases the association between a single soul and the breath has become permanent.

Chapter Eight
The Ego-soul

The ego-soul is an heterogeneous and sometimes obscure body-soul which provides a foundation for stream of consciousness and the center for thought, will, and feeling, in short, the mind. In this way the ego-soul shows a close kinship with our concept of the ego, but it also displays some peculiar features that define it as the source within the individual of thought and will, rather than just being an expression of personality.

The soul of consciousness specializes in perceptions, thoughts, and desires (as does the life-soul) which are the conscious content of the ego. They are often independent, especially when they conflict with other ideas or acquire the character of compulsive notions, compulsive acts, and phobias. This peculiarity of the ego-soul explains why it splits into several potencies, at times assuming an independent and superior attitude toward its owner.

For the most part the ego-soul is described in terse terms that give it an elementary and unequivocal character. That occurs when the ego-soul is presented as simply "the mind" as it is for the Carrier who have two body-souls, one of which is described as a life-soul while the other is called the mind (Jenness, 1943). It is tempting to interpret this simply as the sum total of our psychic states and acts in general, but the term "mind" is too vague to allow such a conclusion. Each case must be examined to determine whether the ego-soul referred to as mind includes all the aspects of the ego-soul listed above, or whether it expresses a single category of consciousness.

In the majority of North American cases where there is enough information about the character of the ego-soul, it is clearly a complex phenomenon which, even if it does not cover everything, does represent several aspects of conscious life. As you can see in the following examples, the ego-soul has in some cases exhibited a particularly wide register.

Among the Greenland Eskimo, the term *isuma* covers temper, thinking, thought, and meaning (Thalbitzer, 1930). The ego-soul of the Kootenay, according to Chamberlain, is the seat of thinking, willing, and feeling. In fact a single word stands for "he thinks, wills, wishes, desires." The Naskapi-Montagnais have a soul-aspect that expresses the mind as "intellect and comprehension," but Speck points out that it is also connected with desire which appears to be its dynamic force.

The Ojibway on Parry Island combine the ego-soul with comprehension, understanding, memory, force of will, and feeling, Jenness says. Among the Cherokee Mooney and Olbrechts found that the soul expresses the mind and the nature of the mind which includes "such concepts as thinking, feeling, being conditioned, being disposed, being in a certain state of mind, and in ritual language, even causation." Finally, the Navajo believe in a particular soul which stands for "mind, will power, volition, reason, and awareness" (Reichard, 1950).

Most Indians believed in several small specialized ego-potencies, but it is reasonable to assume that single ego souls containing only one aspect of the conscious life have occurred, even if these may prove to be relics of a more general ego-soul or the remains of a set of special souls. In some cases an otherwise pronounced ego-soul is connected with physical functions, raising the question of whether it ought to be called an ego-soul. But the Indians did not see the difference we make between physical and psychic, and in the majority of instances of ego-soul in North America, the concept is comprehensive.

The ego-soul generates thought and reflection. Powerful mental activity, for example, characterizes Chipewyan beliefs, Birket-Smith says. Among the Naskapi and the Perry Island Ojibway the ego-soul is associated with apprehension, but the Ojibway stress its connection to understanding and memory; "the soul is the intelligent part of man's being, the agency that enables him to perceive things, to reason about them, and remember them" (Jenness, 1935). Of the two souls recognized by the Menomini, one is "the intellect, which resides in the head" (Skinner, 1912).

The Huron have several ego-souls, one of which is "possessed of reason" while another "thinks and deliberates." The Iroquois have a special soul, functioning "as the means of knowledge, the essence that acquires knowledge." In addition to this intellect-soul there is another, which Hewitt calls "the mind, the intellect." On linguistic grounds he says that "the mind specifically was regarded as that agency, that power of the soul, which could see itself, take cognizance of itself, know itself, hence, the faculty of consciousness. It is used to signify the present thought, the thoughts which succeed one another, the habitual thought or cast of mind, and lastly, the principle of thought, that is, the soul itself."

The intellect-soul among the Creek is called "the good spirit," "his talent," "his ability," "his genius." It gives rise to "thought, planning, and devising," according to Hewitt and Swanton. The Coeur d'Alene believe the heart is the seat of "thought and rightdoing" (Reichard, 1937). Among the Eastern Pomo, *miyuk*, "knowledge," is the name of a soul which is probably an ego-soul (Loeb, 1926). The ego-soul among the Zuni is translated simply as "thoughts" (Bunzel, 1932). The Navajo ego-soul, as it has been described by Reichard, also gives expression to such psychic realities as reason and attention. A differentiated part of this soul is the principle for evil thoughts (and evil actions), conceived as a little concrete substance inside each human.

The ego-soul handles understanding, thinking, and memory. Wherever the intellect is represented as an independent potency, the intellect-soul is included. The Fox, in an exceptional case, say that for words, sentences, and thoughts to be understood, they must enter the mouth of the listener. "We often fail to grasp the meaning of the spoken word. The reason for the failure is that the sense hovered in front of the mouth, and flitted away before finding an entrance" (Jones, 1911). The rule, otherwise, is that the intellectual ego-soul functions as the operative factor in communications between people, meaning that the business of understanding is seated in the ego-soul.

No one could do without the intellectual aspect of the ego-soul, and its value becomes most apparent when it is damaged or lost, a process which can occur in any number of ways. Among the Western Mono, the intervention of supernatural powers can produce a special, abnormal mode. Grayton says a shaman could send a ghost into a person and cause him to go insane. "It entered that man's head, covering up his mind so he knew nothing." The intellect-soul may also be injured if its position in the body is unsuitably altered, according to reports from the Nootka and Shoshone. Boas says that "As long as it stands erect the person to whom it belongs is hale and well; but when it loses its upright position for any reason, its owner loses his senses." Corresponding notions are found in the soul-beliefs of the Wind River Shoshone.

As a rule, however, headache, confusion of ideas, and madness mean the soul has left the body. Mental aberration as a consequence of soul loss occurs all over North America but is most common on the Northwest Coast where ghosts and spirit-animals steal away souls. "Why are you making an uproar, ghosts? You who take away men's reason..." is a passage in a Kwakiutl song (Alexander, 1916). Several of the Indian peoples of the North Pacific Coast, Chamberlain says, thought that "loss of the senses or craziness is caused by the land-otter." But soul-loss can occur as the result of more mundane circumstances, and it is possible to lose one's soul by falling from a horse.

Unfortunately, there is no guarantee that all the cases which result in a loss of senses can be ascribed to the loss of the ego-soul. It is easier to prove that loss of the free-soul results in madness, because in most instances the free-soul plays the role of the ego-soul. I do not mean to suggest that lost mental capacity is always associated with the fate of the free-soul. Indeed in some cases the mental aberration is traceable to the loss of a genuine ego-soul.

The ego-soul is absent when one is mad or partially without the ability to think. But a drunken person is also without reason and the Ojibway have concluded that, "An insane man has lost his ego-soul and, therefore, has no reason. A drunken man, or a man just recovering from a bout of drunkenness, is temporarily in the same condition; his soul moves at a distance from him, so that he consists of body and shadow only and remembers nothing of what occurred during his drunkenness." This can disrupt the next generation. "In his son this disharmony between soul and body may take the form of stuttering, especially if the father lay torpid and memoryless for a day or two after each bout" (Jenness).

In its intellectual aspect the ego-soul supplies the individual with understanding and memory, which seems to be closer to the ego-soul than consciousness. Consciousness is also borne by the free-soul, when it appears as alternating ego-principle, but memory does not appear to form a part of the equipment of the free-soul. It is not at all uncommon for the extra-physical soul to forget the way back to the body, so it seems logical to assume that loss of memory is probably a loss of the ego-soul.

That appears to be behind a well-known myth motif in the Central and Eastern Woodland regions. Among the Coastal Algonquin, the Iroquois, and the Central Algonquin, the profound fear and dread of the dead have nourished ideas about ways to disarm them. A guard on the road to the realm of the dead deprives the recently deceased person of his brain by taking it out or smashing it, which is intended to hinder the dead from thinking of the living and returning to them (Speck, 1935).

But is the myth of the brain-smasher always integrated with the notion of the loss of the ego-soul? Is another soul connected with the loss of the brain, or has this anything at all to do with soul-loss? The first objection is easy to dispose of. The brain is mentioned in Ojibway myth as "the seat of the shadow" (Jenness). But in this case there is a sort of fusion between the shadow-soul, the free-soul, and the ego-soul (Thalbitzer, 1930). Most likely the soul in question here is the ego-soul, not the free-soul. In addition the removal or smashing of the brain has not always been consciously associated with the loss of a soul potency. It is likely that the myth-motif originated among a people for whom the seat of the intellect-soul was the brain (the Menomini), but that through diffusion it afterwards became known among other tribes without the original association between brain and soul being preserved.

The intellect-soul, which activates understanding, thoughts, and memory, must at times be distinguished from intelligence or talent. In the case of intelligence the potency behind the phenomenon explains its existence, and in the matter of talent the potency within the phenomenon explains its strength. The distinction is similar to that between life-soul and life-force. Among the Eskimo on Greenland *isuma* stands for the mind-soul, while *sila* constitutes intelligence (Thalbitzer, 1948).

When thought and understanding are translated in active terms, the ego-soul appears as the volitional soul or will power. The Kootenay, Ojibway, and Navajo adhere to this same line of thought. The Kwakiutl think that people who do not know what they should do have "many minds" (Boas and Hunt, 1902). Among the Crow will-power is at the core of their concept of the soul. Lowie says their word for soul "...is used in speaking of will power and is clearly connected with the word for shadow." Such a connection of the soul's activity to the will also occurs among the Eskimo in the Cape York district. An Eskimo from this region told Rasmussen: "The soul makes you a man. It gets you to will, act, be energetic. It is this which drives the whole of your life, and this is why the body will collapse when the soul leaves it."

The ego soul is also responsible for emotional states. Among the Tlingit the body-soul is represented by the emotive-soul (Lowie, 1922). The Hidatsa soul expresses the nature of a person's disposition; his temper, in a wider sense (Rasmussen, 1935), and that brings it close to the *isuma* of the Eskimo (Swanton, 1908). Among the Creek the life-soul is an ego-soul inasmuch as it gives rise to "sentiments, passions, and feelings of good and evil," while the free-soul is the seat of mental activity and understanding (Curtis, 1909). Among the Ojibway on Parry Island the ego-soul is "the soul that experiences pleasure, grief, and anger."

Not only can the ego-soul govern feelings, but it can also promote wishes and desires. The intellect-soul of the Naskapi, *nictu't (sem)*, also appears as the power which realizes wishes (Hewitt & Swanton). This would be impossible if the Naskapi soul concept had not developed the notion of a powerful guardian spirit. But among the Ojibway, the distant linguistic kin of the Naskapi, the wish-soul is the shadow, a hybrid between ego-soul and free-soul that must assert the ego-potency in its wish-aspect. "Occasionally," Jenness says, "the shadow may divide or become double; one part may wish to co-operate with the soul and body, the other seek to travel or go hunting. The man then becomes a center of conflicting desires. His two shadows contend for the mastery, his struggling soul remains aloof from the body awaiting the outcome of the issue, and the body itself falls sick. There is generally no cure for this condition and the man dies." The psychiatric designation for this condition is, of course, neurosis.

The wish-souls of the Iroquoian peoples are of particular interest. The Huron, Brebeuf says, have a special name for the soul "in so far as it bears affection to any object." This name occurs in such phrases as "that is what my heart says to me," or "that is what my appetite desires." The Iroquois use two terms to denote the ego-soul as wish-soul. The meaning of one term has been distorted while the second term has until recently designated "the mind considered as the seat of sentiment," or "regarded as the agent or seat of desire, purpose, intention, sentiment, of a longing for something" (Hewitt, 1902).

In these cases it is obvious that the wish is regarded as an independent quality in the life-soul. At the same time, among both the Naskapi and the Iroquois, there is a close linguistic connection between wish-soul and intellect-soul. The latter indicates that the wish-soul is a differentiated ego-soul; the former indicates its place close to the life-soul.

The speech-soul also lies on the boundary between physical and psychic soul. Swanton points out that the Haida use the same term for mind and throat, which Alexander finds is "less strange, perhaps, when we reflect upon the importance of speech in any description of the mind's most distinctive power, that of reason." The neighbors of the Haida living on the opposite side of Hecate Strait, the Bella Coola, locate a special life-soul in the throat, which controls the voice (McIlwraith, 1948). It is an independent potency which becomes an owl after death. Although it is more life-soul than anything else, this soul is close to the ego-soul.

The Navajo tell how the first human couple were provided by the powers with the breath of life, mind, and voices (Reichard, 1944). Navajo rituals are heavily dependent upon an intimate connection between sound, speech, breath, and power of movement, and Reichard says that according to Navajo belief, voice, speech, or language constitute a combination between breath and sound. But while the Navajo describe the voice as an essential human quality, it is not certain that they understand it as a real ego-soul.

Seen from several aspects, it seems natural to assume that the ego-soul like the life-soul, may exist as several independent potencies. After all, the absolute unity of the ego does not occur where a dual soul belief prevails. There appear to be two sorts of potencies, inherent and intrusive. Only the inherent potencies, which are congenital and as a rule connected to the individual, are real ego-souls. The intrusive potencies do not belong to the individual, and sometimes exist only momentarily when a certain quality or psychic capacity arises

Even when these potencies have a more permanent character, they may, through the nature of their effect upon the individual, betray their alien origin. Harrison writes that "the ancient Haidas believed that everyone had a number of mice in their stomach, and each mouse represented the wicked and restless soul of a departed relative. A man who was always quarreling and fighting was supposed to have within him a soul which in his former life was addicted to such vices." The effect of that is to blame personal qualities on the activities of intruding beings. "Characteristically enough," Harrison says, "these 'souls' could also be active in dreams. Chief Edenshaw, the superior chief of the Haida nation, calmly told me that on one bright summer's morning, having got up early, he went for a stroll over Rose Spit and came upon some women who were sound asleep. To his horror and great astonishment he saw that their faces were covered with mice. He sat down quietly and watched them. Presently he saw a mouse disappear down a woman's throat, then another, and quickly no less than seven vanished down her throat. Out of the seven that had disappeared only one returned as he had evidently gone down the throat of one of his tribe instead of the throat of an enemy. This left six woebegone souls inside of this most unfortunate woman."

It is also important to distinguish between momentary and constant ego-soul pluralism. The first appears when the will is divided or desires conflict. Pluralism occurs when differing aspects of ego activity are ascribed to the activity of various spiritual potencies. Such ego-soul pluralism occurred among the Huron, Iroquois, and Creek. The Huron and Iroquois believed in the existence of two intellect-souls and one wish-soul, while the Creek believed in a thought soul and a feeling-soul (Hewitt). The split between intellect and wish souls resulted in a sharply defined dualism, though this dualism appears to be secondary.

The dependence of the ego-soul upon the body shows in many ways. The voice-soul, for example, is the power behind a physical organ, it remains in the body, grows with the body, has its seat in the body, and it merges with the life-soul. The Carrier at Bulkley River believe that the ego-soul never leaves the body during its life-time (Jenness, 1943), a view shared by the Hidatsa (Curtis, 1909). According to the Menomini, the ego-soul grows with the body, and when a man has reached maturity, he is completely controlled by it (Skinner, 1913).

Like the life-soul, the ego-soul may have a physical seat in the body. The cognitive-soul of the Eastern Pomo resides inside the body, but it is not known where. Either the localization has always been indefinite, or else it has been forgotten (Loeb, 1926), though as a rule the location of the soul is known. A specialized ego-soul like the speech-soul falls between physical and psychic activity, and may be associated with the throat, but the ego-souls that express mental states are found in the head or in the heart.

Locating the ego-soul in the head or heart seems logical. Among the Zuni "the head is the seat of skill and intelligence, but the heart is the seat of the emotions and of profound thought" (Bunzel, 1932). The soul-beliefs of the Huron are closest to the Zuni, followed by the Creek and the Menomini.

While the head is the only seat of the intellect-soul, the heart may be the point where the intellect-soul and the emotive-soul meet. An illustration of this occurs in Spier's report about the way the Havasupai understand the relationship between mental activity and the body. "The blood in my vein,"one Havasupi explained, "goes into my brain and my heart. When it enters my brain I think what I am going to do. My thought goes on all over my body. It (both blood and thought) causes my whole body to move about."

In most cases, though they come from widely separated parts of North America, the head is the seat of the ego-soul. Sometimes it even has a definite location. The Wintu say it is behind the ear (Dubois), while the Navajo say it is in the back of a person's head. The free-soul is also most often associated with the head, and the intellect-soul and the free-soul often combine with each other. The *navujieip* of the Wind River Shoshone is both ego-soul and free-soul, and in both capacities it is located in the head (Wyman, Hill, & Osanai).

Sometimes this soul has an emotional overtone despite being located in the head. The Shoshone, for example, also experience *navujieip* as a wish-soul, but they locate it in the head. While it is possible to find plausible reasons why the life-soul should reside in the head, it is hard to see why the emotive-soul should be located there unless it has been subordinated to an ego-soul of predominantly intellectual character. But the ego-soul connected with the heart, may be predominantly emotive or predominantly rational. The first is easy to understand because the rapidity of heartbeat reflects the individual's emotional state. A Sinkaietk who has become ill from great sorrow is said to be "broken-hearted" (Spier, 1938).

It is not surprising that the ego which governs feelings has its central seat in the heart. That is the case among the Lenape and

above all among the Huron and the Iroquois. The Huron frequently use the phrases "that is what my heart says to me, that is what
my appetite desires."

The Cherokee say, "Our soul has its seat in our heart. What we
think starts in our heart, and the heart sends our mind out" (Eastman, 1949). A person who is not in possession of all his faculties
is said by the Dakota to "have no heart." It appears probable that
the connection between the intellect-soul and the heart arises from
its connection with the emotive-soul.

What seems clear is that Indian thinking frequently does not
differentiate between the intellectual and emotive even when one
dominates. The emotive aspect of the ego-soul is sometimes less
noticeable when the ego-soul is associated with the head, but
when it is strongly perceptible, if not predominate, it is easily located in the heart, which after all has become the focus for widely
varying psychic and physical functions. Even the free-soul can be
found there.

I might add that when in its intellectual aspect the ego-soul has
its seat in the heart, it is because thought is not understood as an
independent abstraction. As a part of a greater whole it is colored
with emotional qualities, and thinking is judged according to its
moral worth. "You have only spoken with your lips, not from
your heart," says the Lenape Indian when describing someone
who says what he does not mean (Heckewelder, 1821). Among
the Zuni, as I have shown, the heart is the center for profound
thinking. "I shall take it to my heart" means according to Bunzel,
"I shall ponder it carefully, and remember it long."

The Zuni also say that people can communicate with one another through their hearts. "Heart speaks to heart, and lips do not
move" (Stevenson, 1904). In most such cases the ego-soul is both
intellect-soul and emotive-soul. A good example of that comes
from the Ojibway on Parry Island. Here the ego-soul is situated in
the heart, and it is at once intellect, perception, memory, volitional, and emotive-soul; "the soul that experiences pleasure, grief,
and anger" (Jenness, 1935).

The qualities collected in the heart, especially those qualities
which express strength of feeling, will-power, and courage should
be regarded as physical attributes, not as independent potencies,
although their content aligns them with the emotive-soul as a
Menomini legend shows. Here courage and bravery are connected

to the heart. "The hearts of brave men are small, while cowards, who run away when there is fighting to be done have large, soft hearts" (Skinner and Satterlee, 1915). The Sauk once found a fallen enemy who had "only a small piece of gristle" instead of a heart. "The possession of the small heart was what made him the brave man that he was" (Jones, 1911). Among the Western Yavapai a man without fear is said to have a "big heart," while a coward is believed to have a little heart (Gifford, 1936).

No such identity between the potency and its physical substrate occurs in the ego-soul. The Kootenay use the word heart as a collective term for the many and varied aspects of the ego-soul, but they do not say, according to Chamberlain, that the physical heart is identical with the spiritual heart.

The ego-soul has its firmest association with the body when it coincides with the life-soul. This occurs often, but first and foremost where an undeveloped single soul formation has made its appearance without losing the ego-soul aspect. The Athapascans of the Great Slave Lake and the Naskapi are good examples, but it also occurs with a regular dualism in the form of free-soul/body-soul. The Wintu say in describing their ego-soul, "It is your life; it makes you wake up from sleep; it makes you think things; without it you would be like a deaf and dumb person; it is what guides you all the time" (DuBois, 1931). The *niya* of the Oglala is more than life and life-soul. "Its functions during the life of the person are to cause vitality, to forewarn of good and evil, and to give the power to influence others" (Walker, 1917).

The more immediate causes of the connection between ego-soul and life-soul are obvious. Each of the souls gives expression in its own way to the collected vital functions of the individual. The transition between them is therefore natural and unforced. And the more closely the life-soul is welded to the ego-soul, the more it reveals its dependence on the body.

The ego-soul is an exponent of the body's life. But that does not mean it must always be bound to the body. Like the breath-soul, the ego-soul can loose its moorings, at least temporarily, and abandon its body-soul functions. This can occur because the ego-soul includes elements which can release it from its dependence upon the body, especially in its intellectual capacity. One result is that the ego-soul can split into its dominate parts, the emotive and the intellect, as they orient in opposite directions.

Among several eastern American peoples the intellect-soul is intimately connected with the free-soul and often identical, while the emotive-soul, through its association with the life-soul, is firmly anchored in the body. The distancing between the intellect-soul and the body occurs because the intellect-soul is relatively inessential in matters of maintaining life. It is not a concrete entity, it is mobile, and can project itself. When the ego-soul alone represents the body-soul in a dualistic relation, it is bound to the body, but where it operates together with a life-soul it easily assumes a position of secondary importance.

The Navajo believe that very old people have lost their evil mind. An Iroquois can have four or five ego-souls of intellect type at the same time, while on another occasion may be without any. The intellect-soul can be driven away by the storming feeling-soul, says DeQuens. According to the Nootka, the first woman in the world was without an intellect-soul; "hence women are believed to be more flighty and less intelligent than men" (Sapir, 1925). The intellect-soul (and probably the ego-soul in general) is characterized by its abstract and indefinable nature. If it is seldom conceived concretely, that is because it has an abstract character and its limits are vague. In addition it is not dependent upon the body but adapts itself easily to goals far beyond the body and can project itself toward those goals.

A soul that is not absolutely necessary for the immediate functioning of the body, that is abstract and reflects the extra-physical, can quickly and easily sever its connections with the body. It is therefore not surprising that as the soul of light trances and as the absent intellect of the insane, the intellect-soul has demonstrated a far-reaching detachment.

The ego-soul is completely abstract when in mystical meditation it floats beyond the limits of the ego and merges at a higher spiritual level. You may recall how in the peyote vision a Winnebago finds his thought identical with the soul-mass of the cult group. And the Pawnee "conceives it possible for a number of persons to so unite as to think and act as one spirit" (Fletcher, 1904). Such mystical exercise is facilitated by the identical nature of the ego-soul and free-soul. In certain abnormal states of mind (insanity, mental confusion, frenzy), the ego-soul is an extra-physical power that has been lost to its owner. As a rule it then coincides with the free-soul.

This identity between free-soul and ego-soul is just as common as the identity between life-soul and ego-soul. Older sources have sometimes described both free-soul and ego-soul with the term rational-soul. This symbiosis of souls also appears in younger ethnographical investigations.

The free-soul among the Dakota is also "the soul which accounts for the deeds of the body" (Lynd, 1889). The Bella Coola say that during waking hours the free-soul "formulates every thought, no matter how trifling. When a man remembers that he left his fire with insufficient fuel and hurries home to rectify the omission, it is this element which has brought the need to his mind" (McIlwraith). In the psychology of the Bella Coola, the mind is in itself a soul, and there the connection seems to be that "every activity of the mind is due to supernatural causation, the functioning of the spirit." (McIlwraith). The fusing of free-soul and ego-soul means that the ego-soul participates in all the qualities of the free-soul, including its existence outside the body. It is interesting to note that according to the measure in which the newly created soul acts as ego-soul, it assumes a visible, concrete form. Among the Wind River Shoshone the ego-soul is identical with both the life-soul and the free-soul, and it appears as "a black little thing, thin as a hair." The diminutive size of the ego-soul shows that it has has been modeled after the free-soul.

When the identity between ego-soul and free-soul is complete (which among some peoples is always the case, and among others occurs on certain occasions), the ego-soul liberates itself from the body. I said before that the ego-soul has the capacity to split into a body-soul and a free-soul, and that it is the intellect within the ego-soul that is identified with the free-soul. It is certain that whether the ego-soul is split or not, it is the ego-soul dominated by intellectual aspects that is combined with the free-soul.

Of the four causes for this, one is particularly important and that is the quality in the intellect-soul expressed in the phrase "the flight of thought." Thought shows the same or greater mobility as the free-soul. Just as dreams of distant places are interpreted as the journeys of the dream-soul, so the thoughts of remote things (and especially day dreams) sometimes imply the removal of the thought-soul to them. When a Bella Coola Indian thinks of a remote place "his spirit is responsible for the thought and some people even believe that it has traveled there" (McIlwraith). In a popular Tlingit legend thoughts fly forth on the sunbeams like arrows (Garfield and Forrest, 1908). This way of thinking also illustrates how the Zuni mind can absent itself from the body to find out the secrets of other beings (Hagar, 1908). It also throws light upon how in meditation the ego-soul can remove itself from the body. And finally it explains why longing should sometimes be defined as absence of the ego-soul. Among the Cherokee the ego-soul is absent in "acute cases of love sickness, home sickness, melancholy, and dejection" (Mooney and Olbrechts, 1932).

In the second cause the free-soul acts as a principle of consciousness during sleep or trance. The free-soul is frequently the ego of the dream, and because of that it may easily expand to the point where it stands for the individual's collective consciousness. The separable soul demonstrates its connection with self-consciousness by the way in which its absence during sleep, trance, or coma paves the way for such a notion. But if the free-soul in dreams represents consciousness, and the free-soul is lost, which of course sometimes happens, its loss may also imply the loss of the ability to reason.

The third cause is closely connected with the second. If reason is lost, this may imply that the ego-soul is lost. A lost ego-soul must appear as an extra-physical soul, showing the special features of the free-soul. It is possible in some cases that the permanent free-soul comes to coincide with the ego-soul when the ego-soul is lost and has an extra-physical existence.

The fourth cause of fusion between ego-soul and free-soul comes in part from the free-soul being partially independent of the individual. Its double-ganger provides premonitions and presentiments which affect the owner's understanding and thoughts. And the more the free-soul develops into a guardian spirit, the more it will intervene in the sphere of action of the "mind" soul.

If by being anchored to the life-soul, the ego-soul has established its body-soul character and through its ties to the free-soul, it has increasingly freed itself from the body, it has remained an instrument for the psychic resources of the personality. In three ways, however, it demonstrates its limitation. First off it does not always resume all the manifestations of consciousness which remain distributed among other souls (the Wind River Shoshone). Secondly, it sometimes exists only as the researcher's collective term for a number of souls, specialized or not (the Huron). Finally, at least for the Carrier, it functions only as the soul of waking consciousness.

As long as the ego-soul is not the focus for the personality as a whole, ego is a vague concept. A story from a Winnebago shaman illustrates this. "When I had grown up to be a lad, although one not large enough to handle a gun, a war party attacked us and killed us all. I did not know, however, that I had been killed. I thought that I was running about as usual until I saw a heap of bodies on the ground and mine among them. No one was there to bury us, so there we lay and rotted" (Radin, 1923).

Such facts make it clear that the ego-soul may develop in a way which removes it from its direct ego function. What normally expresses the ego-consciousness may be strengthened and may detach itself from its primary function to become a *daimonion* in the individual. This is accelerated when the ego-soul connects with a free-soul that has advanced to the rank of guardian spirit.

The nature of the conception controls its appearance as a more or less independent being operating on its own. Brebeuf says that one of the intellect-souls of the Huron was *oki andaerandi,* "like a demon, counterfeiting a demon." The Naskapi, whose "power of thought" manifests itself in desire, are able to attain the changes they are aiming at by establishing contact with the cause of their thoughts, the soul guardian-spirit, the Great Man, who is stimulated by singing and the beating of drums (Speck, 1935).

The ego-potency here is an attribute of the soul transformed into a guardian spirit that must be placated and satisfied. At the same time it often represents the individual directly, serving as "the seat of the appetites, emotions, and passions, again in correspondence with the traditional terms, heart and mind" (Speck). Among the Ojibway and the Naskapi the ego-soul is, in its volitional aspect, a powerful, half-alien potency. "A weary Indian," Jenness says, "dragging his toboggan up a slope may feel that something is helping him along, pulling on the toboggan with him; it is his soul that has come to his aid."

The Kwakiutl also say that the mind has an independent nature. A Kwakiutl who acceded to his wife's request to keep away from a certain fellow-tribesman said, "then my mind met the wishes of my wife" (Boas, 1930). Nootka belief, reported by Sapir, says that the Creator placed a vertical pillar of ten faces superposed one on top of the other in the breast of the first human being as the principle of consciousness. "If all ten faces look in one direction, the man's will is strong; if five look one way, five the other, he is in a state of evenly-balanced hesitation."

The ego-soul, emancipated as an independent entity within the individual, becomes a power-being. In its most independent form the ego-soul acquires supremacy over the other body-souls and forms a being more or less detached from the individual which controls his ego from a higher plane. It becomes a kind of alien, superior entity, a "conscience."

When the ego-soul is connected with the free-soul/guardian-spirit, the distance is intensified. Among the Bella Coola "a sudden thought is caused by the intervention of a supernatural being," obviously the free-soul in its mind aspect (McIlwraith). Among the Naskapi when someone has eaten human flesh and thereby become a *witigo,* a cannibal, "his spirit grows so strong that they (his enemies) would be afraid to attack him, so a conjuror could destroy him only by sorcery" (Speck,1935).

Independent, detached, and elevated, the ego-soul may easily assume the character of a conscience or at least of a principle of character. Through its dominance over the ego the soul is vested with a social responsibility, and it is naturally judged, according to its actions, as good or bad.

Sometimes to explain the alternation between good and evil people relied on two ego-souls. The earlier mentioned "mentality" of the Bella Coola consists of two parts, "one constantly urging to good deeds, particularly to activity in ritual matters, the other to evil" (Walker). The Navajo believe that "bad and good are both in the mind." The good principle is a sort of conscience and this emerges clearly in the Navajo confession offered in the face of the powers of the universe: "I am ashamed before that standing within me which speaks with me," they say, referring to the good conscience (Matthews, 1897).

The ego-soul of the Coeur d'Alene functions as a conscience with the heart as the seat for "thought and right doing" (Reichard, 1947). And one is probably justified in classifying in the category of conscience the *niya* of the Oglala, inasmuch as its function is "to forewarn of good and evil" (Walker).

The Great Man of the Naskapi, in many respects a fusion between ego-soul and free-soul, is also a conscience, as Speck points out: "An ethical factor is also present in Naskapi soul philosophy, for we learn that as the Great Man becomes more willing and more active in the interests of his material abode, the body of the individual, he requires that the individual tell no lies, practice no deception upon others. In particular he is pleased with generosity, kindness, and help to others."

To the extent that the ego-soul merges with the free-soul, it can also communicate with the individual while he is dreaming. The free-soul in dreams represents the consciousness of the sleeper. Only in its connection with the free-soul can the ego-soul develop into the soul of the subconscious. Through its association to the free-soul, the ego-soul becomes a principle for both conscious and subconscious. This appears in Iroquois and Huron beliefs about messages from supernatural powers, "brought to the knowledge of man by the reasonable soul in the form of an innate desire or in a dream" (Hewitt, 1895).

The Wyandotte mention a special dream-God whose name means "The Revealer," or "He makes the Vision," or "He makes the Dream." Connelley says "he was supposed to have something to do with the supernatural influences that acted upon this life, and he revealed the effects of these influences to the Wyandottes in dreams. All visions and dreams came from him, for he had control of the souls of the Wyandottes, while they slept or were unconscious from injury or disease."

Ragueneau reports that among the Huron and Iroquois the desires of the soul itself could be expressed through dreams, "which are its language." The Huron say that our inner desires become conscious to us "by means of a certain blind transportation of the soul to certain objects," a transportation which takes place during dreams; and we are told further that it is the rational and not the sensitive-soul that is active during dreams.

Clearly the view held by the Iroquois and the Huron about the hidden activity of the soul is a precursor of modern depth psychology. This example is not the only one. Wherever the ego-soul constitutes the principle for the subconscious mental life of dreams, it has become associated with the free-soul.

Other examples come from the Sioux and Shoshone. The *nagi* of the Oglala, which is both free-soul and intellect-soul, "can communicate with mankind, directly or through the medium of a Shaman" (Walker, 1917). The *navujieip* of the Wind River Shoshone, which is at once dream-soul, guardian spirit, and ego-soul, gives the individual advice while his body is at rest. The *mugua* of the Paviotso appears as both conscious and subconscious soul. An old Paviotso told Steward: "I also was interested in women. My soul confessed it. It once said to me in a dream, 'one thing I cannot get away from is love for women. I can get along without other things, but I cannot get along without women.' I shall never be able to outlive this. I found that this was true and spent much time in the company of women."

Probably no soul, except perhaps with the exception of the breath-soul, has a higher capacity than the ego-soul to mingle smoothly with other souls. Among the Wind River Shoshone both life-soul and dream-soul may act as ego-souls, and the breath-soul and the ego-soul form a single conception.

As a rule the ego-soul is a manifestation of the general body-soul, an alternative to the life-soul in a restricted sense. This means that the ego-soul is often found as the concentrated body-soul or as the representative of the body-soul in a dualistic relationship. It has, moreover, physical points of contact with the life-soul, leading to the suggestion that the ego-soul has in a way been a life-soul from the beginning.

Chapter Nine
The Free-soul

While the free-soul, the soul active outside the body, is a single soul concept, it is often embodied in the ego-soul or the life-soul. That is the result of relaxing the strict dual relationship between the souls which has gradually transferred the free-soul to souls of other origin, such as the body-souls.

There are two free-soul concepts. The first is the specific free-soul, a soul which never functions as a body-soul, and appears as an extra-physical soul. It is commonly identical with the soul of dreams. The second is the psychological free-soul which functions as an extra-physical soul. Ideologically it represents a soul which, when not appearing as an extra-physical soul, is either a passive entity, the specific free-soul, or is an active body-soul (life-soul, ego-soul). Every body-soul which is temporarily converted into an extra-physical soul displays in its extra-physical appearance (but never otherwise), the properties that are combined with a specific free-soul.

Of course the specific free-soul is the dominate free-soul, which is also the original free-soul, and is best able to preserve the qualities characteristic of the free-soul. It also possesses features which do not belong to the psychological free-soul. They are connected to the functioning of a free soul, specifically, position and state during periods of passivity. The psychological free-soul may be a body-soul which displays its body-soul properties during extra-physical activity. To understand the correlation between free-soul types and subjective and physical states, it is important to understand the nature of the free-soul.

In its most typical form the free-soul is an extra-physical form of existence. It is best understood as a psychological concept within a strictly dual soul-configuration. In the regular dual soul-system, the free-soul is a shadowy representative of the individual, a commonly neutral mirror image standing in a constant reciprocal relationship. The free-soul appears when the physical person does not appear as an actively operating being, for it is identical with other people's memory-images and recollections of the individual, and with the latter's own impressions of activity while dreaming or in a similar state.

The characteristics of the free-soul include its functioning during passive states (sleep, trance, unconsciousness), its vague contours and fluid nature, its fundamental singleness, and its tendency to form an *alter ego*. From the individual's viewpoint the free-soul in its genuine form is the ego when the life-soul and ego-soul are not in action. In dreams and states of trance one experiences the natural and supernatural worlds through the free- soul, but in a genuine dual relationship the free-soul may also appear consciously conceived. This appears, easily enough, as an alien personality which paves the way for the conversion of the free-soul to a supernatural power and protective divinity.

I said earlier that dreams, trance-visions, and memory images are the basis of the free-soul concept. It is significant that the material from North America shows unequivocally that the free-soul must originally have been combined with abnormal states of consciousness. Experiencing visions, most often in dreams, has been the decisive factor in the evolution of the free-soul.

Two types of dream experiences characterize the free-soul; one referring to the nature of the experience, to the ego sensation, while the other refers to the content of the dream-image. The first, the dream-feeling, emerges directly from the dream-experience assuring the freedom of the dream-ego as it breaks from the restrictions of physical existence. Its genuineness is confirmed by comparing the dream with ordinary waking experience which proves that the dreamer can journey independently of the body.

In the second type, the dream-image, when the dreamer sees himself or persons standing close to him the free-soul appears in its own shape. It is chiefly as dream-image that recollected images influence the idea of the free-soul. The Indians emphasize how dreaming reinforces their belief in a soul separable from the body. One Havasupai, according to Spier, "said that he did not see himself as an actor in his dreams. He sees parts of his body in action and feels their relation to a central core, his personality, just as he does when awake."

In the development of the free-soul, the dream image confronts the ego as it supplies the model for the appearance of the free-soul. For ordinary people the free-soul, for the most part, operates while the body is sleeping. The capacity to see the soul in the waking conscious state belongs only to the shaman.

Because the free-soul has its origin in dreams and trances it appears quite naturally as a pale image of the individual (Arbman). It is, in essence, an image soul, quite literally, reflecting its owner. But the resemblance between the individual and his free-soul is not limited to the outer form because it also reflects individuality or ego.

Morice refers to the free-soul of the Canadian Athapascans as an "alter ego...a kind of double, a reflection of the individual personality." LeJeune says the Indians at Three Rivers "reason about the souls of men and their necessities as they do about the body." Among the Fox the free-soul "has all the physical and mental attributes of the body" (Jones, 1907). The chief free-soul of the Mohave, Deveraux says, "is the 'second self' of a person, and in a way the core of his identity."

Establishing such an identity means that the free-soul cannot come to grief without including the living man. The Bella Coola say if the soul is lost, the owner must die. And McIlwraith makes it clear that death comes from loss of the soul and not the event.

That, of course, places the free-soul among the psycho-physical equipment of the living, and because it is in reality the individual himself, he can scarcely dispense with it (Arbman). Nevertheless, a number of reports show that people believed it was possible to go on living a normal life without a free-soul.

According to reliable reports certain categories of individuals can dispense with the free-soul without injury to their health. Children, it is believed in some quarters, are without a free-soul during their first years of life. Some groups believe that adults can dispense with the free-soul for an even longer period. Sometimes it is thought that certain individuals live their whole life without a free-soul. The Coyukon according to Jette, question whether a white man possesses a free-soul at all. "The prevalent opinion appears to be that the whites are deprived of this protecting devil, and to this may probably be traced the facility with which a Ten'a will murder a white person, if he thinks himself safe from the pursuits of human justice."

However, it is more common for an individual to be equipped with a free-soul from the beginning, but for one reason or another losing it permanently, even many years before dying. Advanced age and crimes against the supernatural are the usual reasons. A Seneca who does not listen to his dream-soul will lose it. "He will be compelled," Converse says, "to live out his earth life bereft of his immortal soul."

Normally, as the representative of the ego outside the body, the free-soul is undivided. It is always the only soul agent outside the body and is not only experienced as an exclusive entity but is also conceived by the consciousness as such. In certain circumstances however, the unity of the concept may be lost.

The metamorphic capacity of the free-soul plays a part in that. The many extra-physical forms the free-soul assumes do not occur simultaneously but alternate so that they exclude one another. This of course proves that it is the *same* free-soul which operates although it shows itself in different forms. If however, these are fixed by a traditional belief in several free-souls, each may appear in a special guise.

Another possibility is offered by the amalgamation of the free-soul and body-soul. The Iroquois in Ontario have two free-souls, because the free-soul has come to coincide with the concept of the ego-soul, which has been divided into several entities. The free-soul is multiplied when coupled with a life-soul concept which is similarly divided into several entities. In this way the Kamia have acquired four free-souls.

Sometimes the free-soul may be doubled if the body-soul imitates its activity as it does in both trance and coma. The Wind River Shoshone have a dream-soul but alongside that they have a life-soul which appears as an extra free-soul.

Finally, there is a free-soul pluralism which is sometimes a consequence of conscious attempts by the religious thinkers to construct new soul-systems. The Wintu doubled the free-soul by leaving room for the physical shadow in their soul ideology. Shamanistic four-soul speculation sometimes led to the creation of one or two new free-souls, reaching an extreme among the Mohave whose four free-souls represent the entire soul ideology.

Probably they were created as instruments for the dream religion common to the Colorado River peoples.

The free-soul is a product of the tension which occurs in a dual scheme where the soul is active when the individual is not. From this it is possible to draw two conclusions. First, the free-soul is only comprehensible as an extra-physical soul, and during its active period fulfills no function as a body-soul. Second, that it has no function for the body when the body's own souls are active. It is only in its secondary capacities of higher potency, double-ganger, and power-entity that the free-soul enters into a relationship with the physical individual.

The relationship of the original free-soul to the body during its passive period poses a problem. Obviously the free-soul must exist when it is not functioning, even though it is at such times superfluous. Yet when the free-soul has been established as a specific soul-entity and has been made the subject of speculation this changes. When one considers that the prolonged absence of the free-soul from the body marks a state of sickness followed by death, it is clear that life and consciousness depend upon its presence in the body. It must therefore exist in the body when it is not active.

The Nomlaki describe the connection between the passive state of the free-soul and its residence in the body when they say that "the spirit stays in our body just like our shadow" (Goldschmidt, 1951). During its existence as a guest in the body, the free-soul is commonly inactive. The most that can be said is that it keeps watch. A Kwakiutl woman declared that "the soul never goes to sleep at night, nor in the day. In the day it stays together with us, and keeps watch over us. But when night comes, and we go to sleep, then our soul immediately leaves us" (Boas, 1921).

The Indians can describe the exact location of the free-soul in the body during its passive period generally assigning it to places associated with the souls of the body, an important circumstance when looking for the origin or cause of the final merging between body-soul and free-soul. For the most part the free-soul is in either the head or in some part of the head or in the heart. In a couple of cases, the Eyak and Achomawi, the free-soul is in the breath, which may indicate a developing single soul (Birket-Smith & deLaguna, 1938).

The head is the seat of the free-soul among the people of the

Northwest Coast and among the Shoshone. The Kwakiutl, say that the soul "always sits on the head" (Boas, 1921) but that is only true during the shaman's curing ceremony, before the soul is pressed into the body. They even mention where the Kwakiutl shaman presses in the captured soul "on the right hand side of the neck" (Boas, 1930).

Among the Bella Coola the free-soul resides "in the back of the neck," where according to Boas, it "is similar in shape to a bird enclosed in an egg." The back of the head and the nape of the neck are mentioned as the seat of the free-soul among the Plains Cree, the latter of particular importance when danger threatens (Boas, 1891). Other much favored locations for the free-soul are the crown of the head and the brain.

Without doubt locating the free-soul in the head occurs because the ego-soul already exists there (the Menomini, Creek, Wind River Shoshone). It is perhaps significant that some of the free-souls located in the head are actually only single souls of a more or less free-soul type. The Lemhi, White Knife Shoshone, and Nevada Shoshone provide examples of that.

It is equally natural to fix the free-soul in the heart as it is associated with the life soul (the Tepehuano) or with the ego-soul (the Cherokee). Where this fusion does not occur the free-soul may nevertheless be connected with the heart through one of the body-souls or simply because there is no place else.

But the heart-soul and "the soul in the heart" are not always the same. The ego-soul of the Nootka and the undifferentiated body-soul of the Havasupai are both called the "heart," but then they also reside in the heart. Sapir points out that the St. George Paiute word for soul is heart and they have a different word for the organ itself. But among the Walapai the life-soul is called the heart, and the free-soul is said to be situated in the heart which means that both souls are located in the heart. It seems almost as if the logic for locating the free-soul has followed the pattern people applied to locating the body-soul. But sometimes the case is quite the reverse as among the Tubatulabal where the life-soul, identified with the breath, resides in the heart while the free-soul, which they locate in the head, is called the heart.

The explanation for that seems to lie in the fact that the habit of referring to one of the body-souls as the heart occurs rather irregularly in North America, and using the same designation for the free-soul is only found in California. If you recall that several Pueblo peoples call their single soul the heart (the San Juan, Cochiti, San Felipe, Santa Ana, Laguna, Acoma) then the diffusion of this idea into California is easier to understand. The Pueblo also believed that the heart is the seat of the soul, and quite likely currents from the Pueblo culture contributed to the development of the idea that the heart is the surviving soul, and since the surviving soul was at the same time a free-soul, the free-soul came to be called the heart-soul.

The free-soul located in the heart also occurs among some eastern peoples such as the Naskapi and Montagnais, among some Southwestern tribes, the Walapai and the Ute (Opler, 1940), among some Californian groups, the Sinkyone and the Yokuts, and among at least two Northwestern peoples, the Spokan (Wilkes, 1845) and the Lummi (Stern, 1934).)

It is possible that anchoring both souls in the heart comes in part from the loss of older concepts. In other cases the connection between heart and free-soul is a late occurring phenomenon connected with the development of a single soul. The Naskapi provide a good of example of that. If we include the Tepehuano and Cherokee then it is clear that the majority of the instances in which the ego-soul is located in the heart offer evidence of single souls with strong free-soul tendencies concentrated in the heart (Parsons, 1939). Typically, when the heart's soul occurs as the lost soul-entity in soul loss, it is almost always a question of either a body-soul, or a single soul with both free-soul and body-soul aspects. In the Pueblo culture, for example, it occurs when the heart has been stolen (Parsons, 1939).

The Indians are not nearly as certain where the free-soul is located when it is in a passive state. The Athapascans in Canada say the free-soul is "invisible in time of good health, because then it is confined within its normal seat, the body" (Morice, 1911). On the Northwest Coast descriptions are often most general. The Kwakiutls say that "the body is the house of the soul" (Boas, 1922). The Chinook and the Cocopa of the Southwest say with great conviction that the entire body constitutes the seat of the free-soul (Gifford, 1933). The Fox, finally, seem to believe that the free-soul never enters the body. It is called "the outside soul" and is conceived of as a guardian outside the individual (Michelson, 1925).

The free-soul fulfills its actual function only when it appears outside the body as a replica of the living individual; an extra-physical ego. As an interior soul it scarcely fulfills any function. It is also self-evident that this copy of the individual appearing outside the body, despite its identity with the individual, does not have the same properties. In the first place the free-soul is often indifferent. The Walapai, call it *matkesa* or empty body (Kroeber, 1935). Furthermore it belongs to the supernatural world and therefore bears a different nature than the individual. From a psychological viewpoint these properties derive from the fact that the free-soul usually appears during sleep and trance in the abstruse world of the dream-vision.

This free-soul does not represent a physical presence but rather gives expression to a more ethereal airy and sometimes misty conception. Because of its human form and its delicate substance, the free-soul is generally represented as a shadow which is why it is often referred to as a shadow or a shade soul or a shadow spirit. Thalbitzer says that the name of the free-soul on Greenland, *tarrak,* "may mean both reflection and shade or shadow." The free-soul of the Coyukon, *yega,* signifies picture or shadow (Jette, 1911). The free-soul of the Carrier, *bitsen,* is described by Jenness as "reflection in water, shadow cast by the sun or moon, ghost or apparition of a living person."

The surviving free-soul of the Tlingit is characterized with a word which, according to Swanton, signifies both image and shadow. The Algonquin Speck says, generally associated the free-soul with the shadow. The free-soul of the Montagnais is compared with the shadow, as Le Jeune pointed out. Shadow and image are the words used for the free-soul among the Coastal Algonquin from the Micmac in the North to the Delaware in the South. The Cheyenne call the free-soul, "his shade or shadow" (Grinnell, 1923). Indians of the Southeast, the Choctaw, for example, believe in a free-soul which may be rendered by shadow, shade or the like (Swanton, 1931). The Catawba refer to the free-soul with a name that expresses the concepts of the ordinary shadow and mirrored image at the same time (Speck, 1939). The *nagi* of the Dakota, Riggs reports, signifies "primarily the *shade* or *shadow* made by any material thing in the sunlight." And the free-soul is also characterized as a shadow among a number of Northern Californian groups and Southwestern tribes.

But there is no mention of a shadow-soul of free-soul type

among the tribes on the southern Plains; the Shoshone, Piman, and Pueblo peoples. This may be in part because among these groups the single soul either already existed or was in the process of development. But the habit of comparing the free-soul with the shadow does not always presuppose a strictly dual soul-belief as the following examples illustrate. The Wind River Shoshone make no comparison between the free-soul and the shadow, but the Paviotso in Owens Valley, whose soul-belief is practically monistic, liken their soul to a shadow (Steward, 1933). What they presumably want to indicate is the free-soul character of the soul concept they hold, for rarely is the original life-soul compared with the shadow.

In the final analysis the misty image of the individual has occurred more frequently in the northern than in the southern parts of North America. There the shadow has not only lent its form, but its gray hue to the appearance of the free-soul. And yet despite that, the soul may also appear as a brightly colored being, it may change in size, or it may assume the form of an animal, a plant, or an inanimate object.

The color of the free-soul sometimes coincides with that of the shadow, inasmuch as it is a dark soul. LeJeune says that the Algonquin "represent the soul of man as a dark and somber image." Among the Quileute "the outside shadow," the free-soul, is somewhat darker than the inner soul, according to Frachtenberg. The Lemhi say that the "spirits of Indians are darker than those of white men" (Lowie, 1909). Dixon says that the free-soul of the Maidu is gray in color, while among the Cora a recently deceased person appears in the shape of a black man (Preuss, 1912). The color black in North America is frequently the color of death. It is therefore easy to understand how among the Hamilton Shoshone and among the Paranigat Paiute in southeastern Nevada "death caused the soul to turn black."

Generally however, the Paiute imagine the soul as red. Their linguistic kinsmen, the Gosiute, hold a similar belief, saying that the soul, which leaves the body, is red or white (Steward, 1941). However, most often the free-soul is the color of fire or light, both hues indicating the affinity between the soul and the supernatural world.

The *inua* of the Eskimo may appear according to Alexander, in the form of a light or a fire. Olson says the Quinault have seen the soul rise up out of the body of a human being looking like the full moon. These same Indians say they have seen the soul of someone who has just died "flying through the air like a ball of fire, throwing off sparks and making a crackling sound like burning spruce twigs."

Speck says that when a Chinook is at the point of death "the soul resembles fire, and sparks fall down, and it seems like a firebrand." Speck also says that according to Naskapi belief, "the soul-spirit often appears as a spark of illumination" when it glides out of the mouth of a medium or a shaman who is in a trance. Tanner reports that lightning flashed when the soul left an old Naskapi Indian. As a matter of fact, notions of the soul at times leaving the body as a spark or ball of fire occur in the whole of the northeast. Speck makes it clear that this has nothing to do with shooting stars, however much a shaman might connect lightning to the soul in the course of his conjurings.

The dream-soul of the Iroquois has the appearance of "a small spark of fire," Converse says. From old sources we learn that the Tuscarora and the Cusabo (of the Muskhogi group) believe the soul leaves the body of a dying person in the shape of a spark or a flame (Swanton, 1946). It is the soul of a dying individual that the Blackfoot describe as "a ball of fire" (McClintock, 1910). The free-soul of the Omaha, which floats over the ground, is surrounded by a glimmer of light, a halo, according to LaFlesche, while Curtis says that the free-soul of the Mandan is the color of light and transparent. It should be pointed out here that the Wahpeton Dakota identify the will-o'-the-wisp over swamps as the spirits of the dead, but that "when a man sees a will-o'-the-wisp and is not frightened by it, he is looking at his own spirit which has temporarily left the body as it will do permanently at death" (Wallis, 1923). The Skidi Pawnee liken souls to small stars but this is the result of astral speculation and myth-formation in this society (Dorsey and Murie, 1940). Among some other peoples, the Shawnee, Zuni, and Navajo, for example, it is the life-soul that produces light.

The free-soul may also change in size. Crawley says that the diminutive soul arises from the memory-image of a human being, and that "the brain, using its experience of size and distance, prefers to see a man at such a distance that his size is equal to the size of an object that can be fully seen in the hand." It is true that the shapes seen in dreams as well as other hallucinatory states such as alcoholic delirium, often assume a diminutive form. On Greenland according to Boas, the life-souls associated with separate physical organs are very small.

Most of the material on the size of the free-soul comes from descriptions of the way in which a shaman restores a soul to the body. It must be small enough to be held in the cupped hands of the shaman or to fit into a moccasin or a gourd or a tube. All instances of the soul conceived as a miniature being come from the Northwest Coast, the Plateau, the Great Basin, and the Central Woodland because those were the places where shamanistic soul restoration occurred.

But what does this manikin look like? Among the Kwakiutl and Kathlamet (Chinook) the free-soul is likened to "a small bloody ball" (Boas). However, among the Kwakiutl it generally looks like a human being and less frequently like a bird. The Haisla, who belong to the Kwakiutl, say that "a soul is the exact image of a person, but it is only as big as a fly" (Olson, 1940). Similar ideas have occurred among the Nootka. Boas "heard several Indians maintain that they had seen the soul caught by the shaman, who let it march up and down on a white blanket."

The Quinault say that a man's soul is "ten inches in diameter, while the soul of a woman is still smaller. It looks like a tiny baby, yet looks like fog" (Olson, 1936). The Bear River Athapascans in California describe the soul (probably the free-soul) as "a small creature about two feet high, and strictly human in appearance, dress, and actions" (Nomland, 1938). The Shoshone also conceive of the soul as a miniature being, and both the Nevada Shoshone and the Gosiute, believe the soul is the size of a pea (Steward, 1943). The transparent soul of the Lemhi Indians is ten inches high (Lowie, 1909). The free-soul among the Wind River Shoshone is "very thin and one inch high."

Souls are also dynamic. The free-soul of the Kwakiutl Indian shrinks to the size of a thumb when the shaman displays it in his hand, but when placed on its owner's head it grows until it fills out the entire body (Boas, 1921). A Kwakiutl woman explained that "in the daytime it is small, but when we are asleep, it is big, when it travels about where it is going" (Boas). Among the Chinook if the runaway soul of a sick person is brought home by the shamans, and they notice on the way that the soul is shrinking, this may mean that the restored soul will not fill out the body and the person will die (Boas, 1893).

"Now your soul fades away," the Cherokee say in a magic formula intended to deprive an enemy of his life, "your spirit shall grow less and dwindle away, never to reappear" (Mooney, 1891). The Fox run the risk of the free-soul becoming too large and turning its owner into a murderer (Michelson, 1925).

The supernatural capacity of the free-soul refers to both quantitative and qualitative changes of shape. The free-soul may appear in a non-human shape assuming the features of some animal, a conception which most likely originates in dreams and visions, and is closely akin to the notion of the guardian spirit, which in the same hallucination looks at once like a human being and an animal (Lincoln, 1935; Lowe 1935, 1951).

Seldom does the free-soul appear as a four-footed beast, and though the Kootenay believe that the free-soul may appear as a bear, and for the Navajo it sometimes assumes the form of a mouse, it more commonly appears as a reptile, an insect, or other mite. The Haisla and the Kwakiutl see it sometimes in the shape of a worm. Among the Iroquois, the Plains Shoshone and the Cahuilla, it appears as a snake or a lizard. The Cahuilla may also see it as a grasshopper, as do the Navajo.

The free-soul also appears, as it did for the Greeks, as a winged being; a bird or a flying insect. Such occurrences are strikingly few and the majority are on the West coast. The Tsimshian and the Southern Paiute conceive of the free-soul as a butterfly (Boas, 1910). The Kwakiutl sometimes say simply that the soul flies (Boas, 1921). The White Knife Shoshone say only that it reminds one of a bird (Harris, 1940). If a Bella Coola Indian faints, his soul has flown away. "The shaman hears its buzzing wings, which give a sound like those of a mosquito" (Boas, 1892). The Huchnom (the Yuki, California) say that thunder is caused by "the flight of some Indian's many-winged spirit up to heaven, flapping its pinions loudly as it ascends" (Powers, 1877).

When the appearance of the soul is described as a bird, it is generally a smaller bird. The Huichol identify it as a little white bird and the Luiseno describe it is a dove (Lumholtz, 1904). The Kootenay believe that the free-soul can show itself as a tomtit or jay (Chamberlain). The Kwakiutl think that the owl represents both the deceased person and the free-soul of the living individual as a double-ganger. There is nothing strange, of course, about the notion that a fugitive, delicate free-soul should assume the shape of a bird or other winged being, and it seems likely that peculiar dream experiences such as the sensation of hovering or flying have stimulated the development of this popular concept.

What is more difficult to understand is how the free-soul, as it does among the Kootenay and the Wind River Shoshone, can assume the form of a flower or a tree (Chamberlain). The Naskapi describe their guardian soul as having developed from the free-soul as a flower (Speck, 1935). In some cases the free-soul appears as an inanimate object. It is easy to see how among the Kwakiutl and the Shoshone in Nevada and at the Great Salt Lake, the free-soul is represented as a ball of eagle's down for the fine light feathers mimic the ethereal nature of the free-soul.

But among two Salish tribes, the Bella Coola and the Spokan, people believe that the free-soul resembles, "a thin bone shaped like a maple leaf." The Spokan believe that the free-soul appears as a bone in its capacity as surviving soul, perhaps based in the notion that bones are the visible remains of the deceased and serve a symbolic role. The Nevada Shoshone liken the soul to a hailstone (Steward, 1941). LeJeune says that when an Algonquin wizard wishes to kill an enemy, he sends his guardian spirits after the latter's soul, which then sometimes looks like a stone.

The most important of the non-human forms in which the free-soul appears is without doubt theriomorphic. Not because the deceased person in the shape of an animal is a continuation of the form assumed by his free-soul during his life-time but because the free-soul in animal form and the deceased person in animal form have the same psychological (hallucinatory, illusionary, incidentally associative) cause.

In both cases it is impossible to distinguish between the animal as the form in which the soul or the ghost is manifested and the animal as the dwelling of the soul or the ghost. That the soul always appears as soon as it leaves the body is connected with the fact that it usually personifies an independently operating liberated spiritual substance.

Any determination of how the free-soul functions must be based upon the extra-physical appearance of a soul without considering whether the soul is a free-soul or a body-soul. But at the same time it is necessary to be aware of the correspondence between the state of the body and the nature of the extra-physical soul. The best course is to analyze how the free-soul functions in light of the physically conditioned states in which it is active.

The dream-soul, a free-soul type that executes the actions of the dream, undoubtedly constitutes the purest and most important free-soul. It has nothing in common with the body-soul since the body-soul never appears in dreams.

The most typical function of the dream-soul is dream wandering, perhaps best characterized by Nomland's lines from the Bear River Athapascans: "Dreams were believed to be the recollections of experiences which the freed spirit of the sleeper had encountered. When an event occurred, of which the sleeper had dreamed, he always said, 'That is what I saw when I dreamed'." In dreams the soul is liberated from the limits set by time and space, and the idea of the soul wandering in dreams can be identified in every corner of North America. The soul which lives the experiences of dreams is, in a dual soul scheme, an independent free-soul, without contact with other souls.

Dream wandering produces a drama whose content is determined by the dreamer's experiences or an outsider's observations. The dreamer experiences the events from within, while the observer describes the form in which the soul makes its exit from the sleeper and how this exit takes place. A Haisla Indian reported that when a fellow-tribesman was asleep, "queer white wood-worms would come out of his nose." (Olson, 1940). Similar experiences most likely convinced the Tubatulabal that the dream-soul leaves its owner at night through the ears (Voegelin).

Through the influence of tradition internal and external experiences are welded into a consistent interpretation of the dream action as the respective experiences of the observer and the dreamer are made to agree with each other. Two Iroquois hunters were waiting for dawn beside a little brook in the wood. "One was drowsy and half asleep, when his companion, who was watching the eastern sky, saw a small spark pass from the mouth of the sleeper and float in the air to the edge of the stream, crossing it on a silvery willow leaf which was drifting to the opposite bank. Hovering there for a moment as if confused, it finally entered the skull of a small bird which lay on the bank and disappeared. The watching hunter did not disturb his companion, and when at sunrise he awoke, he related a strange dream that had come to him."

In the dream he had "in a great light as if with wings" floated in the air to a distant country where an ocean extended from horizon to horizon. In a silver canoe he voyaged over the great waters to the other shore, where a big eagle awaited him. The bird bore him to its home "whose pearl-white dome touched the high sky above the gray clouds." Seldom can an outsider read the experiences of the dream from the events in the world of reality. It is the dreamer who lives the experiences of the dream.

A Sinkaietk shaman who in a dream sees the free-soul of another person, distinguishes it from a real man because it is "going fast without walking." The gliding movement of the free-soul in the dream-vision frees it from the inhibitions of daylight consciousness, while the quickness of the free-soul seems to reflect the short period of time during which the dream action takes place (Wolf, 1919).

Most narratives of dream journeys are a stereotyped repetition of the same thing: the soul wanders about in a world that looks like our own, but whose figures reveal their supernatural origin by their fantastic behavior. "You do the most impossible things," say the Wind River Shoshone. The Thompson River Indians say that "the soul of a person who has a nightmare is nearing the beginning of the trail leading to the world of the souls" (Teit, 1900). In de Angulo's view the Achomawi are more conventional believing that in the evening the free-soul departs with the sun and returns with the dawn. But the dream-soul does not always return. Many dangers await the wandering soul. If it wanders to the realm of the dead the dreamer falls ill or dies later on (Greenlee, 1944). Other dangers threaten. A malevolent shaman may seize the opportunity to snatch the dream-soul, and its owner upon awakening is either ill or insane (Spier, 1938). If the soul of a sleeping Kwakiutl Indian "goes too far away and comes not back again, the man remains in bed asleep and is dead" (Boas, 1921).

An untimely awakening may leave the soul no time to return to the body. If a Paviotso Indian, according to Park, is awakened too suddenly his soul does not return, and unless the shaman cures him, he becomes sick and dies. The Cahuilla will wake an ordinary sleeping person, for the dream-soul "knows it and can return instantly." But they take care not to waken a sleeping shaman. "His spirit has gone so far away and is so very busy that it cannot return immediately" (Hooper, 1920).

Moreover, a soul recalled too hastily may perhaps not find the right way into the body. "Sometimes," one Kwakiutl explained, "the souls come back the wrong way, when they return and then the soul is hurt when it comes quickly and goes in crosswise or upside down. Then the soul is not strong enough to come out where it is held and the man at once looks sick" (Boas). In cases where the victim does not fall ill or die, the soul loss may at first manifest itself in dreamlessness.

LeJeune says if the Indians in New France "cease to dream, they say that their soul has left them; if the Devil arouses their fancy, their soul has returned." A number of Canadian Athapascans were convinced that death must gradually result from prolonged absence of the dream-soul (Mason, 1946).

There is some risk in experiencing the body as a separate entity, for if you perceive such a distinction the dream must be regarded as a premonition of death (McClintock, 1940). But as a rule the emergence of the dream-soul concept implies the beginning of a change in the relationship between the free-soul and the individual, in which the free-soul becomes easily understood as an independent being, an event which begins the dissolution of the intimate association between the free-soul and the individual.

This dissolution is enhanced by the fact that in dreams the individual does not merely experience himself in the shape of the free-soul, but feels the free-soul as a separate object. A Wind River Shoshone sees himself acting in dreams in his own shape or in the shape of an animal. The orientation of the ego becomes confused and the dreamer sometimes identifies with the soul, and sometimes sees it detached from his ego. "How did I get here? How can my spirit get back to my body?" the Walapai Indian asks (Kroeber, 1935).

Dream wandering is a spontaneous act of the dream-soul, and in the majority of cases is independent of the waking self. Anything positive performed in the course of the dream wandering is a result of the soul exhibiting its own will and capacity.

Probably the chief positive function of the dream-soul is its role as cognitive-soul, spying out events and developments in distant places and in the future. It finds out "what you're going to do," a Kaska told Honigmann. The explanation of a Kwakiutl shaman concerning the behavior of dream-souls in dreams is also illuminating. "In the morning when it is nearly daylight, they come home to the owners of the souls. And then they tell where they have been and what they have seen where they have been all around our world, and that is what we call dreams, the news that is told by the souls when they come back to us" (Boas, 1921).

Tylor says that the theory of the dream-wandering soul is one of the alternative interpretations that North American Indians apply to the mysteries dreaming. The other is the theory concerning "a visit from the soul of the person or object dreamt of." The instances of such dream-visits are legion but unless it appears as one object among others, observable to the dreamer, it has no function at all, other than producing speculation. For example, the Mohave say that it is the dream-soul that sees the free-souls of others in dreams (Deveraux, 1937).

Where the free-soul as dream-soul appears as a guardian spirit half-emancipated from its owner, the free-soul provokes the dream. The free-soul of the Bella Coola, for instance, "is the cause of dreams which are desired as a means of foretelling the future." (McIlwraith). The guardian soul sometimes appears as a being alien to the individual's ego in these dreams. If the dream-soul is the experiencing ego of dream adventure, this implies a reduction of its proper function. Du Bois says emphatically that the Wintu, who believe in dual souls, do *not* associate dreams with any belief in the free-soul leaving the body.

Here the dream function of the free-soul has lapsed. That eliminates the free-soul, unless it has an essential function to fulfill in states of trance or sickness. The Yokuts, who experience the events of dreams through the heart (soul), have a single soul (Grayton, 1948). Several other tribes, the Cherokee, the Sanpoil-Nespelem, and the Klamath, which also do not believe in a dream wandering soul believe in a single soul.

The dream-soul may occur as a free-soul in practically all situations of extra-physical soul activity, but it is only in the dream experience that it stands alone as a free-soul. In other cases it shares its function with souls which are primarily body-souls which can also appear as free-souls and temporarily assimilate conceptual elements belonging only to the dream-soul.

The free-soul appearing in states of trance displays this mixed character. In a lighter trance (the trance of waking consciousness) the dream-soul plays scarcely any role at all while the ego-soul and the double-ganger are more evident.

In deep trance it is the dream-soul or the body-soul which bears the individual's consciousness. It is always one of these souls that in the moment of visionary ecstasy, particularly during the procedure of shamanizing, wanders about outside the body. When the trance is not too deep, as in the fasting vision, a free-soul appears which is commonly identical with the dream-soul. But when the trance is so deep that the individual appears to be dead and cataleptically stiffened, then that individual may have been abandoned by some body-soul.

The vision appearing to the fasting individual may often be combined with the extra-physical appearance of the free-soul. For example, among the Plains Cree the free-soul might, according to Mandelbaum, leave the body in a vision and journey about with the guardian spirit. In this case, as it was among the Wind River Shoshone, the contact with supernatural powers has been mediated by the free-soul. This is generally the same as the dream-soul for the fasting vision is much like a dream. Only in exceptional cases does it acquire dimensions of depth. An Ojibway Indian who had visited the sky during a fasting vision woke up and "found that three more days had passed away. During this time my body had lain there motionless as a corpse; only my soul had wandered so freely in the air. Then I breathed, sighed, and moved about like one waking from a deep sleep" (Radin).

The deeper trance, however, is clearly connected with a shaman practicing medical skills. In the state of ecstasy the shaman's soul frees itself from the body in order to seek out and fetch the soul of a sick person who has gone astray. Generally, this therapy corresponds to soul loss during sickness. Not only during the technically induced ecstasy does the shaman carry on his medical activities. Thanks to his labile psychic equipment he can also use his supernatural capacity during other states of absence. For instance among the Bear River Indians, shaman spirits were said to travel during dreams, faints, and trances, during the training dance for new shamans, and the curative dance for the sick" (Nomland, 1938). In this case, because a high degree of identity obtains between different twilight states, Nomland is referring to the dream-soul.

If the Hidatsa have a soul "that is active in dreams and visions," it means that no distinction has been drawn between the psychic states (Curtis, 1909). The character of psychic absence here outweighs individual differences. It is the free-soul, and not those of the body, that have drawn the greatest interest.

But when one focuses on the states of the body, the distinction between normal sleep and trance becomes natural. Still another circumstance must be taken into consideration. As a rule, the shamanistic act (in connection with curing soul loss) requires such pronounced psychic concentration that the medium's state of absence contrasts strikingly with other twilight states. In some cases there is a direct correlation between the apparent lifelessness of the body during the trance and the appearance of the body-soul as a free-soul. This makes it probable that the body-soul's abnormal mode of activity has been stimulated by the situation of the body. In other words, the lifelessness allows the liberation of the body-soul and its appearance as the incarnation of the individual outside the body.

All the evidence points to this interpretation. The Wind River Shoshone assume that every person has a dream soul which can detach itself from the body, but in the case of the shamans the body-soul is also separable. The necessary prerequisite for this differentiation between two free-souls is, as I have tried to show, that a distinction has been drawn between the light unconsciousness of sleep and the heavy unconsciousness of the shaman's trance. The dreamer lives, breathes, moves; but the shaman sunk in ecstatic trance appears to be dead. A Lemhi doctor who was curing soul loss "went into a trance, ceased breathing, and was like dead while going in search of the lost soul" (Steward, 1943).

The trance state is therefore tantamount to death. The consequences of this for Indian modes of thought are two. In the first place, during his soul's excursion the shaman reaches the realm of the dead, or it is at least within his power to get there. In the second place, the body's soul may be absent from the body and appear as a free-soul. The dream-soul is not actualized if the body-soul functions as a free-soul. The freed body-soul is no longer a body-soul but represents the person's consciousness and individuality outside the body. Among the Cocopa, who have both body-soul and dream-soul (Gifford, 1933), the body-soul is the soul which leaves the body during the trance state and the evidence for that is the inhibition of vital functions which means that the soul connected with them leaves the body and appears as an extra-physical soul.

While in a trance the shaman thus dispatches the dream-soul or, if the vital functions are evident, the soul responsible for all the manifestations of life. It should be remembered that the shaman does not always send his own soul after the fleeing soul of a patient. Among some of the peoples on and in the vicinity of the Northwest coast, especially the Coastal Salish and Northern Californians, as well as among some Western Shoshone groups, the shaman might dispatch his protective spirit instead of his soul. Among some groups near Puget Sound, such as the Lummi, Snohomish, Quileute, and Quinault, the shaman follows his guardian spirit, but probably only in dramatic pantomime.

Deep trance is qualitatively close to the psychic twilight state associated with a coma. The two states also resemble each other in the way the soul can reach the realm of the dead...evidently a consequence of the view that the complete stupor of the individual is equivalent to death. On the whole the shaman has the same experiences, whether he has fainted or intentionally gone into a trance. It happens that in the vision which defines his calling, the free-soul of the shaman is carried away to the realm of the dead to be initiated into the secret healing art. The psychic twilight state corresponding to this flight of the soul is identical to the twilight state of trance.

As coma and trance are qualitatively equivalent in respect to the depth of the absence and also because they mediate the same visionary results, one might expect that either the dream-soul or the body-soul should operate outside the body in both states. But in a great number of cases it is a pure free-soul, (of dream-soul character) which appears during unconsciousness.

Definite instances of the body-soul taking over the role of the free-soul are few. Moreover, loss of the body-soul does not always prevent the free-soul from remaining active as the representative of the ego-consciousness in the state of lethargy. In many cases the acting soul constitutes a single soul, frequently of predominantly free-soul type. A careful investigation of these cases appears to show that a free-soul assimilated into a single soul has given rise to notions of soul flight.

If this observation is correct, and I offer it here with every reservation, then it affords still more confirmation of the view that in the majority of cases the pure free-soul is the soul which has freed itself from the body during coma. It is therefore also probable that everywhere in North America it was originally the only free-soul during both coma and trance. The appearance of the body soul in this function is a secondary phenomenon resulting from progressive speculation.

In both trance and coma the functioning free-soul (whatever its origin) frequently represents the ego-principle of the individual, and often the form in which he appears. Both the shaman, who has voluntarily visited the realm of the dead, and the person in a swoon, who has involuntarily done the same (perhaps in a coma so profound that relatives have already taken the body to its last resting place), tell, on their return to life, of their experiences in the state of lethargy in the first person. But just as in dreams, the free-soul may in the states of coma and trance be conceived as a potency with shifting relationships to the individual.

The Blackfoot, Flat Tail, felt his "spirit starting for the Sand Hills" (McClintock, 1910). "You feel yourself going away" is the Navajo way of describing the sensations of the ego in the moment of dying (Wyman, Hill, and Osanai, 1942). The soul of the Yuma in the unconscious state (actually a body-soul), behaves as if it had nothing at all to do with the ego. If its owner has lost consciousness it departs and acts like a being with a will of its own. "The soul goes up with the dust caused by the fall and hovers above undecided whether to return" (Forde). But even a genuine free-soul may exhibit the same inclination when in a similar situation. The penchant for independent action always characterizes the extra-physical soul and is one of the chief prerequisites for its development into a guardian spirit for the individual.

Normally the soul's appearance as a free-soul is combined with some sort of twilight state. The separation of the soul takes place in a light trance, a state of waking consciousness, allowing the individual to cross the frontier to another, abnormal form of consciousness. That also occurs in various states of sickness, especially those which are combined with mental weakness. The person may apparently be in a state of normal consciousness, but has nevertheless taken a step into another world. Yet during the states of lethargy proper and in light trance the individual may experience himself in an extra-physical form of existence. The sick person is seldom in the same situation. Soul loss is the rational explanation for an abnormal state.

Insanity, loss of memory, shock, and physical disease are all blamed on the loss of a soul. According to Indian terminology, everyone whose behavior departs from current standards of conduct is insane. The causes of such insanity are broad. Sometimes the disease is caused by a meeting with a ghost. Sometimes it is the result of enchantment by mystical beings, though that is not always accounted as a disease and many madmen are believed to be vessels for the will of higher powers. Nevertheless, in some quarters it is held that a demon can make a person demented by getting control of the ego-soul. It is sometimes fatal for a person to have a dangerous guardian spirit. Insanity may also be a consequence of the ego-soul being shifted from its position or it may be traced to the loss of the ego-soul or the dream soul.

There is nothing remarkable about insanity being connected with the loss of the free-soul. In accordance with the nature of the dual soul system, the free-soul appears outside the body whenever the body's souls are deprived of their normal function. In this connection the free-soul becomes an alternating principle of consciousness. If the free-soul does not return to the body, the person may suffer a markedly reduced ability to comprehend or understand. He becomes strange or in a number of cases goes completely mad. The degree of mental aberration is sometimes related to the distance between the lost soul and its owner. "Once in a while," a Nomlaki said, "people get nervous or dissatisfied, and Indians claim that is when the spirit goes out and comes back. The shadow of a crazy man goes far away from him and he doesn't know anything" (Goldschmidt). The loss of the free-soul is of course not always connected with insanity. Still the frequency with which it is cited as a cause is striking.

It is less common for mental debility to be blamed on the loss of the ego-soul. Nonetheless, in many cases the identity between the lost soul and the ego-soul should be suspected as a cause. Among the Puyallup and Nisqually it seems quite clear. However, everything in such cases indicates that the free-soul function of the ego-soul is secondary.

Loss of memory, another form of mental weakness, is connected with the loss of the ego-soul in its memory aspect. The concept is not, however, clearly developed outside the mythology, and the ego-soul is presumably imitating the function of the free-soul in insanity.

Finally, soul loss diagnosis may be applied to an imagined or actual sickness which refers only slightly to mental weakness. Two types of disease occur, one the result of a momentary mental twilight experience, the other a result of physical disintegration. In both cases the sick person is awake and in both cases the soul must be returned or the patient will die.

In North America it has been commonly believed that the free-soul can exist outside the body without the immediate loss of consciousness or normal vital activity. If the free-soul has attained a high degree of independence its appearance outside the body need not entail any risks for its owner. However, if the extra-physical activity of the free-soul is the result of having found itself outside its owner as the result of temporary mental or physical trials, then the person will be in danger until the soul has been restored.

The notion that a shock may separate the free-soul from the individual is also widespread in North America. Psychologically, the idea is easily understood. For some short moments during extreme fright or when experiencing a slight confusion, the soul is driven out of the body. "The spasmodic contraction of the muscles is enough to expel it," say the Bella Coola (Clements, 1932). An old Cheyenne woman said, "I was so badly frightened that I saw my shadow" (Grinnell, 1923).

Seldom, however, does one see one's own soul in a waking vision without suffering dangerous consequences. Such a shock may cause loss of consciousness, paralysis, or some other illness. It is believed that the fatal effects may be felt, even if the victim does not at first suffer any ill-effect. There is no lack of descriptions of such eventualities and not even a shaman is immune.

An old Achomawi shaman who sustained a slight concussion when his buggy collided with a motor-car, later said his soul had been left at the scene of the accident and he had to return and call it back to him. In the cases sketched here it is as a rule the regular, permanent free-soul which is believed to have been lost. One must not, however, exclude the possibility that in one case or another it may have been the body-soul.

Steward distinguishes between two causes of disease among the Shoshone in Nevada, "intrusion of a foreign object, which is usually, but not always, indicated by an acute pain; or loss of the soul, which is usually indicated by unconsciousness." It seems to emerge from this that soul loss as a cause of illness was diagnosed in cases in which the victim was unconscious, and under varying circumstances the same diagnosis may have been applied to all, or at least the majority of diseases. A mild illness which grows worse and leads to loss of consciousness and death may at the outset have been diagnosed as soul loss. The life-soul may, after the pattern of the free-soul, be the chief actor in a soul loss drama, and just as the free-soul leaves the body when the individual is lying unconscious, so a specialized life-soul leaves its organ when the individual is paralyzed or in pain.

That the concept of the stolen free-soul may be influenced by the pattern of the life-soul is shown by the soul beliefs of the Kamia. As I have shown, a Kamia Indian may have no fewer than four free-souls which have taken over the functions of a vanished life-soul. "A person with more than one soul might become ill from the theft of one, but would still live" (Gifford, 1931).

Among other peoples the same rules apply for soul activity during illness, but always with reference to the life souls. The specialized life-soul is better fitted to such situations than any variant of the free-soul. Therefore it seems reasonable to assume that at least in one case, the Kamia, the appearance of the free-soul in connection with ordinary illness has been modeled after the pattern of some organ-soul. However, from a broader perspective the extra-physical activity of the specialized life-soul in such cases of illness is an imitation of the activity of the specific free-soul in connection with illnesses combined with an abnormal state of consciousness.

It should be noted that the general life-soul does not abandon the individual in case of ordinary illness. If it leaves the body in states of trance or coma, it is because in such states the individual sometimes shows such barely perceptible signs of life that he is regarded as dead. It is understandable that if one of several life-souls leaves the person and vital activity is weakened, it nevertheless continues at other points. In all cases in which the life-soul is reported to be missing during ordinary illness, it is not the general vital principle that has left the body, but one of the specialized organ-souls.

A good example is presented by the soul-belief among the Greenland Eskimo. Every limb of the body is provided with a soul and a pain in one of the limbs implies that its soul has departed. Since the soul is not necessary for total vital activity, its loss, as a rule, is not a great misfortune (Thalbitzer, 1930).

It should come as no surprise that among an Indian group, such as the Coastal Salish in Canada, both souls are able to fulfill the functions of the free-soul (Barnett, 1938). The probable explanation is that only the specific free-soul has found adequate expression.

The extra-physical soul has until now appeared to researchers as a single soul concept, psychologically as well as ideologically. But the ideologically unitary nature of this soul is only apparent. Psychologically, on the other hand, one is justified in speaking of a single free-soul idea. And the older ethnological investigators make a point when they characterize the extra-physical soul as the most important soul-concept among native peoples.

Chapter Ten
Mystical Extensions

A mystical extension is best understood as a real or imagined substance directly connected with the individual and bearing his essence. It is not a repetition of the individual himself, it is a part of him. If a replica of the individual, his shadow or his image, is placed in a mystical relation to him, it becomes an expression of him and is then conceived of as a free-soul.

The free-soul is the person as a mystical totality, whereas the extension only partakes of this totality. Even if the resemblances are striking, the differences are more essential. The free-soul is the individual, the mystical extension is a part of the individual in the same way as a heart or a hand are a part. And while the free-soul is necessary, at least in the long run, for existence, the mystical extension is frequently unnecessary.

Because of their resemblance to the free-soul, the shadow and the image may sometimes be interpreted as free-souls, and that may also occur for the name which is a mystical extension when it is understood to characterize the whole individual. That the life-soul may also combine with a mystical extension offers a paradox which will come clear as I develop these ideas in detail.

The concrete extensions afford the best and most reliable examples. Of course, each part of the body bears the individual's essence, and they continue to do so even after their eventual separation from the rest of the body. This notion forms the basis for a good deal of black magic which uses such elements as the nails, the saliva, the after-birth, a single hair and so forth, to attack the individual to whom these elements belonged. Even the ashes from a funeral pyre contain the individual essence of the deceased person which explains why the bones of the dead have often been used as instruments in North American Indian witchcraft.

Among the most important extensions are the blood and the hair. In North America the blood, curiously enough, has played a rather unimportant role as an incarnation of the individual's essence. Blood brotherhood, for example, has been extremely rare (Tegnaeus, 1952). Yet the blood has not been entirely without significance as individual essence. The Huron used to mix their blood with that of a slain enemy to acquire knowledge of the approach of enemy forces to avoid surprise attack. The Keres believed it was possible to impersonate an individual by rubbing oneself with his blood (Parsons, 1939). But while many Indian peoples consider the blood to be the seat of mystical qualities, the Ingalik think of the hair as a mystical entity. It must not be burned or cut if its owner suffers from hemorrhages (Chapman, 1921), and Holmberg reports that among the Tlingit, the shaman's hair must never be cut.

The Sinkaietk believe that the individual risks his life by letting his hair fall into an open grave (Spier, 1938). From the Omaha Fletcher reports that "the hair of a person was popularly believed to have a vital connection with the life of the body, so that anyone possessing a lock of hair might work his will on the individual from whom it came. By custom the hair, under certain conditions, might be said to typify life."

In their four soul system the Dakota include a tuft of hair from the deceased. They believe the tuft of hair is a mystical part of the individual maintaining his existence after death (Lynd, 889). The Luiseno use the same word for hair and spirit according to DuBois. Spier found that the Diegueno had strict rules about hair. "Hair clippings, if not used in the manufacture of the cord with which the hair is bound, are burned, for should their owner die he would cry to see his hair blowing about. Another reason for burning them, and nail parings as well, is that a shaman may use them to cause their owner to become insane and die. A man gathers his wife's combings for this reason and also because the shaman may attract the wife."

In all of these cases the hair is a mystical extension of the individual; that it finds a place, secondarily, in the soul beliefs is the result of shamanistic speculation. The hair may be referred to as a spirit, but it does not fulfill any soul function. It is important here to distinguish between soul and essence, and to note that not even a physical potency such as the life-soul is thought by many North America Indians to have its abode in the hair.

That the deceased and their extensions sometimes share identity is another matter. Among the Dakota, Ojibway, and Cree the hair of a dead person is regarded as an adequate representative for the person in the ritual usages after death. The reason is clear enough. The hair is a substitute for the living, concrete person, and the tender feelings that were once given to the physical individual are now transferred to his representative made of hair. It is called the "spirit bundle."

Consequently the hair becomes invested with an independence that it lacked when its owner was alive, and it shares this property with other extensions. Teit says that for the Thompson River Indians, "the toe or finger nail, hair of the head, or any bone of the body of a dead man, may assume the form of a ghost, and pursue persons." The "hair-soul" of the Eastern Dakota shares this notion and becomes after the ritual for the dead "a roving and restless spirit," according to Lynd.

Concepts like these are connected with the scalp of the dead person, which is a complete representative of its former owner. In the Southwest especially, it is given a remarkable personal coloring, for there the scalp lives, screams, makes its wishes known, accepts sacrifices; indeed, even coitus is practiced with it.

Concrete extensions also include excrements and secretions, especially in Western Canada and the Yukon, the same regions which produced legends of excrements that speak and give warnings (Bogoras, 1902). The Ingalik say that "the afterbirth is a part of the body, and you would not want to destroy it, just as when you cut yourself, you wipe off the blood with shavings and place the shavings in the fork of a tree" (Parsons, 1921-22).

Chapman writes that the Ingalik believe that "special virtue" resides in the secretions, as well as in other parts of the body such as the hair, heart and so on. "The sputum of a consumptive must not be burned, for it will take away some of his vitality. Old people sometimes put their spittle into the mouths of children to bring them good luck." The Kwakiutl also believe that spittle is a part of the person, and a wizard who has collected a dose of another person's spittle can kill him with it, according to Niblack.

The Sinkaietk regard the shadow, perspiration, saliva, hair, and underclothes in the same way. An enemy who had collected any of these appurtenances was in a position to destroy their owner. The sequence is reported in a matter-of-fact fashion: "The victim lost his property, fell into consumption, and died" (Spier, 1938). Among the Diegueno, "a shaman may gather the dirt in which one spits and place it on a red ant nest so that the victim will die of tuberculosis. Or he may gather the dirt which has been urinated on, or the feces, thus stopping the functions of the bowels."

In these cases excrements are regarded as extensions of the individual, not as souls. But among the Cherokee, who have as we know a well-developed single soul concept, the soul and the essence inherent in the excrements were, by all the evidence, considered equivalent. In a black magic formula designed to annihilate, the sorcerer says: "Your spittle I have put at rest under the earth. Your soul I have put at rest under the earth. When darkness comes your spirit shall grow less and dwindle away, never to reappear." He then buries a tube containing the victim's spittle and some worms among the roots of a tree which has been blasted by lightning. The victim "feels the effects in himself at once and, unless he employs the counter charms of some more powerful shaman, his soul begins to shrivel up and dwindle, and within seven days he is dead."

The third and last group of extensions comprises objects or living entities that through contact with the individual partake of his essence. As a rule only those endowed with supernatural powers, and especially the dead, can incorporate foreign objects with themselves in this way. A manifestation of this is the custom of destroying a person's property after death. The objects, Bendann writes, which most frequently came into contact with the individual, especially clothes and personal possessions, "are so saturated with his personality that they are regarded as primarily identified with the deceased." As early as 1884 Fletcher wrote that the Oglala believed that the clothing of a dead person "partakes of the individuality of the person."

The sphere of death extends over the objects and the living persons in contact with the deceased. The result is that the dead person drags the living with him. This effect can be counteracted with methods such as sacrificing parts of one's body to the deceased; a finger joint, for example, or a lock of hair, which like the finger-joint, represents the whole of the mourner (Bendann).

The remarkable thing about all such cases is that through the substitution of his own extension, the living individual ceases to be the extension of a deceased person. But such participation may also be transient, particularly when the person in the cult plays the role of the god and partakes of his nature. An external cult symbol is sometimes used to facilitate the transformation. For example, the kachina dancers in Cochiti, "think that in putting the sacred mask on their head they take on the holy personality" (Dumarest, 1919). Such transformations often take place in the mythology, frequently in connection with some ritual act. In the tradition concerning the Bear Woman scattered throughout the Indians from the Northwest to the Iroquois, a woman is transformed into a bear by putting on a bear-skin.

Seldom does a concrete extension gain currency as a soul. The extensions which are of a more immaterial nature, such as the shadow, the image, and the name, may sometimes figure as free-souls. This seems to be the result of their ethereal substance and the bewildering resemblance to the free-soul (in appearance or significance), and they come close to the conception of the free-soul.

The Shadow

Your shadow is a part of you, it has your characteristic contours, and it is in constant, direct contact. Because of that, the shadow evolved into an ordinary free-soul as well as a double-ganger. That occurred in various places around the world and among the Indians of North America. Rarely is the shadow considered as a natural phenomenon. Only here and there has closer reflection led individuals to relate sunlight and shadow. "When the sun shines, my shadow shows; when it ceases to shine perhaps it returns to my body," a Havasupai explained. And a fellow-tribesman said, "I think my shadow goes to the sun, because it fades as the sun ceases to shine" (Spier, 1928).

The shadow, for the most part, is understood as a mystical entity. The Wind River Shoshone boast of having conjured up shadows of themselves, which their enemies shot without injuring them. But as a rule the shadow has a mystical quality, even if its appearance does not betray anything uncommon or unexpected.

The shadow, independent of the individual's actions, follows him and imitates his actions, and in essence becomes a mystical extension of him. Examples of this occur throughout North America but are particularly abundant among the Salish.

To the Bella Coola the shadow is an extension of the individual, and that emerges clearly from their fear of the shadows of mourners. Boas says of these mourners that "their shadows are considered unlucky, and must not fall on any person." The ghost, which after death works mischief in the surroundings of the living, seems to be identical with the shadow (Drucker, 1950).

As I pointed out earlier, the shadow seems to have functioned as a mystical extension of the individual among the Cowichan too, though it was also given the character of a soul. The shadow among the Sinkaietk was associated with sweat, hair, and spittle, and was not permitted to fall in an open grave (Spier, 1938). Of the Algonquin peoples, the Ottawa and Atsina saw the shadow as a mystical extension. The Ottawa believed is was possible to kill a person by drawing pictures of his annihilation on his shadow; and according to Curtis, the Atsina classified the shadow among the mystical potencies which had attained soul-dignity. In the Southeast the Cherokee understood the shadow as a mystical extension (Mooney and Olbrechts, 1932), and the Hidatsa and Arikara regarded the shadow in the same way. But while the Arikara see the shadow as almost a spiritual entity, the Hidatsa include the physical shadow among their souls.

For the Paviotso the shadow has a particularly broad effect, appearing to incorporate everything it falls upon. "If a person's shadow passes over a frog by day or night (moonlight), the frog will follow that person and get in bed with him" (Kelly, 1932).

Among the Pomo the shadow was part of the person. The Coast Central Pomo identified the shadow with the spirit, one of the many mystical spirit-beings of animism (Loeb, 1926). A Navajo told of how he was terrified by an encounter with a ghost while on horseback on a moonlit night. The terror was particularly acute because he thought he was being chased by his own shadow.

In some of these examples the shadow also occurs as a soul, and a number of investigators have regarded shadow and soul, above all the free-soul, as identical. But that is seldom the case, for the shadow-soul and the shadow are different things. Even though the free-soul is often referred to as the shadow, or is represented as a shadow, that does not mean that the ordinary shadow of everyday experience is identical with the free-soul. What they mean is that the appearance and airy consistency of the free-soul are shadow-like.

Sometimes the body-soul is also likened to a shadow, and although this is less frequent, it should be remembered that all souls are close to the shadow, because of their fluid, semi-immaterial nature, and at least for some, because of their temporary extraphysical appearance. For example, the Oglala refer to the free-soul with the same word they use for the shadow, but the Oglala also say that the life-soul, "like a shadow," dwells with the person until death, and that the guardian spirit, *sicun,* "is like one's shadow" (Walker, 1917). The Hidatsa classify the ego-soul as one of man's "shadows" or souls, according to Curtis, and the undifferentiated body-soul of the Choctaw is, like the free-soul, characterized as a shadow.

But a resemblance to the shadow does not imply identity with the shadow, and indeed, as the source material shows, there is often a clear distinction made between the shadow-soul (the free-soul conceived as a shadow) and the shadow. The Haida, for example, have different terms for soul and shadow (Swanton, 1929). The Kwakiutl liken the free-soul to the shadow, but they draw a clear distinction between them (Boas, 1921). The Sinkaietk distinguish between the shadow and the freer shadow-soul, because the movements of the shadow and the body are inseparable, while that is not true of the shadow-soul (Spier). The majority of the Quileute say that the shadow "has no connection whatsoever with any of the souls" (Frachtenberg, 1920). The Penobscot, according to Speck, appear to share this view. For the Blackfoot the free-soul assumes the nature of the shadow, but is not the shadow (Curtis, 1911).

The Wind River Shoshone do not consider the shadow in their soul conceptions. Steward says that neither the North Shoshone nor the Gosiute in the Great Basin consider the shadow to be an independent phenomenon, connecting it neither to the soul nor the ghost. Nor do the Sinkyone question the distinction between soul (free-soul) and shadow. Nomland says that "souls appeared like shadows of their owners but fresher and younger looking."

The River Patwin have different names for soul and shadow,

making it clear that when they say "shadow" they mean the physical shadow. In addition, Kroeber says that is not possible to show any direct connection between soul and shadow among the Walapai, even though the free-soul is described as a shadow. The Havasupai draw a terminological distinction between the shadows of animals and men and those belonging to plants and other objects, but none of these shadows bears any relation to their soul beliefs (Spier).

These examples are unequivocal enough, and yet the free-soul and the physical shadow do, in some groups, merge to form one conception, a fusion that gives the free-soul substance. In such cases the shadow appears as the visible manifestation of the free-soul, identical with the free-soul (Arbman). This implies that the shadow can provide a way to express, to a far higher degree than might a regular mystical extension, the individual's conscious personality, his ego.

However it would be a mistake to conclude that the shadow has given rise to the idea of the free-soul, or that the free-soul was at first identical with the shadow. On the contrary, the free-soul has developed out of inner experiences and was not originally a detached double, but the person. The shadow must, if it is a free-soul, function as a double. How often, then, does the fusion between free-soul and shadow occur? The question is not easy to answer. For one thing the information is so scanty that it is hard to develop any clear impression. And even if the free-soul is called the shadow, this does not mean the two are identical. The following cases, however, strike me as indicative.

Osgood reports that among the Kutchin the shadow is conceived of as an independent spirit, obviously a free-soul. Among the Slave "death was recognized as the loss of the individual's shadow." (Honigmann, 1946). Jenness assures us that the Sarcee regarded the shadow and the soul (the free-soul?) as identical. The Ojibway on Parry Island consider the shadow-soul, referred to as the shadow, as invisible, but it is sometimes described in such a way that it appears to be identical with the real shadow (Jeness). Among the Fox the outer soul, which "is like a shadow in the daytime," may well be identical with the shadow, according to Michelson. Among the Iroquois in Ontario the shadow appears to have been one of the free-souls. The "outside shadow" of the Choctaw, which always follows the person, also appears to be the shadow functioning as a free-soul (Swanton, 1931). One of the free-souls among the Wintu is, as we have seen, nothing other than the physical shadow, and for the Yuma, the shadow appears in the role of the free-soul.

Among these examples, the soul concepts of the Mandan constitute a special case. Their four souls have *all* been represented as real shadows. The body-soul directly coinciding with the shadow in such a fashion has not been reported from any other quarter. Curtis made the observation that the word for soul, common to all the four souls, does not signify shadow but "has grown to be identified with the shadow of man."

The Atsina, Mandan, Hidatsa, and Cowichan, invest the shadow with the dignity of a soul without identifying it with any of the true souls, most likely the product of four soul speculation.

Identifying the free-soul with the physical shadow may have special consequences. Either the shadow-soul is developed into a double-ganger, or it becomes automatically a double-ganger if identification occurs. By double-ganger I mean a relatively independent free-soul which may leave its owner when awake without causing any ill-effects.

The Polar Eskimo, according to Rasmussen, regard the soul as an immortal essence which follows us as our shadows follow us in the sunshine. The Ojibway hold similar views. "When a man is traveling his shadow goes before or behind him; normally it is in front, nearer to his destination" (Jenness). The Wintu free-soul also follows its owner on a journey, staying perhaps a half or a whole day's march behind (DuBois, 1935). The chief among the free-souls of the Mohave, "the real shadow," stands behind its owner, according to Devereux. The shadow-soul becomes a real double-ganger when it is freed from its owner's movements, or when it changes its activity from a passive companion to an active, dynamic spirit protecting its owner. For example, the shadow of the Ojibway is not only a companion, but also a spirit which during its owner's waking hours may be wandering far away.

The Soul Represented in Pictures

The human image, represented in the single plane of a photograph, or a painting, or mirrored in the surface of water, may, like the shadow, reveal a great deal. Three dimensional representations may of course have the same effect, but usually only single-plane images are identified with the free-soul.

Levy-Bruhl says the image is more than a reproduction of the original and is in fact a mystical extension of the individual. From this it follows that if the image is destroyed, the person it represents will die. No understanding of soul belief is necessary to understand this connection, but the image, like the shadow, is reminiscent of the soul, particularly the free-soul.

Everywhere in North America the image bears a mystical relation to its original, but there is no precise information describing the nature of this relationship. Perhaps that is because most of the research was gathered when an Indian was either being painted or photographed. But even when Indians have been directly questioned about their views of the nature and import of the image, nothing definitive arises. It is of particular interest to see how the image glides from mystical extension to free-soul. In a number of cases the material throws light only upon individual behavior in front of the camera or easel, but in others it offers glimpses of the ideology behind the behavior.

While the photographer or the painter runs no great risk (because the danger does not lie in making the portrait but in the mystical connection between the picture and the original) it is still dangerous to have a picture of a person who has died in your possession. The Southern Ute destroy pictures representing deceased persons (Opler, 1940), and the Zuni also remove such pictures, probably because they give rise to a perilous longing for the dead (Parsons 1916). The Blood, too, are afraid of such pictures (McLean, 1892). Among the Dakota only persons who have dreamed of ghosts dare to draw them, and it is said that such a person draws his own spirit as it will look after death (Dorsey 1894). What this offers is a glimpse of both the free-soul and the mystical extension.

Nelson reports that the Eskimo at Bering Strait "believe that persons dealing in witchcraft have the power of stealing a person's *inua* or shade, so that it will cause him to pine away and die." Nelson himself was taken for a stealer of souls when he set up his camera in a village on the lower Yukon. At his request the headman of the village was given permission to peep under the black cloth and when he saw his kinsmen in the glass, flung off the cloth and shouted, "He has all of your shades in this box!" Panic ensued, and all the Eskimo rushed into their houses.

Paul Kane's experiences painting the peoples living around the Strait of Georgia and Puget Sound were similar, though the motives varied. Among the Chinook, Kane's skill was ascribed to a supernatural gift. "I found," Kane writes, "that, in looking at my pictures, they always covered their eyes with their hands and looked through the fingers; this being also the invariable custom when looking at a dead person." A Nootka Indian kept careful watch on Kane, to ensure that he did not paint his fellow-tribesmen, and as a consequence expose them to "all sorts of ill luck." When Kane threatened to paint his portrait if he would not leave him be, he promised not to cause any further trouble.

Among the Cowichan, Kane met an Indian wearing a medicine-cap which he wished to draw. Its owner resisted because he did not wish the cap to be drawn unless he was drawn with it, "for fear it might be deprived of some of its magical properties." A woman, whom Kane had painted, died shortly after his visit, and the Indians assumed he had caused her death. A Snohomish Indian whom Kane had sketched was absolutely serious when he asked if he was risking his life. The Indian stubbornly followed Kane about until, in order to get rid of him, Kane took out a copy he had made of the drawing and tore it up in his presence, pretending that it was the original. Kane also painted a Cayuse Indian who was afraid that the picture would be handed over to the Americans, whom he hated bitterly. He feared that if the Americans had his picture it would "put him in their power." Kane was forced to flee with the portrait, which the Indian, "the most savage I ever beheld," wanted to throw into the fire.

Kane had similar experiences among the Ojibway and Saulteaux. An Ojibway girl from Lake St. Clair refused to sit for him, although her father insisted upon it. "Her repugnance," Kane says, "proceeded from a superstitious belief that by so doing she would place herself in the power of the possessor of what is regarded by an Indian as a second self." On another occasion Kane made a sketch of a Saulteaux Indian and the model's tribesmen laughed so at the picture that the man demanded that Kane destroy or at least hide it.

Other Algonquin tribes have reacted, according to the statements of other writers, in the same way. The Pottawatomi do not want to be photographed, and they smash the cameras of any photographers they encounter. The Cheyenne shared this attitude, as Grinnell points out, "because they believed that when the picture was taken away, the life of the subject was taken away too, and the actual man would die. They regarded a photograph as the man's shadow." McLean says the Blackfoot "seemed to feel that part of their personality left them and was reproduced in the photograph."

Another celebrated painter of Indians, George Catlin, had similar experiences among the Iroquois and Sioux. At times he is in complete agreement, and yet at other times he is completely at odds with the experiences of other painters and photographers. An Iroquois chief said the painting would "make him live after he was dead," a viewpoint that is rare among the Indians.

The keenest attention was aroused by Catlin's art among the Mandan. They felt, he says, that "I had made *living beings,* they said they could see their chiefs alive, in two places; those that I had made were a *little* alive...they could see their eyes move, could see them smile and laugh, and that if they could laugh they could certainly speak, if they should try, and they must therefore have *some life* in them." Catlin also says they thought a painting "took away from the original, something of his existence," so that his life could be destroyed, or so that after his death he would have no peace.

Another of Catlin's models was a medicine man who all the time he was being painted sang the "medicine song which he sings over a dying patient, looking me full in the face until I completed his picture." When Catlin had left the Mandan village, he was pursued and accused of causing, through his "medicine," a young girl to fall into a death-like coma. "The picture which you made of her," he was told, "is too much like her. You put so much of her into it, that when your boat took it away from our village, it drew a part of her life away with it."

Like the Mandan, the Dakota Sioux believed that after death they would be more at peace if no picture of them existed. Nevertheless, an Indian who survived the death of one of Catlin's models appreciated finding the deceased preserved, "alive" in Catlin's portrait gallery. The Sioux do not seem to have had any unanimous view of what consequences might follow having a portrait painted, and that is clear from the conflicting opinions which arose at a stormy council meeting held during Catlin's stay among the Dakota. One Indian said Catlin had "taken our chiefs away, and he can trouble their spirits when they are dead! If he can make them alive by looking at them, he can do us much harm! You tell us that they are not alive yet we see their eyes move, their eyes follow us wherever we go, that is enough!" But one medicine man was delighted to have had Catlin paint his portrait. "I am very glad to see that I shall live after I am dead," he said and then added, "but I know that this man put many of our buffaloes in his book for I was with him, and we have had no buffaloes since to eat." However much opinion may differ over the consequences of having a portrait painted, one thing remains clear; there is no difference between the picture and the model.

Later reports confirm this view among the Sioux. Densmore tells of a Teton Dakota who, having been given a picture of President Wilson, sent a message to the president in which he said he felt that the president had been his guest during the time he had had the picture with him. Dorsey says that the Dakota aversion to having their pictures taken is explained by their belief in several souls. "I have been told," Dorsey says, "that for many years no Yankton Dakota would consent to have his picture taken lest one of his *wanagi* should remain in the picture, instead of going after death to the spirit land."

The older Wind River Shoshone still refuse to allow themselves to be photographed. In the majority of cases they offer no reason, but in the opinion of some, a person is "shot" when photographed and does not live long after. Older persons among the Ute also refuse to let themselves be photographed as "this makes a person die quickly." Photographing the mourning ceremony of the Diegueno destroys its aim, leaving the spirits of the dead bound to the earth instead of being set free to go to the realm of the dead (Davis, 1919). The Zuni say that a person who has been photographed must die (Parsons, 1916). Lumholtz tells us that two Piman peoples, the Papago and Tepehuano, fear having a part of them carried off by the photographer.

The Indians believed that being painted or photographed led to death, and furthermore, that by binding the dead person to his old existence during his lifetime, it gave rise, indirectly, to ghostly disturbances. Of primary interest, however, is the association between the picture and the person. It is believed that it is the "life," the capacity to live, which has been transferred to the picture and not the life-soul itself. In this way the picture participates in the person's nature or becomes identical with that soul which has the capacity to appear outside the body. The picture oscillates between several shifting, vaguely defined significances: it is a mystical extension (the Blackfoot, Mandan, Papago), spiritual essence of floating import (the Chinook and others), free-soul (the Eskimo, Ojibway, Cheyenne, Dakota). But always they see in the picture an individual essence connected with the original, now as a free-soul, now as a mystical extension.

A final confirmation of this comes from Indian pronouncements on the content of the mirror image. Here, too, free-soul and extension form the alternatives. "See-soul-metal" is what the Naskapi call the mirror in their language. The designation used for soul is identical with *atca'kuw,* the shadow-soul (Speck). From the Cheyenne Grinnell reports that "in early days when little trade mirrors were first received, many people refused to look into them, because they would see their shadows, and bad luck would follow." Some of the Shoshone in Utah claimed that "some men had mirrors on their walls in which they captured men's souls when they slept" (Steward, 1943). On the other hand, Kelly tells us the Paviotso viewed with "great hilarity" the suggestion that a reflection in the water might be the soul.

Names

The name customs of the North American Indians, the ways in which they used names, and the conceptions connected with them are so numerous and varied they could provide material for several books. What I wish to establish here is the relationship between individuals and their names. The question is whether a name is an extension of the person or a soul.

The significance a name has for the individual varies greatly in different parts of North America. Birket-Smith reports that among the Caribou Eskimo "names are looked upon as a rather separate part of man." Among the Inland Salish, "a name was regarded as a part of the individual."

Loeb says the Pomo believed the name was an intregal part of the being. Spence found that among the Mexicans the name "was regarded as part of the individual, and through it the ego might be injured, a common belief in both Americas."

Mooney, too, stresses the wide distribution of this belief. "The Indian regards his name, not as a mere label, but as a distinct part of his personality, just as much as are his eyes or his teeth, and believes that injury will result as surely from the malicious handling of his name as from a wound inflicted on any part of his physical organism. This belief was found among tribes from the Atlantic to the Pacific, and has produced a number of curious regulations in regard to the concealment and change of names."

This does not imply that all names participate in their owners' nature. The names of the Havasupai "are mostly nicknames or meaningless words," says Spier, "and they have no special emotional or religious significance." The result is that a Havasupai does not hesitate to reveal his name, perhaps because it expresses few personal qualities.

The transitory nature of names emerges in other ways. For example, the loss of the name does not necessarily mean that sickness and death will follow. A father (among the Athapascans) can transfer his name to his son. A warrior can give his name to a brave youth, and names are changed upon moving to a higher age category, usually in connection with visions or (on the Northwest Coast) upon contracting to marry.

Many people change their name after a relative dies; either because they bear the tabooed name of the deceased, or they want to prevent the dead person from finding his relatives, or because the deceased has been attached to the person's name. In all of these cases, the name may be renounced without ill-effects for the bearer. When the name is transferred to another, the characteristics associated with the name accompany it, otherwise the transfer would be meaningless.

Clearly the name is not always an intimate and inviolable part of the individual. On the contrary, the name sometimes has a loose connection with the individual, and even if it contains something of his essence, it may be disposed of or communicated to others at any time. Yet at the same time a name may be so identified with the individual that it becomes inalienable.

There is, however, a vast difference between the name as an attribute and the name as a permanent, essential soul. As I have said, the Havasupai do not attach any deep significance to the name, while the Inland Salish regard it as a mystical extension. This difference shows how a name can be used as a covering for different realities, providing a simple system of classification for human qualities. The material everywhere shows that names are also used to distinguish people socially, as an external form for a supernatural capacity, as a paraphrase for the essence of the individual, and as an expression for the soul that sustains the whole of this essence; the free-soul. This means that a name has no independent existence, but exists only in association with existing qualities and entities. To name an individual after a dead person implies, that the deceased once more appears among the living.

It is well-known that many Indian peoples give their new born babies or their as yet unnamed fellow tribesmen names based on some striking quality which characterizes them. Many North American Indian peoples are of the opinion that by assuming strong names, they ensure vitality and strength. Boas says the Central Eskimo believe that a sick child becomes healthier if it is given a new, more effective name. The Eskimo at Bering Strait assume new names in old age to strengthen their flickering flame of life (Nelson, 1899). A sick Naskapi changes his name in order to get better, Jenness says, and he also reports that among the Ojibway: "So weak did they consider the bonds uniting the shadow, soul, and body of a young baby that the Parry Islanders refrained from spreading the news of its birth until it had received a name, through fear that an evil *manido* might steal and destroy its soul. A good name, they believed, focused the attention of the baby's shadow on its significance and gave it strength and power throughout the duration of its owner's life. A poor name correspondingly weakened it and sometimes caused the child's death." "Names," one Ojibway said, "seem to have lost their power today, but formerly a good name ensured a child long life."

Kroeber reports that an old Atsina gave his name to a youth with the words: "I give you my name in order that you may have as long a life as I." Among the Blackfoot Wissler says, "there is the feeling that the name carries with it some power to promote the well being of him upon whom it is conferred." And among the Eastern Dakota Wallis says, "the name given the child helps it to grow and to become strong."

The qualities represented by and implicit in the name often come from a deceased ancestor who bore the name, according to

Pettitt. The name may also be associated with supernatural power, and the Kwakiutl Indian who receives supernatural power from a supernatural being assumes both the power and the name of the spirit conferring it, according to Boas. Among the Pawnee a man on the warpath often assumed a new name, "believing that it would contribute to the success of the expedition" (Dorsey and Murie, 1940). The Navajo believe, Reichard says, that "names are full of power, ritualistic items of tremendous value." In times of need, he says, a Navajo relies upon the innate strength in his name.

In each instance a quality is transferred with a name. Whether the connection comes from the mystical power of the name, or from the connection of the name with spirits and the dead, are problems which go beyond this discussion. But at all events, it is not the name as such which is the origin of the quality. Loeb says the Pomo believe that "the mana given in connection with a name comes from the person who bore the name, and not from the meaning of the name."

A name which brings a particular quality to an individual only represents that quality. There is, however, usually another name based on a personal aspect which characterizes him both as a person and an individual. This is the name which mourners change after the death of a relative, that the murderer conceals after committing the deed, and that the patient relinquishes during or after an illness in order to prevent the dead or other evil spirits from seizing him. Apart from thwarting soul-snatchers, it may cheat intruding spirits seeking a host (Reichard, 1928). But above all, this is the name that one is careful not to mention to outsiders, even if they belong to the individual's social group.

A certain shyness about saying one's name, as well as the names of others, occurs all over North America. This behavior, reminiscent of the rigorous taboos about the names of deceased persons, is so general that it almost appears to be a psychological pattern for the whole of native North America. However the matter is not so simple. There are important exceptions to the rule, especially in two great culture areas, the Northwest Coast and the Plains. There the fear of mentioning the name is less pronounced because the name was more a title than a personal name and was part of the system of privileges which characterized Northwest culture (Benedict, 1923).

In the Plains culture, with its sensitiveness to military prestige, names were used freely on particular, socially sanctioned occasions (Lowie, 1923). This occurred when a warrior returned from a victorious battle and his name was shouted out over the whole camp. This custom was so strongly rooted that it even overcame the fear of the names of dead persons, and among the Cree the names of famous warriors "were recalled and pronounced long after their deaths as a means of perpetuating their glory" (Mandelbaum, 1940).

Even among some tribes outside these culture areas, there were freer attitudes about using names, though perhaps as a result of influence from European-American culture. The Copper Eskimo mention their names without inhibition (Stefansson, 1914). Freeland says the Pomo did not believe that a name could be used as "a source of power over a man," but Loeb believes that the use of a person's name had a magic affect upon its bearer.

If we disregard the exceptions, it was probably normal not to pronounce the name in front of strangers, either by the bearer or by any of his relatives (other than possibly in a whisper). Even in the closest family circle, a reserve name might be used (Schoolcraft, 1851). The motives vary. Among the Hopi one who pronounces a name is overtaken by death, in other cases it is the person whose name has been pronounced who suffers.

But while the belief that mentioning a name brings misfortune to the person named is at times vague, the belief becomes more definite in specific cases. The Navajo believe that a name becomes worn out by use, and when that happens its owner will be accorded less respect. The Chinook and the Makah believe that if a name is stolen, its bearer falls ill and dies. The Arapaho say that a stranger will get the whip hand over someone by knowing his name. The Apache believe that allowing a stranger to know your name places you under a hidden power.

Behind all these explanations is the fear that the person will be exposed to the arbitrary will of another or be ruled by another. Frazer saw the name taboo as an instance of contagious magic. Swanton rightly says that for an Indian, his name possessed "sacred character" since it so "perfectly expressed his inmost nature as to be practically identical with him." The name interprets the essence of the individual; it incarnates him, it epitomizes him as a person. Yet for all of that the name need not have anything to do with belief in a name-soul as some folklorists have suggested. In certain areas the concealed name has been a soul, in others not, and the latter is the rule.

Such notions come close to the edges of soul belief. It is clear that if the name includes the essence of the individual, the person's ego *in nuce,* it may easily become a symbol for the extra-physical ego of the individual, his free-soul. Sometimes a name may acquire an existence of its own outside the individual, so that it approaches, but to judge by all the evidence, never wholly coincides with the extra-physical soul.

In several North American Indian communities children are not given names until they have attained a certain age. The Eskimo in western Canada do not give their children names until they are ten or twelve years of age when their soul takes possession of them (Stefansson, 1913). The Wishram and Klikitat wait up to two years before giving their children names, for naming a child too early might cause the child to die (Krober, 1925). Among the Yurok, children may be six or seven years old before they are given names. The Karuk, too, wait several years before naming their children because then if the children died young, "they would not be thought of by their names" (Krober). Nor did the Wintu give their children names at a tender age for such a measure might cause premature death (DuBois, 1935).

The Havasupai have a different approach, only naming their children after they have begun to prove humanly interesting, usually after one or two years, though sometimes waiting as long as five to seven years. Spier says this means that "the need of a name awaits the creation of a personality." The Yuchi name the child on the fourth day after birth, a number which coincides, as Speck points out, with the four-day journey between the realm of the dead and the world of the living. That is significant because the Yuchi believe the child is a reincarnated ancestor.

The custom is so ancient that it would be vain to seek its original motives. Two basic motives can, however, be distinguished, one social, one religious. The first implies that the individual is not in the social sense a person until reaching a certain age. The giving of the name, as Charles points out, is a dramatic act intended to introduce the individual into the process leading to socialization and enculturation. The name is meant then to express the essence of the individual.

The second motive may be that name and soul belong together so that the name cannot be conferred until the soul has arrived. But it is also possible that the social motivation is primary, and that the practice of conferring the name later has given rise to the belief in the development of the soul. For that to happen there must be an intimate relationship between name and soul as is the case for the Eskimo.

One of the risks with naming a child early is that the child may get a name which, as he grows, no longer fits. In such cases, among the Eskimo on Greenland and Hudson's Bay, the Ingalik, the Ojibway, the Saulteaux, the Eastern Dakota, and the Modoc, the child howls until it gets the right name. Clearly the name is necessary for the health of the child, and at the same time it constitutes an independent something outside the individual. The conception most closely corresponding to this description is the free-soul. It is believed in the majority of the cases mentioned here that the child cries because it has not been given the name it bore in its previous existence, although that may not apply to the Dakota and Modoc.

The dead person who provides the name is like a free-soul in relation to the newborn child, reincarnated at the moment of naming. While not putting too fine a point on this, it does nevertheless appear probable that the name here has an existence as the bearer of the individual's free-soul. This existence disappears once the name has been "incorporated" into the person named.

From a number of peoples in eastern North America come examples of reincarnation connected with adoption after a death. Le Jeune describes the Algonquin on Allumette Island: "When he who has passed away has been raised from the dead, that is, when his name has been given to another, and presents have been offered to his relatives, then it is said that the body is 'cached,' or rather, that the dead is resuscitated." Sagard says that among the "neutral" nation closely related to the Huron, dead chiefs are brought back to life when their names are given to persons who have their virtues and qualities.

When the Pueblo confer a name it is customary to let the child breathe in the essence with which the name is associated, leaving the impression that the breath-soul is functioning as a single soul which the child receives with the name. The Hopi even go so far as to name a child that has died nameless so that it can live among the souls in the realm of the dead (Beaglehole, 1935). It is interesting to note that among the Mexican Aztecs and Maya the *nagual,* reminiscent of the free-soul, comes into existence through the name (Spence, 1910).

Of course the effect is to suggest that receiving a name may also imply receiving a soul. The identity between name and soul is most clear where the belief in reincarnation is strong. Yet it is not definite in other cases, and it is sometimes non-existent. A Kickapoo baby, for example, gets two names, one for his soul and one for himself (Charles). After the naming, the identification of the name with the free-soul seems to disappear.

The name may, however, be firmly associated with the free-soul during the lifetime of the individual and in certain cases develops an actual identity. There would seem to be three forms of permanent connection between name and free-soul. The first is frequently called by its owner's name, because in a genuine dual soul relationship it is the individual in an extra-physical form. But as soon as the free-soul is conceived as separate from the individual, as an emancipated soul, its connection with the name ceases. In the second, the name binds the free-soul to the individual. This process expresses the magical power of the name, and it also demonstrates the belief that through naming one deprives someone of their soul. In the third case the name is sometimes a mystical symbol for the free-soul. This implies that the name functions as a free-soul (the name-soul). It no longer designates the individual but is an independent being with the substance and qualities of the free-soul; in short, a kind of personality.

The name-soul presupposes a fusion between soul and essence, though in practice this change of import seems to have occurred rarely. In North America, as far as I know, only the Eskimo have a regular name-soul, though like many other North American people, the Eskimo believe that a child's name reincarnates some previously existing individual. Here the identity between name and soul is evident. By identifying soul and essence in the name, the Eskimo manifest a peculiar historical evolution without parallel in North America, but not even among the Eskimo is the free-soul always identical with the name.

On East Greenland, according to Holm, the name, *atekata,* is "of the same size as a man and enters the child at the moment when a finger dipped in water is passed over the child's mouth,

the names of the dead ancestors being simultaneously pronounced." The name here is an independent reality of free-soul
type, and it is, like the free-soul, essential to the individual. "Care
must be taken not to offend the 'name' in any way; for then he
may desert the man, who is then sure to fall ill."

It is understandable that Thalbitzer identifies the name with the
most prominent soul, apparently the free-soul. The linguistic import of the name seems to indicate that the name was originally
the designation which bound the soul to the individual. Its identity
with the free-soul is in this case secondary.

On West Greenland, according to Birket-Smith, "the name is a
mystical, independent part of the person, and after death the name
roams about restlessly, until it is once more attached to a new-
born," a notion quite like those in East Greenland.

Kroeber says that among the Polar Eskimo the name, after
death, ascends, into the air. The Eskimo on Baffin Island believe
that a reincarnated person retains the name from his former existence (Boas, 1901). The name has the position of a free-soul
among the Central Eskimo, an assumption supported by the fact
that a child who dies before being named is not mourned (Turquetil, Rasmussn, 1929).

Finally, Rasmussen reports that among the Netsilik Eskimo, "It
is as if a name had its own particular soul acting quite independently of the body's soul, and this soul is for the benefit of all
who have the name. According to some people, this means that
the soul of the body, the real fountain of life, is the one that makes
mankind human, while the soul of the name merely makes it generally strong, keeps it up and protects it." Even if the name here is
not the free-soul, which is, however, by no means impossible, it
has soul qualities.

The Eskimo name-soul was originally a mystical extension,
which has more or less become identical with the free-soul without losing its original character. It would appear, nevertheless, to
be the free-soul which is always predominant.

Chapter Eleven
The External Soul

On the boundary between soul and mystical extension lies the so-called external soul, an enigmatic phenomenon, closely connected with the conception of the life-symbol and the life-token. The term external soul is a trifle misleading, but general acceptance dictates retaining it. What is an external soul? First and foremost every soul appearing outside the body to which it belongs may be regarded as a kind of external soul. This applies especially to the free-soul.

All across North America Thomson has recorded a large number of instances where the notion of an external soul occurs. For clarity I have divided the source material into myths, legends, and popular beliefs.

Boas, in his discussion of myths, says that the concept of an external soul, "the mythic notion of the 'life' which is kept outside of the body," occurs with particular frequency on the North Pacific Coast and in California. The Northwest Coast seems to be the center with Northern California, the Mackenzie Plateau, and Great Basin areas as offshoots. But it is also found on the Plains, in the Eastern Woodlands, and in the Southwest.

A Bella Coola tradition tells how a twin dies as a result of an eagle consuming the heart of a salmon; evidently the heart is, or includes, an essential part of the twin's life. The Kwakiutl have a legend of a female giant who was repeatedly killed and always came back to life. She did not die until a great spruce tree in which her life was preserved had been shot.

The motif of the external soul occurs in different versions of the legend of the Bear Woman. The Chilcotin say that the Bear

Woman used to carry a little basket which she sometimes hung on the roof of her house. When her brother put a bullet through the basket, she fell down dead for she had kept her "life" in the basket. Curiously enough, her external "life" had to be killed three times before she disappeared from the world of the living.

An interesting episode from the description of the long battle with the Bear Woman throws light upon the relationship between (the supernatural) individual and the external soul. We are told that the basket with the woman's 'life' was thrown into the fire in her absence and began to burn. She immediately began to scream and rushed back to the house, but before she got there the "life" had been consumed, and she fell dead to the ground (Farrand, 1920). In a corresponding tale from the Bella Coola, the Bear Woman is invulnerable "since she had taken her heart and lungs from her chest" (Boas).

A Tillamook tradition tells how an old hag was killed and cut into pieces, but nevertheless came back to life. Blue Jay, the culture-hero of the Oregon Indians, knew what to do: "You must not take her body but take her hat. You will find a small, long thing in the top of her hat. That is her heart. You must tear that and throw it into the sea, then she will be dead (Boas). A narrative from the Kathlamet (a Chinook group) describes a supernatural being who carried his life in his little finger. As in some other well-known myths, the external soul is not removed from the body but is located in a peripheral, insignificant part.

The legends of the Algonquin also locate the external soul in an obscure part of the body, commonly in the heel or in the toe. And so the heel of Achilles turns up in a Penobscot tradition: when the heel is shot, the heart preserved there is also shot (Speck, 1919). The Wawenock, a tribe in the Abnaki group, believe in a supernatural being who carries a piece of gold in his mouth. He once put it down to be able to drink, it is said, and a hunter took advantage of the opportunity to steal it. The spirit then cried: "My friend, please do give me back that gold...that is my life" (Speck). The Central and Plains Algonquin have two narratives with an external soul. In one we are told of an evil magician whose heart is on a remote island (Algonquin, Ojibway); the other, common to the Cree, Ojibway, Arapaho, Atsina, and Blackfoot, is identical with the widespread tradition of the Bear Woman, but here her "life," her heart, is placed in the little toe.

The Ojibway say that one could only kill her by wounding her in the toe with a needle (Jones, 1916).

The Algonquin Arapaho have a tradition about dwarfs who had their hearts hung up in their camp while they were away. A person came to visit and saw the hearts. "He took an awl and pricked each heart. Out on the prairie the dwarves dropped dead." The same story occurs in two variations among the Wichita (Dorsey and Kroeber, 1903).

In a Modoc legend we are told how an old man who fed on human flesh kept his life in a mortar (Curtin, 1912). The Jicarilla Apache tell of two bears who "preyed upon the people, who were unable to kill them, as they left their hearts at home when off on their marauding expeditions." While they were out marauding, Fox cut their hearts into pieces. "The bears, aware that their hearts had been tampered with, rushed with all speed to rescue them but fell dead just before they reached Fox" (Russell, 1898).

A Navajo myth relates how the Coyote—the trickster and culture hero—once fell to the bottom of a canyon and was dashed to pieces, but... "he did not, like other beings, keep his vital principle in his chest, where it might easily be destroyed. He kept it in the tip of his nose and in the end of his tail, where no one would expect to find it; so after a while he came to life again." The Navajo also have preserved the legend of the Bear Woman. Here she takes her "life" out of her body when she goes out to fight, and puts it back in its usual place after the struggle is over (Matthews, 1887).

The mythology of the Pueblo also reveals stories describing an external soul. In the Zuni origin myth a woman from a hostile tribe is shot at with arrows but does not die for she has her heart in a calabash rattle (Parsons, 1939). And the Hopi tell of a girl whose life has been taken by wizards because she resists their courting. But her breath had been transferred in a mysterious way to a wheel adorned with feathers, and from here it was later returned to the body (Voth, 1905). The story is consistent with Hopi belief that the breath is identical with the single soul.

If the external soul motif is a common element in the Indian store of legend, how common is it in popular belief, how often does the external soul occur as an experience or imagined reality in the present? The supernatural beings of myth and fairy tale may place "the life" outside themselves, but can humans still do so? Frazer found but a single genuine instance of the external soul in North American popular belief and practice. He reports, citing Jacobsen, that the shamans of the Alaska Eskimo sometimes take a sick child's soul out of its body and keep it in an amulet, which for safety's sake he conceals in his medicine-bag. Which soul the shaman takes, is not mentioned.

The concept of an external soul projected upon existence after death also seems to appear to occur among the Ingalik. A baby which dies is wrapped in bark and buried in the wood under a spruce sapling. "As long as the tree lives, the spirit of the child lives, too, under its protection. The spirit dies with the tree" (Parsons, 1921-22). The mystical participation lies in the closeness between the tree and the child, both in age and locality and that allows the tree to guarantee the life of the external soul.

A Cherokee tradition which seems to be based upon an historical event is also worthy of note. A Cherokee war chief once exposed himself boldly to his Shawnee enemies, who shot at him without wounding him. The Shawnee chief then had his men shoot into the branches above the warrior's head, and the Cherokee chief fell down dead. Before the battle he had placed his "life" in the top of the tree (Mooney, 1900).

The Pueblo often connect the belief in the external soul with the belief in witches. Among the Nambe a witch in modern times kept "a little stone, which was her bad heart" in a bag. When the bag was thrown into the fire and consumed the woman died. The same fate also overtook other witches when their "hearts," which were kept in the same way, were burned (Parsons, 1929).

When a Zuni Indian named Nick was accused of witchcraft, he got drunk, started brawling and was beaten. "When he came to, he boasted, being still drunk, that he would not die because his heart was in his toenails and he was wise, that is, a witch" (Parsons, 1939). The Zuni also use clay dolls to magically stimulate a woman's fertility. The doll, called the "baby," is handed to the woman by a kachina dancer. Parsons was once shown such a doll whose beneficial influence had given a woman a son. The doll "was being kept carefully as 'the heart' of the child. Were anything to happen to the doll or were they to sell it, the child it brought would not live." James has shown how the corn-cob fetish among the Zuni functions after the death of the individual as a reservoir for life, a kind of external soul. Among the Cochiti,

San Felipe, and Hopi the maize fetish is the heart of the deceased or a substitute heart. The owner of such a fetish is said to live as long as the fetish wishes (Parsons).

What this comes down to is that in myth and popular tradition, the legendary figures and heroes are equipped with an external soul which in the majority of cases is identical with the life-soul. People today are sometimes in spiritual contact with objects which constitute or contain some mystical extension of the external soul, but seldom is such an entity an external life-soul, unless its human counterpart has at least in part been removed to a supernatural sphere.

It is self-evident that if the external soul is identical with the life-soul, then the life-soul exists outside the body and it cannot form part of the equipment of ordinary living people. The life-soul of the Eskimo child is not so firmly attached to the body and therefore provides an exception.

What is characteristic for the external soul does not lie in its supposed soul-nature. The external soul is a projection of essence, which has only secondarily acquired the value of a life-soul. That notwithstanding, the mythology describes the life-soul as combining its functions with those of the external soul. This comes clear when you consider that the external soul is called the life or the heart, and that the individual is invulnerable as long as it is not in the body.

As a mystical extension, the external soul comes close to the concept of the *nagual*, or Guardian Spirit and sometimes even merges. It also shows a strong connection with the concept of the life-token and with other blended conceptions

Like the external soul, the life-token constitutes a projection of the life-essence, but without carrying weight and significance for the life of the individual. The life-token does not guarantee the life of the individual, but it shows its mystical identity with him by succumbing at the same time he does. In a number of cases its state reflects the degree of the individual's happiness and well-being. A good example of this occurs in the notions connected with the birth tree regarded as a life-token. Hartland, who has dealt more comprehensively and in greater detail than any other writer with the problems connected with the life-token, distinguishes between two kinds of life-token: those that have some original connection with the hero and those which are arbitrary.

Common to both types, Hartland says, is the belief that the life-token "is part of the substance of the personage whose welfare it indicates. It is the converse and essential correlative of the External Soul." What is important here is that while the external soul is frequently a life-soul, the life-token is never anything more than a mystical extension.

In mythology and in legend the concept of the life-token occurs in all parts of North America. The story of the Iroquois hero, Dekanawida serves as an example. "He departed southward, first assuring his mother that in the event of his death by violence or sorcery, the otter skin hung with the head downward, in a corner of the lodge, would vomit blood" (Hewitt, 1907).

In a Modoc legend a doctor with remarkable powers had a life-token, a wooden comb which he hung up when setting off on a journey. "If this comb falls," he told his mother, "you may know that somebody has killed me." The comb fell, and the mother then knew her son's fate (Curtin, 1912). The Mohave tell of the twin brothers who before going hunting hung a quiver in the hut and a hair from each of their heads over the door. They told their wives that if the quiver fell this would be a sign that they were dead, and if the hairs were snapped this would signify that they were dying (Bourke, 1889). There are other tales as well, a plant that withers, or a pot that boils, or a digging stick that breaks to signify that the hero is imperiled (Leach, 1950).

From the evidence it is clear that a typical life-token has no points of contact with soul-beliefs. But there are, as Hartland has pointed out, transitional forms between life-token and external soul. Such a transitional form is the Haida concept of the thread of life, represented both in legend and in popular belief. The Haida believe that every person and every animal is provided with a thread of life. "In a grizzly bear story the male bear goes hunting, and in his progress unwinds a thread of life, one end of which is fastened in his den. When this thread stopped unwinding, his wife knew he had gone as far as he intended and was about to return. Desiring to kill him, she cut the thread" (Swanton, 1905). In other narratives the life-thread reveals a person's state, and may, when tampered with, change the course of its owner's life. Among the Haida two conceptions, the life-token and the external soul, have merged.

The external soul is also closely connected with a peculiar notion among the Bella Coola; the tally post. This concept falls within the circle of ideas of the totem-pole culture, but the fundamental concept, the reciprocity between the individual and an external object whose appearance determines his health and duration of life shows a connection with the external soul. "The tally post, which looks like a totem-pole, is placed in the celestial realm of death by the Supreme God himself, and is raised when a child is born. "As long as the post remains upright and straight, firmly fixed to the ground, its owner continues to be strong and prosperous, and has success in all his undertakings; if it becomes loose, or is crooked, he ceases to succeed" (McIlwraith, 1948). The condition of the life-pole thus determines the condition of the individual. But the life-pole does not constitute an immutable destiny. Anyone can straighten their pole, and a shaman can travel to the other world and straighten a sick man's falling pole.

Some of the Bella Coola believe that the tally post is always, invisibly near the individual and brings good luck. McIlwraith says this conception is secondary and has arisen through a fusion between the tally post and another entity, the guardian-soul. The same vacillation between celestial being and an essential substance located near the person characterizes the concept of "the wash basin," whose function is almost identical with the life-pole. "There is a firm belief," McIlwraith writes, "that an individual's fortune in life depends upon the activity of spirit, tally post, and wash-basin."

Other peculiar notions have developed around the idea of an external soul, but exploring them here would move this too far from its central theme. What has emerged emphasizes that the boundary between soul and essence may often be vague.

Chapter Twelve
The Nagual and the Guardian Spirit

In *Nagualism* the guardian spirit is closely identified with the person to whom it belongs and, above all, shares in its nature. The concept appears fully developed in Santa Ana where every individual possesses a guardian spirit, *tsayotyenyi,* from birth. This spirit "looks after his ward during his lifetime, protecting him from harm and keeping him from doing wrong. At each meal the person offers *tsayotyenyi a piece of food* before tasting it himself." In several places when the individual dies, the *Nagual* follows the soul on its journey to the other side (White, 1942).

In a more common version, the death of the guardian spirit is fatal for the individual. The sorcerer of the Caddo has the owl as his guardian spirit. "Whenever a bird is shot, there in the corresponding part of the witch's body will be a hole or bruise" (Parsons, 1931).

The concept of power loss, or spirit loss is common for the Indians at Puget Sound and for a number of Salish groups on the Plateau in the interior, but it occurs sporadically outside the Northwest. Where the belief exists a supernatural power has intervened in place of the free-soul, and its activity conforms to the pattern of the free-soul, except during power loss when the guardian spirit replaces the free-soul because it has become indispensable.

The shaman depends upon his guardian spirit to fetch a soul from the realm of the dead, because it performs better than the free-soul. The connection between the guardian spirit and the individual allows the individual to participate in the nature of the guardian spirit. Among the Shuswap, according to Teit, twins have the same guardian animal; the animal of which their mother dreamed; a black bear, a grizzly bear, or a deer.

Among the Central Algonquin a person suffers because his guardian spirit is suffering (Radin, 1944). A Crow who had ghost-medicine "made a noise like an owl, went out of the smoke hole, and returned to the tent" (Lowie, 1922). The Wind River Shoshone believe that a person acquires the abilities of the animal whose form the guardian spirit has taken.

The image of the guardian animal is often found drawn on the breast of a sun-dancer, among the Basin Shoshone. Steward says that "swift birds gave the power of fleetness, mountain sheep the power to climb rocks, wolf, bear, and other pugnacious animals the power to fight, insects the power to hide." The Lemhi shaman imitates the voice of his guardian spirit when he is healing the sick, and a Bannock with bear power imitates his guardian spirit when he has been wounded and needs help.

The Pawnee who has been instructed in the mysteries of bear-medicine and received the bear's blessing must be careful not to become wrathful around his kinsmen, for then the canines of the bear begin to show (Dorsey, 1906). And the Tarahumare sorcerer who unexpectedly meets a bear exclaims: "Do not harm this animal, for it is I" (Hartman, 1895).

These examples show that in order to share in the power of his guardian spirit, a person must sometimes strengthen the contact with the spirit by imitating it. Imitation sometimes merges into transformation when the power of suggestion is strong enough. This form of *Nagualism*, not at all uncommon in North America, falls into three types. In the first the person identifies with the guardian spirit through ritual, the transformation occurring when wearing a mask or animal skin. The Laguna woman who dons a wolf's skin is transformed into her *nagual*, which is a wolf (Parsons, 1939). This belief in metamorphosis is prominent in the beliefs of the bear-medicine clan in California and among the Pueblo. In California bear-doctors, shamans who had the power of the bear and who could transform themselves into bears, were common (Krober). As bears they were a danger to those round about them, and they killed persons whom they found disagreeable. If they were killed in their bear form they came to life again. The Indians believed that the bear shamans acquired their skills by putting on bear-skins; but they are not always sure whether the man under the skin is a human being or a real bear. Some accounts, however, describe how the man disguised as a bear is transformed in the course of the bear-dance into a bear (Grayton, 1948). The same sort of bear-*nagualism* occurs in the Southwest. "Of all the curing societies, Keresan, Zuni, or Tewan, Bear is the particular patron," writes Parsons. "The doctors or shamans are called bears; by putting on the bear paws which lie on the altar the shamans impersonate bears, as the paw is the equivalent of the mask. It is believed that shamans have power literally to turn into bears, just as bears may divest themselves of their skins and become people" (Parsons).

In the second instance the transformation may be mystically induced by an act of will, without any external requisites such as animal hides and masks. In most cases the person establishes identification with his guardian spirit through sheer force of imagination and hypnotic power while playing its role. The Yo-kuts testify that transformation to a guardian animal takes place "under conditions of great stress" (Grayton). It does not appear however, that the person undergoing transformation becomes possessed by the spirit (Stewart, 1946). The Nootka tell of young men who in connection with their puberty-fasting and guardian-spirit quest join the wolves, when, "after a time, body and soul have changed into the likeness of these beasts," according to Johnson. He also says that a Penobscot or a Passamaquoddy shaman, after deciding what should be done, "turns himself into his guardian animal and goes off to do what he wishes." The Ojibway warrior calls to the animal which is his guardian spirit when he has been wounded and assumes its form to make good his escape (Densmore, 1929). A Teton Dakota who has dreamed of an elk leaves the footprints of this animal behind him (Densmore, 1918). And an Iroquois sorcerer was able, if hard pressed, to turn himself into his guardian spirit, commonly an owl (Hewitt, 1895), because in southeastern North America owls are temporarily transformed sorcerers.

Finally, in the third case the individual survives death by assuming the shape of his guardian animal. This belief has been recorded from diverse parts of North America, and it shows that the boundary between transformation and transmigration may be quite plastic.

When the soul and supernatural power merge into a single

concept, they form the guardian or power-soul, a spiritual entity whose essence is leavened with supernatural power. The free-soul of a medicine-man bears his power (since the free-soul is the medicine-man himself). Among the Carrier "powers in the animal or spiritual world captured and imprisoned human shadows. After recovering their shadows the individuals became imbued with special gifts of foresight and of healing not granted to the ordinary layman" (Jenness, 1930).

The power-soul is a personal guardian spirit to which the person is subordinate, and it often operates as independently as an ordinary guardian spirit acquired from without. It helps and supports, watches over and punishes its protege, and it sometimes receives sacrifices from him, but at the same time it has functions which connect it with the free-soul of dreams and visions. That the soul can develop into an independent power-being is not new. Mauss stresses that it is difficult to distinguish the soul from the guardian spirit, and Mensching says that the notion of the guardian angel has emerged from the same group of concepts as the free-soul and the external soul.

In North America the soul most qualified to develop into a guardian spirit is the free-soul. The more independent a soul can become, the more it merges into a spiritual principle coordinated with the individual and yet emancipated, a being that is beside or over its human counterpart. The free-soul never slips its moorings from the individual, but it easily becomes distanced and develops into a being with a will and with powers of its own. That puts the free-soul/power-soul in the same order as the spirit beings of nature, but because it is bound to its owner, this power-soul assumes the character of a guardian spirit.

The free-soul, in changing to a guardian soul, does so as either a dream-soul or as a double-ganger. In dreams the subject and object of the action coincide. The dream-soul, in reality the dreamer himself, is suddenly seen as the being one is dreaming about. The dream no longer comes from the experiences of the dream-ego but reveals a half-alien being, reminiscent of the dream experiences in North American cases of guardian-spirit quest. There the guardian spirit inaugurates the dream, just as the dream-soul does, and, like the dream-soul, it figures in the dream and changes shape between animal and man. That in turn makes the fusion between dream-soul and guardian spirit seem natural.

The double-ganger, the active free-soul of the conscious, divorced from the activity of its living prototype, has even greater independence than the dream-soul, and it ends up in the category of guardian spirits. It is also possible for the life-soul and the ego-soul to become guardian souls. Nor should it be a surprise to see the ego-soul in certain situations assuming some of the trappings of a guardian spirit. In the living individual the ego-soul has little to do with vital functions and is therefore more easily freed from the body. And in strength of feelings, endurance of will, and the sway of reason the ego-soul may show a tenacity and span suggesting superhuman resources and potential.

It is, however, difficult to show what role the ego-soul may have played in the origin of the guardian soul. The guardian soul is certainly a principle of character and conscience. But whenever the ego-soul appears to form the core of the guardian soul, it has in reality merged with the free soul, meaning, that the free-soul is the basis for the guardian soul.

The guardian soul is a power-concept associated with the individual, even if in its origin it is only a soul. I find it likely that the guardian spirit served as model for the conception of the guardian soul. And though that is difficult to prove, the connection between the objectified dream-soul and the guardian spirit experienced in dreams points in that direction. But a power belief like *nagualism*, with its connection between the individual and the guardian spirit, is even more significant as a factor in forming patterns. *Nagual* and guardian soul may in the long run become almost identical concepts, but the individual can never be transformed into his guardian soul. The fusion that may occur between the guardian spirit and the soul is generally one-sided, the soul assuming the essential qualities of the guardian spirit, while the guardian spirit absorbs few of soul's qualities. Nor, does the appearance of the guardian soul imply that the guardian spirit has been ousted from its position, for one who has a guardian soul may also have a guardian spirit.

In North America, the prerequisite for having a guardian soul is the capacity of the underlying soul-concept to become independent of its owner. It must develop will and feelings of its own, allowing it to leave the body of its own accord, to wander about or follow its longing to journey to the realm of the dead. But the free-soul also returns to its owner of its own accord, and probably in the final analysis the travels of the emancipated soul conform to the causes and course of disease. When the soul operates as an independent being outside the individual, it frequently serves to forewarn of coming events, particularly when danger threatens.

The guardian soul of the Bella Coola causes its owner to recollect, just in time, important things he has forgotten; "his spirit is always striving to pierce the future and obtain information for him, however indefinite. In retrospect it is easy to believe that one felt a warning, and that provides proof that the spirit, the cause of thoughts, has supernatural ability." In addition, sudden pains and physical changes give symbolic hints of misfortunes that will occur (McIlwraith, 1948).

Instances from other quarters show the same trend. The shadow of the Ojibway, says Jenness, is "the eyes of the soul, as it were, awakening the latter to perception and knowledge. It often causes a twitching of the hunter's eyelids, informing him that he has seen game ahead. When a man feels that someone is watching him, or near him, although he can see no one; it is his shadow that is warning him, trying to awaken his soul to perceive the danger." Since the shadow is a soul at considerable remove from its owner, it is not surprising that it sometimes plays a less central role in the welfare of the individual.

An aging Ojibway no longer perceives any warning impulse, "for people tend to lose it as they grow old" (Jenness, 1935). The neighbors and kinsmen of the Ojibway, the Plains Cree, also believed in the soul's capacity to forewarn. "Only when danger threatened did a man feel the presence of his soul along the back of his neck" (Mandelbaum, 1940).

Closely allied to this is the soul's function in communicating knowledge. Sometimes the person receives the information as an inner certainty, a premonition of coming events, but often enough the soul speaks to the person. On such occasions if the free-soul is not far enough removed from its owner's personality, the respective egos of the soul and of the individual alternate with each other. Among the Wind River Shoshone it functions, like the guardian spirit, as a guide and counselor. From the Naskapi Speck reports that "when the soul-spirit of man is strong and active, he believes that he may expect continual direction and guidance in all affairs."

In this way the soul gives instructions, especially for the hunt

(Speck, 1935). These instructions, which are generally given in dreams, must be followed; for "cessation of revelations as to when and where to go for game, how to proceed, and how to satisfy it when it is slain, would result in the loss of a powerful and far-seeing guide, the individual's 'Providence,' and a doom of failure and starvation" (Speck, 1924). The same belief occurs among other Algonquin tribes, especially the Fox (Flannery, 1939). The large soul of the Fox watches over the life-soul (Michelson, 1925). And the free-soul of the Oglala controls the actions of the individual. (Walker, 1917).

This powerful soul that intervenes in life, like a power coming from without, is generally a benevolent guardian spirit. The "Great Man," the guardian soul of the Naskapi, is solicitous of its protege's welfare. "It is the Great Man of the teacher that makes him strong and wise, of the leader that gives him fertile schemes and influence over others, of the successful hunter who garners game for him, of the warrior who garners enemies for him. By the same explanation, these people explain the power of leaders, inventors, and wealthy men among the whites" (Speck, 1935).

The Bella Coola thinks in the same way. "If a man prospers in his ventures and has success in life, it is due, not to his own efforts, but to the activity of his spirit. When a man acquires wealth with little labor, he knows that his spirit has been constantly trembling at the back of his neck; when he is unfortunate, that it has become inert or sluggish" (McIlwraith). The Mohave divide happiness and wealth between two souls. The one, called by Devereux the "power soul," decides the social position of the individual both in this world and in the world to come. "It gives general good luck, special powers (especially shamanistic powers), luck in love, for example, but can also bring unhappiness and bad luck." Concerning "the soul through whose agency one acquires wealth," Devereux writes that "it never causes trouble and its sight augurs success."

Among the Fox, according to Michelson, the large soul remains with the corpse, and "it seems as if it guarded the body," until the body has decayed to see that it is not disturbed. Jette says that among the Coyukon, the free-soul has become a dangerous guardian spirit "The *yega* is a protecting spirit, jealous and revengeful, whose mission is not to avert harm from the person or thing which it protects, but to punish the ones who harm or misuse it, and to visit them with the calamities most dreaded, sickness and death either of the offender, or his near relatives." Above all the *yega* avenges the death of its protege.

But the guardian soul also punishes the one it is protecting when its wishes have not been fulfilled. If among the Wind River Shoshone a shaman does not follow his guardian soul's instigation to steal the souls of other people, he will be overtaken with misfortune. A worse fate, according to Ragueneau, will be the lot of the Huron who does not carry out the wishes of the soul active in dreams: if this soul "be not granted what it desires, it becomes angry, and not only does it not give its body the good and the happiness that it wished to procure for it, but often it revolts, causing various diseases, and even death" (Jesuits). And a Naskapi or Iroquois who disobeys his guardian soul must acquiesce when it abandons him (Speck). The Naskapi also lose their guardian soul when the they grow old. Curiously enough, the guardian soul then enters the service of another (Speck).

The relationship between the individual and the guardian soul is particularly significant. The psychic attitude varies from religious veneration to the exploitation of the guardian soul for magical purposes. In its special function the guardian soul is helper and protector. But from a wider point of view it is an awesome, dangerous being much like the spirits of nature. The guardian soul or spirit of the Bella Coola is said to be "small, but of great power, since it belongs to the world of the supernatural; in fact, the spirit of a man is not a mortal, but a supernatural being" (McIlwraith).

The guardian soul of the Naskapi behaves almost like a possessor (Stewart, 1946). The guardian soul of the Ojibway frightens animals with its whistling, (Jenness) and the free-soul of the Iroquois is "sharp-sighted by night, specifically carnivorous" and has "the ability of uttering sounds, speech, sometimes resembling the whistling or the trilled note of the cricket, and sometimes resembling that plaintive and doleful exclamation so largely used and imitated in the chants of death and of public and private condolence and mourning" (Hewitt, 1895). The power-soul of the Mohave is "sacred and dangerous" according to Durkheim and Mauss. The Nomlaki believe that a man's guardian soul "may bother him or may help him during sickness" (Goldschmidt, 1951)

The Penobscot call the soul "goodness," the Creek call it "the good spirit," and the Naskapi Montagnais designate it as "the Great Man," but these names mean a great deal more. Everything is done, chiefly through sacrifices and prayers, to please the guardian soul whether one is addressing one's own guardian soul or that of another. A Coyukon who has killed a person and is therefore menaced by the latter's avenging *yega* can easily avoid danger "by cutting open the body of the victim, and devouring a small piece of his liver." After that the *Ten'a* has only the human avengers to deal with (Jette). The Naskapi hunter "proceeds toward further communion with his own soul-spirit by smoking tobacco in his stone pipe," his intention being "to feed the soul" (Speck, 1924). A particularly solemn occasion in the adoration of "the Great Man" arises when a bear has been killed. "Then they throw a wooden spoonful of the grease with some meat into the fire for the *Mistapeo,* the Great Man, to satisfy him. And they drink it using a wooden spoon to satisfy their *Mistapeo.*" After describing how in outbursts of rage the "rational" soul of the Onondaga is thrown out of the body, de Quens says, "That is why, on such occasions, they usually make a present to restore the rational soul to the seat of reason."

But religious behavior easily merges into magic, and it is possible by magic to strengthen one's guardian soul. Among the Bella Coola, "after the termination of a long period of continence, a person's spirit is so strong that his friends place their hands on the back of his neck in order to absorb some of the power radiating from his spirit. Ancient myths record how the mere force engendered in a man's body by lengthy abstinence was enough to kill an enemy, as if his spirit had been driven from his body by a sudden start." A Bella Coola who had been continent for a whole year could walk on the surface of the water (McIlwraith).

Speck points out that among the Naskapi "musical action is regarded as a means of strengthening the Great Man of the individual," because the Great Man is stimulated "by singing, drumming, and rattling" (Speck). The guardian soul may be exploited by its "master" to perform any number of tasks. It can invade the body of a strange person at the bidding of its owner to find out what that person is thinking and planning, or to injure him or make him ill.

While the power-soul rarely goes off on such missions the

guardian soul as free-soul is frequently used by a shaman wishing to recover the soul of a sick person. Among the Mohave it is the specialized power-soul, and not the ordinary free-soul, which is sent to catch the absentee soul (Devereux).

The tendency to develop into a guardian-soul or power-soul characterizes the free-soul concept all over North America. In some quarters it results in limited concepts of the guardian-soul, especially among the Coyukon, Bella Coola, Naskapi, Iroquois, Huron, and Mohave. In all of these cases the guardian soul fulfills the functions of the free-soul, though that is less true of the Naskapi, where it appears more as the ego-soul.

But does everyone have a guardian soul? McIlwraith says that among the Bella Coola every man or woman, whether rich or poor, chief or slave, has a guardian soul. But does the well-developed guardian soul belong chiefly to the shaman? It is he, after all, who can use magic to increase its power (McIlwraith). It is he who can journey to the realm of the dead. The Coyukon-shaman, after all, has a guardian spirit that is superior in power and resources to the ordinary kind, and that pattern occurs frequently.

Chapter Thirteen
Preexistence and Incarnation

Indian thinkers not only speculated about the contents and mutual relationships of the various souls, but they tried as well to answer questions about the origin of the soul and its human incarnation. They also believed in preexistence, especially in so far as it emerged as a natural consequence of reincarnation.

Information from Indian sources is relatively limited, but they do sem to have believed that both body-soul and free-soul derive from a creative god. It is, after all, common for the breath of life to be conceived as proceeding from the creator and returning to him after death. Even without that connection the origin of the soul is ascribed to the creator or the culture hero. The Bella Coola and Wind River Shoshone believe that a Supreme Being is the giver of life and the life-soul. The Sauk refer to their creator as "he that gave us life." The kinsmen of the Sauk, the Fox, believe that the life-soul is a gift of the Great Spirit.

In the majority of cases Indians speak of the creation of life but Goddard says that the Supreme Being of the Bella Coola "made a soul for each of those about to be born; one of the minor gods fashioned its face; and a goddess rocked it, and sent it below to be born." The dream-soul of the Sinkaietk, according to Spier, is believed to have come from God. The Fox, Michelson says, believe that just as the Great Spirit provides the life-soul, so the culture hero supplies the free-soul. The sky god Skan of the Oglala has given man the whole of his psychic equipment including the life-soul and free-soul (Walker, 1917). The Wind River Shoshone describe the free-soul as the gift of the supreme god. For some groups, the question of soul origin has not produced an established belief. The Cherokee, for example, have never had any definite view in this matter (Mooney & Olbrechts, 1932)

Where direct statements fail to provide an answer to such questions, the mythology reveals that the creation of the first humans and the events of the primeval cosmic era are repeated in the occurrences of later epochs, and that the souls of the first man and modern man are believed to have had the same origin. Matthews recounts a Navajo myth concerning the first human beings. "It was the wind that gave them life. It is the wind that comes out of our mouths now that gives us life." Unfortunately, however, myths of man's creation are rather rare in North America. One of them, and one of the best, is the origin myth of the Thunder Bird clan among the Winnebago.

If, however, a high divinity is believed to have created the world, it is natural to expect that he will also be credited for having given man his soul(s), even if that is not directly stated. But there is a danger in reconstructing a belief based only on what appears to be logical. To be sure, the origin of the soul is often referred to the god who is also the creator of the earth, but even subordinate divinities may collaborate in the act which creates the soul, as the Navajo believe.

However in a couple of cases, it seems justified to deduce the origin of the soul from the characteristics of the supreme being. He is often referred to as the Breathmaker or Master of Life. The first of these terms, which has been used by some Muskhogean peoples (the Creek, Chickasaw, Seminole) of course speaks for itself. The second term, the Master of Life, which has for the most part been given to the creator of the Algonquin (and which in the literature is most frequently found as the designation for the supreme god of the Lenape), presumably refers to the god's capacity as the giver and guardian of the soul.

In some cases, among the Cree, the Micmac, and the Cahita, the supreme deity is called "the Master of Life and Death.".Here one is often justified in suspecting Christian influence upon the conception of the deity. But the truth of the matter would appear to be that the title in question has from time immemorial attached to the high divinities of a number of peoples, and that it has been applied by Europeans as a technical term for corresponding gods in other tribes, independent of whether the figure behind the concept was the result of Christian speculation.

There is no lack of evidence that the title in some quarters is of ancient origin. Brinton says that "among the Michoacan the epithet of the chief goddess of their cult was, The Sustainer of Life." The highest divinity of the Aztecs was Tonacatecutli, God of Our Life. And in the Muskoghean tribes, His name was The Master of Life." The Northern Algonquin call their Supreme Being Kitci Manitou "Master of Life," or in their words "Thou who hast mastery over life." Cooper says that this designation for a supreme god dates back to pre-Christian times.

As a rule the Indians of North America believe that the spirit has its ultimate origin in the deity, either through creation or partial emanation. In a couple of cases, it is true, the father of the child has been credited with begetting the soul as well as the physical embryo, but these exceptions are few and are probably the products of a speculation designed to fill a gap in knowledge of the souls.

A soul that is commonly believed to derive from the gods is not an ordinary profane creation. Whether it is believed to be a gift of the deity or an emanation of his being, it belongs through its origin to the supernatural world. Yet its effect need not be supernatural in the same way as mystical power

The supernatural origin of the human soul comes clear when connected to the idea of preexistence. Not the preexistence a reincarnated individual has had in a previous earthly life, but the preincarnative existence, a person's life before being incarnated on earth. "Man" stands here for individual reality, which from the psychological view point is the extra-physical soul, the free-soul, which represents the ego in the pre-incarnative state.

Some investigators, feel that a belief in preexistence is natural for early societies, but this view does not always hold water. In North America the Achomawi and the Southeastern Yavapai have no notion of preexistence. DeAngulo says that no Achomawi has ever asked where the souls of the newly born come from. The reason this has not been a common problem lies in the lack of interest in such a theoretical question, if only because it was so irrelevant to considerations of the present.

Boas agrees, pointing out that "except in instances where there is a well-developed belief in transmigration, there is no clearly formulated concept of the places and conditions in which souls exist before birth." Boas also says that believing in the soul as a substance renders possible the belief that the life of the soul is independent of the life-course of the individual. But he also says that the extent to which the belief in a previous existence emerges from this background, it is necessarily connected with the concept of rebirth.

The belief in preexistence has occurred wherever people have enquired about their origin, but it has not usually been conceived of as a previous incarnation. Here even if the immediately preceding forms of existence have consisted of incarnations, there is a still older, pre-incarnative existence. The dead, said the Saulteaux Indian, Fair Wind, "have been on this earth once, and before that they were sent from above to come on this earth" (Fewkes, 1896).

This pattern of pre-incarnative existence occurs in practically all parts of North America, but the locations vary widely. Among the Pueblo peoples of the Southwest the realm of the dead in the underworld is the place where the unborn dwell. But that does not mean that the newborn are reincarnated from the dead who dwell there. According to agrarian Pueblo ideology the underworld is also the place for the renewal of life and is the original home of humanity, a belief common to agrarian Indian communities across North America. The Hidatsa also regarded the underworld as the place where humans were generated, though they distinguished between that place and the realm of the dead.

Even when pre-incarnative existence occurs in someplace other than the underworld, that place frequently houses the dead as well. The Salish at Shoalwater Bay locate the realm of the dead for adults in the underworld, but the souls of children are gathered at the rising sun, from which they came. Some Athapascan groups in Oregon believe that at death men return to the goddess in the South (Dorsey, 1889).

According to the Miwok, man's soul is quite familiar with the way to the realm of the dead, "for it has been that way before. We don't know when, but we all say that we all of us come from there. Even our little children know that trail" (Hudson, 1902). As I pointed out above, the Pueblo realm of the dead is also the place of origin of their souls. Where the prenatal original home does not coincide with the realm of the dead, it is nevertheless located in places that are similar. The Ingalik believe that "there is a place filled with the spirits of little children, all impatient to be 'called,' to be born into this life" (Chapman, 1921).

In the depths of the forest there is, according to Kwakiutl belief, a mysterious house. "Since one of the performances held in this house," Goddard says, " was that of giving birth, it was probably believed that from this house all generation of men, animals, and plants took place."

The Indians in the north-westernmost United States have a "baby land" where the unborn children live and play before they come to the earth (Underhill, 1945). The Chinook children, according to Ray, lived before birth, "a quite definite existence" in the sun, the daylight. In the Montagnais tradition, Speck says, children come from the clouds. According to the Eastern Shawnee, unborn children live on the little stars of the Milky Way, but they also believe that they live together with the creator, "Our Grandmother" (Voegelin, 1936).

The Mandan, Weid says, appear to have believed that newborn babies are incarnated stars, while J. O. Dorsey reports that a dying Omaha, who belonged to a buffalo clan, would be told: "You came from the animals. And you are going back." Dorsey connects this pronouncement with the notion of descent from the totem animal. Fletcher, however, emphatically denies that any such conception existed. Nor is it possible to find any support for Dorsey's view.

What the Omaha meant was that before birth people lived among the totem animals of the tribe. While the concept of people occurring as an incarnation of a totem being is not well-developed in North America, we do know that other supernatural beings often allow themselves to be born as humans. These individuals are then invested with a mystic nimbus, appearing as shamans, sorcerers, twins, etc.

The tradition of mystical origin is intended to endow one with a higher authority, to sanction religious leadership or to motivate spiritual gifts. Supernaturally equipped persons (medicine-men) and individuals associated with peculiar circumstances (twins) constitute two categories whose mystical qualities are explained by their having lived a prenatal life or being incarnated spirits. In those communities in which the chiefs occupy a sacral position, among the Natchez for example, it is believed that they possessed a privileged preexistence (Swanton, 1911).

Narratives of shamans who before their human incarnation had been spirit-beings are known from many parts of North America.

Mercier tells of a Huron shaman who declared that he had lived as an *oki* (spirit) under the earth together with a female spirit. Both, possessed by the desire to become human beings, had finally concealed themselves near a path and taken up their abode in a passing woman. She gave birth to them too early. The shaman lived, but his female partner, with whom he had fought in the womb, came to the world still-born.

The Central Algonquin and the adjacent Sioux believed their-shamans were thunder-beings in a previous life. The Menomini think that "some babies are actually *manitous* in human shape, as in the case of thunder boys, who are nothing less than these powerful god beings come to earth for a while; or girls who personify one of the sacred sisters of the eastern sky." In such cases even the name of the person preexisted, and no other name can be used (Skinner, 1913). The reserved character and meditative behavior of a child is decisive evidence of supernatural birth, Skinner says, and the same notions presumably existed among the Ojibway and Pottawatomi. The Fox, as mentioned earlier, also believe in the preexistence of certain individuals as *manitous*.

The Winnebago and Eastern Dakota, belonging to the Siouan peoples, believe that shamans are humanly incarnated thunder-birds, or at the least supernatural beings who attend these thunder-ers. Nowhere is the speculation concerning human preexistence so subtle and sublime as in the notions of the preexistence of the Dakota medicine-men. Pond has produced a splendid account of their ideas on this subject. He writes: "The original essence of these men and women, for they appear under both sexes, first wakes into existence floating in ether. As the winged seed of the thistle or of the cottonwood floats on the air, so they are gently wafted by the four winds, *Taku-skan-skan*, through the regions of space, until in due time, they find themselves in the abode of some one of the families of the superior gods by whom they are received into intimate fellowship. There the embryonic shaman remains till he becomes familiar with the characters, abilities, desires, caprices, and employments of the gods. He becomes essentially assimilated to them, imbibing their spirit and becoming acquainted with all the chants, feasts, fasts, dances, and sacrificial rites which it is deemed necessary to impose on men." This is how medicine-men become "wakanized" and prepared for their mission.

An echo of that occurs in the belief of the Mohave shamans that "they were present in spirit form at the beginning of the world, at the time when all power, shamanistic and other, was established and allotted" (Krober, 1910). Some Dakota shamans declare that their supernatural powers derive from the time when they existed as twin-partners in a previous life. (Dorsey, 1894). Here the medicine-man's capacity is attributed to the property of being a twin. Not only are twins considered to be supernatural in many quarters, they are also believed to have a supernatural origin, inasmuch as before their human birth, as the Akwa'ala say, they exist in a spirit form in the spirit world

The Northwest Coast tribes believe, Chamberlain says, that in their prenatal state twins live together as salmon in salmon-land. The Teton Dakota locate their prenatal home in a special land of twins (Dorsey, 1889), as do the Yuman tribes. The Mohave and Cocopa say twins come from a mountain landscape, the Akwa'ala describe a mythical village off to the northwest.

The Mohave, according to Deveraux, probably believed that only the first and foremost of the four souls, the real shadow, had a preexistence. They say that these twin-souls "have always existed in heaven and have no father and mother." Twins among the Cocopa are not begotten by the husband of the mother but have "supernatural paternity." When they reach the age of three or four years, they assume the names they bore in heaven.

Future human beings are often given the opportunity in their preexistent life to choose the people they wish to live among on earth and the women of whom they want to be born, Schoolcraft says. An Iowa shaman, Skinner reports, "inspected many tribes before he decided to be born an Iowa. He declined the Winnebago because they smelled fishy, and so he circled around until he discovered the Iowa. They suited him because they were clean, kept their camps swept up, and sent their women a long way off to menstruate. He came down and entered a dark lodge with a bearskin door, and after quite a stay, he came out."

An ethnocentric viewpoint also decides the future Dakota shaman's choice of parents. He does not, for example, want to be born of a white mother, partly because he wishes to have Dakota customs and dress, and partly because his kinsmen the thunderers would kill him if he became white and thereby ignored their instructions (Wallis, 1919). Mohave twins do not wait particularly long for incarnation. "One life is all they want," said Devereux's informant. The twins of the Akwa'ala, on the other hand, accept several incarnations (Gifford & Lowie).

Not all may choose their fate. Preexistent Ingalik children, for example, wait impatiently in their world to be called to the earth. "As one is called, the rest slap him, through jealousy and impatience, and the marks of their rough treatment persist" as birth marks (Hudson). Among the Yokuts the babies who are to be born wander in silence in a long column along the road from the land of the dead to that of the living (Chapman, 1921).

Opinion about the soul's entry into the embryo and its role during the development of the embryo is divided among North American Indians. Some Eskimo imagine that children, like eggs, live in the snow and creep into the womb, while the (free-) soul of a Tlingit is not reincarnated until the body with which it is to be united has been born (Boas, 1940). The Mackenzie Eskimo have a number of incompatible notions concerning incarnation. One says that the soul, *nappan,* comes with the water when the mother drinks or from the ground when she urinates. Another says that the child gets a soul at the same time as it is born. And a third says that the soul comes at some time during the pregnancy, "how or when she does not know" (Stefansson, 1914).

The breath of a child to be enters a Tanaina woman like a cold puff of wind, according to Osgood, while the soul of the Haisla is often the spirit of an uncle which takes possession of the child's body even before birth (Lopatin, 1945). The single soul among the Sanpoil is already in the embryo, according to Ray, and among the Plains Cree the free-soul takes up its abode in the body at birth (Mandelbaum, 1940).

The Naskapi receive their "Great Man" during the embryonic stage (Speck, 1935) and according to the Shawnee, "a soul goes to earth and jumps through the mother's vagina and into the body of the child through the fontanelle just before birth" (Voegelin, 1936). Jones writes that the Ojibway believe that "the Manitou on the other side of the world" delivers their souls to people before their birth. The Fox maintain that the life-soul is with the human embryo during embryonic development, while the free-soul remains outside the mother and does not enter the child until its birth (Michelson, 1925).

A survey of all the material shows that contradictions and inconsistencies are frequent, beliefs being made to conform with the nature of the problems which arise. The single soul among the Sanpoil, for instance, enters the person in the embryonic stage (see above), but in another connection it is said that a deceased person is incarnated in a newborn baby when it receives its name. Is it too bold to see in this discrepancy a reflection of an older soul-belief with dual souls? On the whole, the material favors the assumption that, if a dual soul concept exists, the body-soul appears as soon as the embryo shows signs of life, while the appearance of the free-soul may be fixed at some arbitrary time, even long after the birth of the child.

In this connection it is interesting to consider a rather uncommon version of the soul's attachment to the embryo. Its import lies in the fact that the soul is neither given by the deity nor is it preexistent, but produced by the parents on copulation. In an older account of a journey by the English captain Jonathan Carver (1780), there is a remarkable statement that according to the Sioux (probably the Eastern Dakota) the soul is delivered by the father of a new-born.

"The Indian children," Carver writes, "always bear their mother's names; and if a woman who has had several husbands has had children with each of them, they are all named after her." The reason for this custom is that the soul the children inherit is the work of the father, while the body is the work of the mother. If the information is correct, and Carver did not misunderstand his informants, these Sioux, though perhaps under pressure from their white interlocutor, offered what appears to be a secondary and not fully reasoned motivation for the the custom.

The concept produces speculation among the Cherokee where "there is no clear concept as to the origin of the soul of the child. The majority of the informants say that they do not know, they have never thought of it." The keenest of the shamans, thought that it came along with what went to form the body of the child and was therefore secreted by both the individuals concerned in the act (Mooney & Olbrechts, 1932).

According to the Mohave, "souls spring from the state of 'aliveness' after conception has taken place" (Deveraux). Evidence that the child is believed to have an active soul during the embryonic stage shows in the Indian notion of fetal consciousness and the belief that the child feels and thinks while in the mother's body. Sometimes this consciousness is intensified to the point of precognition and prophetic clairvoyance.

A Bella Coola child that cries in the womb is believed to have an excellent intellect (McIlwraith, 1948). A shaman from the Great Bear Lake district declared that before his birth he had seen a star which revealed to him all the medicines that have power over man (Osgood, 1933). The Chipewyan embryo warns its mother when she is approached by an evil spirit (Birket-Smith, 1930). The unborn Lummi Indian hears what his future relatives are saying and thinking, and if they have evil thoughts in their mind, he leaves them before his birth (Stern, 1934).

The Saulteaux say that in former times they had consciousness during the embryonic stage and were certain about what earthly life would be like, a prophetic capacity that was one of the signs of magic power. Such things are now rare. A Saulteaux did, however, tell Hallowell that "four nights before I was born I knew that I would be born. My mind was as clear when I was born as it is now. I saw my father and my mother, and I knew who they were. I knew the things an Indian uses, their names and what they were good for." Such certainty occus when a person believes they have earlier lived among human beings.

The unborn Fox child understands what his mother is saying and abandons her if she proves to be quarrelsome (Michelson). The Winnebago shaman who is sent down to a woman's womb from his preexistence, retains his consciousness both at conception and during the entire embryonic period, according to Radin. The Wahpeton shamans know everything about their future existence before they are born (Wallis, 1919).

Devereux, writing about the four free-souls of the Mohave, says that "in the fetal stage they follow the actions of the mother and dream of 'how to be born.' The souls of fetal shamans, however, dream of how *not* to be born, that is, how to kill their mother during parturition."

Information concerning the life of the soul in other respects during embryonic development is sparse. The Choctaw believe that the embryo has a delicate soul that is easily lost if a pregnant woman crosses a rushing stream, the soul of the embryo remaining on the bank she has left, meaning its life will accordingly be brief (Swanton, 1931). The Lenape hold the view that the soul of an unborn child follows its future father on his hunting expeditions "romping and playing about the bushes, invisible to mortal eye."As game is scared off by this activity, it is customary to fasten a miniature bow or a miniature mortar to the father's clothes, so that the spirit of the child to be has something to play with and will not be tempted to leave the father's side (Harrington, 1913). Exactly the same notions and customs exist among the Menomini (Skinner, 1925).

The events after the incarnation, and especially at the actual moment of birth, have been dramatically described by a reincarnated Winnebago shaman. "Then I was brought down to earth. I did not enter a woman's womb, but I was taken into a room. There I remained, conscious at all times. One day I heard the noise of little children outside and some other sounds, so I thought I would go outside. Then it seemed to me that I went through a door, but I was really being born again from a woman's womb. As I walked out I was struck with the sudden rush of cold air and I began to cry" (Radin, 1923).

After birth the soul-life of the child is characterized by two peculiarities: an advanced consciousness and a fragile life spirit. Both of these correspond to the status of the ego-soul and the free-soul. The newly born is sometimes considered, especially in northwestern North America, to possess a child-consciousness, which allies him with non-human beings. He speaks the language of baby land, Underhill says, and Spier and Sapir say he understands the language of some animals.

The Yuchi believe, according to Honigmann, that four days after the birth the child overcomes its spirit nature and becomes a real human being. It is believed that small children, not least the newly born, possess the mind of an adult, especially intelligence and understanding. Little children clearly remember the course of their previous life. The older among them recognize objects they have used earlier and are able to describe their previous life. The youngest are thought to display that by crying until they have been given the names they bore in their earlier existence.

There is other, equally direct testimony to the spiritual maturity of the child. Among the Tillamook, Boas says, "newborn children were believed to be wise and to know the thoughts of every person." An Ojibway baby weeps because it wants to see its father, information obtained by the shaman from questioning the child's ego-soul (Jenness, 1935).

Sometimes prophetic gifts are ascribed to the new-born. The Chinook rely on a guardian spirit to understand crying children. A Menomini child who is a reincarnated thunderbird "is able to prophesy rain with accuracy, because coming from above, it has inherited the knowledge of overhead affairs," Skinner says.

The fragile child-soul runs the risk of being lost to the body, and as a rule it is the free-soul that finds itself in the danger zone. And though the free-soul of a Bella Coola child is considered to be so weak that it cannot leave the body, in the majority of cases it is precisely because of its weakness that the free-soul may find itself outside the body. Though it occurs sparingly in North America, there is also the fear that by exhausting his own soul, the father may also exhaust that of the child. The father of a new-born Ingalik child must refrain from chopping wood for a period of twenty days and must be careful to avoid violent movement. "If he leaves the house a pair of scissors or a scrap of tin or some other metal is placed upon the breast of the child as a kind of shield to protect its soul" (Chapman, 1921).

The Puyallup and Nisqually believe that the child and not the free-soul is the weak link. A child loses its free-soul when playing about by itself in the bushes and the grass, as it is not strong enough to prevent the soul from fastening to the thicket (Smith, 1940). The Ojibway consider the child's shadow-soul to be "peculiarly sensitive," and they therefore watch with anxious solicitude over the little one, whose soul is experiencing the world around it, experiences which make the child smile without our perceiving the cause. So that the free-soul will not be lost during these expeditions, one must not throw hats or other objects against the cradle, nor put questions to the child, nor leave wounded animals during hunting excursions which causes the child to suffer out of sympathy for the animal.

A Menomini mother blackens her child's face with ash to prevent the soul from falling behind on walks, or even being blown away, Skinner says. The newborn Lenape child is thought not to have a firm footing in this world, and its little spirit is easily stolen by the dead. In order to deceive the ghosts, the child is disguised in adult clothes and is hung with fringes and rags, so that it looks as if it were bound to the earth, Harrington reports.

The Navajo also believe that the child-soul is weak and therefore must be strengthened with the help of ritual, Reichard says.

The free-soul may also decamp if the child does not feel at home. If the child is insulted or mishandled, whether it is an ordinary child, a "spirit-child," or a twin—its soul goes back to the land of spirits from which it came. Ordinary children, but especially children of supernatural origin, long for their former home, the realm of the dead or the spirit world, for some time after their birth (sometimes many years), and they may perhaps return there. Among a number of tribes in the Woodland country or its immediate vicinity the soles of the children's moccasins are pierced so that in the event of their wishing to return to their spiritual abode, they may not be able to undertake the long, rough journey (Skinner).

But as the child grows, the soul develops. The free-soul of the Bella Coola child is weak and feeble when the child is born, but it grows in strength with the body. The most interesting contribution to the belief in the changes occurring in the soul as it grows older during the childhood of the individual come from the Eskimo. They say that the souls of babies are fragile. Thus the Eskimo of Baffin Land and Hudson Bay believe that "if the souls of children are not strengthened by those of a deceased friend, they are apt to fly away or to lie down," Boas says.

The Mackenzie Eskimo hold a similar view. The soul, *nappan,* is so weak and inexperienced after birth that the mother of the child calls upon a deceased relative to take possession of the body (Stefansson, 1913). Owing to the weakness of the body-soul during childhood, the deceased, generally an ancestor, continues to manage and protect the child, and this bond between the child and its protector is so intimate that the latter is thought to utter everything that the child says. But gradually "as the child grows up, the soul with which he was born, the *nappan,* gradually develops in strength, experience, and wisdom, so that after the age of ten or twelve years, it is fairly competent to look after the child and begins to do so." No further scruple is felt about punishing the child (Stefansson).

Children, who are incarnated spirits, slowly lose their spirit nature and become more ordinary human beings. When the Menomini child, who is an incarnated thunder-spirit, "has grown to a man's estate less care need be used, for his earthly mind will then have more sense and will prevail over his thunder spirit," Skinner says.

Four days after his birth the Yuchi child has overcome his spirit nature. Twins, according to the Cocopa, who are of supernatural descent, "change minds" at the age of thirty years, resolving to become like ordinary Cocopa and to marry (Gifford,).

The soul's development in stages during the different epochs of human life is also well known to the Zuni, who compare the life-course of the human soul and that of maize, Cushing says.

Chapter Fourteen
Various Body Souls

The Indians have in some quarters conceived of the body as an element distinct from the soul or souls, which means they have made the relationship between the body and soul (both free-soul and body-soul) an object for analysis.

Older theory, represented chiefly by Wundt, says that the soul among early peoples is identical with its substratum, yet it seems that in North America they were for the most part distinct entities. Such a dualism between body and soul never, in early peoples of the Old World, becomes a philosophically deepened idea. There the dualism is simpler, an expression for a self-evident insight, an observation. Neither cosmic nor ethical doctrines have been based upon this natural dichotomy.

The North American Indians have, on the other hand, more or less consciously conceived such a dualism between the souls and the body. To begin with, there is no evidence to the contrary. Among the Fox, who believe in the continuity between the free-soul of the living individual and the spook-ghost of the deceased, it is possible that the corpse is the free-soul, but there is no identity after death between the soul and body (Michelson, 1925). When the Yurok refer to the phenomenon of soul loss as "body loss," as Spott and Kroeber report, presumably they mean simply that loss of life is also loss of the body. And while the activity of the free-soul may imply a weakening of the opposition between body and soul, this opposition is not eliminated.

The proof that the Indians must have believed in the dichotomy between body and soul is both indirect and direct. The indirect proof occurs in special conceptions and complexes of ideas from which dualism may be deduced as a tacitly understood (though perhaps not consciously apprehended) principle. Incontestably, all belief in soul-activity implies the division between body and soul. The belief in a surviving soul, like the belief in the free-soul, must inevitably lead to the separation between body and soul. The mere existence of a free-soul operating on its own as an ethereal substance, liberated from the sleeping body, seems to presuppose the dichotomy, as does the theory of soul incarnation referred to above.

Evidence of this dichotomy comes from the Indians. The body is frequently represented as a covering for the soul. The body is the house of the free-soul, the Kwakiutl say, while the free-soul of the Bella Coola, according to Boas, is like a bird enclosed in an egg, and "if the shell of the egg breaks and the soul flies away, its owner must die." The Lenape, Harrington reports, say that "man has a spirit, and the body seems to be a coat for that spirit." According to Wright, death implied to the Choctaw that the soul threw off its outer covering, "as the snake sheds his skin." The Navajo use the phrase, "you leave your skin" to describe the soul's departure at death.

The psychophysical dichotomy here is conscious and invites reflection. The dualism between soul and body is obviously as old as the soul belief itself and conditioned by the same causes. The destruction of the body after death, and the conviction of continued independent existence, have been the chief factors in the origin of the separation between the physical and psychic.

At death, say the Oglala, the body "rots and becomes nothing" for "anything that has a birth will have a death." Souls are unborn and consequently do not die (Walker, 1917). The Quileute and Ojibway pay little attention to the existence of the body for it decays after death. At the cremation of the corpse the soul of the Pomo Indian is freed from the perishable body, Powers says, and the Winnebago believe that the lack of a body is the chief peculiarity distinguishing a dead from a living person.

Presumably the dichotomy also had other causes. The experiences of the free-soul at a distance from the body have meant a good deal, while the impression of pulsating life-souls has played a lesser role as a body-soul interacting with the body.

Not only do Indians distinguish between the soul and the body, but they also have a definite notion about the nature of the relationship between the soul and the body. Indians believe that the soul is supreme and dominates the body which it animates. The causes of the soul's predominance are its immortality, the body's perishability, the independence of the soul, and the body's dependence on the soul.

The notion of the body's death and the soul's continued life inspired the idea of the dichotomy between soul and body. In practice, the demise of the body sometimes signifies that it is dissolved into the elements of which the universe is composed (the Navajo, according to Reichard), or that its constituent parts are strewn over the earth and fertilize it (the Klamath, according to Spier). The surviving soul is not atomized. It represents the total persona of the living human being after death. The perishable character of the body arises from the fact that it does not exist independently. The body is a dead, incoherent mass, to which the soul imparts life and coherence. The soul, on the other hand, exists independently of the body.

The body-soul constitutes no exception even though it may manifest a certain freedom as the following instance from the Bella Coola shows. "It is generally considered that a person dies if his life leaves his body. In contradiction to this, though the discrepancy seems of slight importance to the Bella Coola, is the belief that it ascends at the winter solstice to the gathering of the supernatural beings" (McIlwraith, 1948) A still greater emancipation from the dependence upon the body is shown by the body-soul when, among some peoples, it appears more regularly as a free-soul.

The specific free-soul, the dream-soul, is bound to the body as a condition of the latter's existence. In its essence, however, it is an independent spiritual entity, which may depart from the body without feeling any dependence upon it. Ragueneau provides the following instance from the Huron. "When, during sleep, they dream of something that is far away, they think that the soul issues forth from the body and proceeds to the place that is pictured. During all that time they say, however, that it is not the sensitive soul that issues forth, but only the rational one, which is not dependent upon the body in its workings."

The relationship between soul and body is rather one sided. It is said that the body cannot exist without the soul, whereas the soul can do without the body. "The body needs the (free) soul, but the (free) soul does not need the body," the Thompson River Indians say, according to Teit. The soul is "what gives us life," say the Nomlaki. "When it is gone, we are gone, it just leaves us like a broken automobile" (Goldschmidt, 1951).

The general rule is that if the life-soul leaves the body, the latter is dead. But the free-soul may also have dominion over the body, for it makes the body cohere according to the Kwakiutl (Boas, 1921). Speck says says the Naskapi understand it as the leader of the body in the same way as the engineer drives a locomotive. The Canadian Athapascans, Morice reports, believe that in times of health and well-being, the free-soul is enclosed in the body. When the person becomes sick, however, it has left its dwelling. The body's helplessness, when it has been deprived of the free-soul, shows clearly in the Bella Coola belief that the misfortune which afflicts the body arises because the free-soul has left, McIlwraith says.

Generally speaking Indians believe that the body is more dependent upon the body-soul (especially the life-soul) than upon the free-soul, and that the free-soul is more independent of the body than the body-soul. No soul, on the other hand, is directly dependent upon the body, even if the death of the body implies that the existence of the life-soul ceases. What they are saying is that the affairs of the life-soul are no longer of interest once man continues in a new form of existence.

In two ways, however, the body binds the souls to itself: it functions as their base and it constitutes the form of the active individual. It is also possible to localize the free-soul to the body where it remains during its passive period. Sometimes, however, it shows its freedom from the body by keeping its distance. The important thing to note is that though the free-soul is an independent entity, its function binds it to the body.

Incarnation, which is an expression for the will of supernatural powers, restricts the free-soul's freedom of movement, relinquishing its grip on the free-soul only when physical death approaches. Then the extra-physical soul is attracted magnetically to the realm of the dead as the Orpheus-like traditions show.

There can be no doubt that the Indians regarded the body as the outer symbol for both person and personality. But the perishable body has never represented the individual self, though it merges with the free-soul which bears the individuality of the person, during the twilight experience. The human form, the body, has therefore become something of a strait-jacket for human content, the spirit, the free-soul.

The theoretical dichotomy of body and soul recedes into the background when the free-soul is experienced as the subject's ego and person. The following two cases are typical: one illustrating the weakening of the body-feeling when the free-soul is operating, while the other throws a more definite light upon the interdependence of the free-soul and the body at such moments.

In the first case when the individual experiences himself as a free soul, when he functions outside his body, the assurance that he is far away from his body does not always occur during the experience, but is often felt after awakening. In dreams or in a state of trance man is in his totality. The body's existence is not realized by one who experiences himself as a free-soul unless the waking consciousness steals into the dream-fantasy in the form of sober reflection, as McClintock discovered among the Blackfoot. Unconscious or dead persons who in extra-physical form cannot realize that they are cut off from real life, illustrate the weakened body feeling in the free-soul experience.

In the second case Jenness tells of a Carrier Indian who, unaware of his death, traveled on the road to the realm of the dead until he suddenly became aware of his situation and returned to his body. A Babine Indian following the same fatal road suddenly discovered that he was naked, whereupon he turned back, Jenness says. The Navajo knows that he is dead when the flames from his campfire rise straight up into the air in spite of a strong wind (Wyman, Hill & Orsani). In the last-mentioned case, the body-feeling is obviously of no consequence.

In a Winnebago tradition we are even told that a couple of slain Indians had no notion of their fate although they saw their own dead bodies, and received no replies from their wives when they addressed them. Not until they saw their relatives lamenting over their bodies did they understand that they were dead (Radin, 1923).

In other cases the circumstances have not been quite so extreme. A Winnebago shaman told Radin that in a previous existence he became convinced of his death when he saw his dead body. It may be added that the dead person's ignorance of his state may occur because the memories of earthly existence have been effaced during the individual's journey to the realm of the dead.

The unreflected association between the free-soul and the body is sometimes seen in the possibility of reading the experiences of the free-soul from the body and vice-versa. The commonest case occurs when the experiences of the soul leave traces on the body. The Lillooet shaman exposes a thief by holding his free-soul to the fire. When the soul in the shaman's hands is scorched, its owner shrieks (Teit, 1906). The Thompson River Indians believe that "the soul of a person who has a nightmare is nearing the beginning of the trail leading to the world of the souls," Teit says.

The Ojibway maintain that a baby's smile reflects the experiences its free-soul meets on its wanderings, according to Jenness. If a Pottawatomi dies of an unknown wound, Gregg says, those around him believe that his soul has been wounded in an encounter with an enemy on its dream-journey.

Sometimes the body's experiences are reflected in the states of the soul. The free-soul of the unconscious Ojibway who has been shot shows the same wounds as the body, according to DeSmet. The dream-soul of the Cahuilla knows what is happening to the body although it is far away and reacts immediately if anyone attempts to wake the sleeper, Hooper says.

In summarizing the conceptions of the relation between soul and body held by the North American Indians, it is clear that these substances are not only distinguished entities, but through the process of incarnation have become united in an association in which the body binds the soul, but where the soul is nevertheless the dominant partner regulating the reactions of the body. Based on premises of early soul belief, this functional relationship must be regarded as the only one possible. And yet, in practice the body now and then unintentionally appears as the center of the personality. Such occurrences, while not acknowledged by the Indians, are in practice inescapable.

I have shown a number of instances in which during dreams the feeling of the ego is both associated with and detached from the free-soul. But when the dream-soul does not represent the ego, and the ego-soul of the waking consciousness does not function, a third entity, the individual present through the body, represents the ego-experience. The same thing occurs if both the ego-soul and the free-soul, as is the case among the Naskapi, exist as guardian beings outside and above the individual, either in dreams or in waking consciousness.

There are also times in the waking state when the normal ego-soul does not function. Psychic resources can be reduced by mental disorder, loss of memory, and by loss of the ego-soul. An Ojibway, for example, who gets drunk, chases his ego-soul from his body leaving the individual realized through his body, the physical person, as the only actor (Jenness, 1945).

Earlier I pointed out that by leaving the body the free-soul may expose the latter to accidents. This notion, which is a consistent application of the free-soul idea, is often replaced by another, which reverses the causality but is perhaps more realistic. In one instance an Achomawi shaman, who had been run into by a car while riding in a carriage, was told by his guardian spirit that "his shadow had been knocked out of him when he fell out of the buggy" (deAngulo, 1926). In other words, the bump to the body was the cause of the soul being driven away.

But perhaps the body shows its dominance over the souls to a higher degree than in the above cases when its unchangeable association with the individual during his lifetime is contrasted with the notion, occurring especially in northernmost America, that the soul (as a rule one of several life-souls) is alienable and may be exchanged for another soul of the same type. The best known instances of such an exchange have been given by Egede and Cranz based on their work among the Eskimo. Egede says, for example, that a damaged soul could be exchanged for the soul of a little bird. The Eskimo on Greenland had a whole set of life-souls, and the loss of one of them did not necessarily entail any serious consequences. The shamans regularly replaced older, worn-out souls with new ones. The same notion of the shaman's ability to exchange souls occurs among the Chokchee who also believed in the existence of a number of body-souls.

South of the Eskimo region the life-soul is more firmly associated with the individual, perhaps because the concept of plural life-souls is not as pronounced as it is among the Eskimo. According to information from the Ingalik, Tsimshian, and Cheyenne, a life-soul may be strengthened through the infusion of the life-soul of another, dying individual. Wilkes tells how the medicine-man among the Carrier, after the death of a fellow tribesman, catches the spirit of the deceased (the life-soul?) and blows it into a living person, who thereafter "takes the name of the deceased in addition to his own." This was not, however a soul exchange.

The Zuni, who locate the soul in the heart among other places, consider death to occur when "the heart wears out. Medicine men," Bunzel says, "can fix it up when they come to cure, and it will go for a while, but sooner or later you will have to get a new one." That process is the first rite in the society-initiations of the Zuni, and it is obviously the physical heart and not the soul associated with the heart that they are talking about.

Curiously enough exchange of a free-soul occurs among the Cowichan when a sick shaman replaces his lost free-soul with the free-soul of another which he has captured (Boas, 1894). This is possible because the Cowichan believe that people have several free-souls. Where a normal dual orsingle soul belief exists, the free-soul exchange does not occur.

Frachtenberg does report that among the Quileute souls "may be taken off or put on in exactly the same manner as a snake sheds its skin," but what he refers to here, is presumably the capacity of the regular free-soul, the ego-soul and one of the life-souls for extraphysical activity. For he also says that "the souls of a person are his individual property and may not be sold." Furthermore, Underhill says that the coastal Indians of Washington believe that a sick person will die if his soul is replaced with that of another.

Just as the free-soul or the life-soul can operate for a time outside the body without the health of the owner being jeopardized, so a strange soul may take possession of a person without risk to the person's life as long as the possession is nor permanent. The soul of the "possessed" person (his free-soul) need not have departed from the body beforehand. The Mackenzie Eskimo is, as I have shown earlier, "possessed" during the first years of his life by the spirit of an ancestor without his own soul being ousted. On the contrary it is able to grow in both maturity and wisdom (Stefansson, 1913).

Among the Bella Coola, McIlwraith says, an individual whose soul has entered into another is said to "become mad, try to eat dirt, and die," but if the "possessed" is a dancer of the Kusiut Society, "the entry of a strange spirit into his body does not inconvenience the dancer, although he senses its presence."

The Nootka, on the other hand, say the soul of the "possessed" is frequently absent. Sproat says that "if the soul has migrated and entered in any other form or body, and the soul of this other form or body does not in turn migrate to the one which has been bereft, this latter first becomes weak, and then sickens, and finally dies if the soul is not brought back."

The Eskimo believe, according to Thalbitzer, that the shaman is possessed by his guardian spirit when he has dismissed his free-soul. And among the Nootka, Sproat adds, an evil strange spirit takes advantage of the opportunity provided by the absence of the soul (evidently the free-soul) to possess the person.

The above instances presuppose the body as the element which represents the continuity of the individual. And though from the Indian point of view it is impossible to ascribe such a function to the body, it is in actuality little more than a container for the soul.

Chapter Fifteen
Interplay Between the Souls

In the full-grown, healthy human being the dual soul apparatus, with its interesting interaction between different soul agents, is intensively active. That activity is conditioned, from the psychological viewpoint, by the body and its physical condition. Interplay occurs in two main forms: as alternating action and as cooperation. The alternating or reciprocal action between the souls takes place according to the state of the body, while cooperation between them is indirectly dependent on the body's circumstances.

Reciprocal action between the free-soul and the body-souls has, as I have shown, given rise to a belief in dual souls. In a reciprocating action the individual's life and his ego alternate with the state of consciousness depending upon the state of the body. In a regular reciprocal action life-elements and ego-elements (the elements which together form the individual or the concept of the person) are represented by the life-soul and the ego-soul during waking consciousness and by the free-soul during dream-consciousness.

When the person is awake and physically active, his body-souls fulfill the functions which characterize the living individual: life, motor capacity, understanding, feeling, and will. But all these functions disappear when the person is dreaming and physically passive, replaced by the dream-soul, which is a dematerialized form of the person and is only actual during the dream. In this unreflected and regular dualism, the relationship between the souls causes no problem.

But the nature of this reciprocity soon becomes a subject for reflection and deliberation. The free-soul is an independent entity, separate from other soul-entities while the life-soul and the ego-soul continue to function in relation to various states of the body. But the connection between the potencies is complicated and to understand them it is important to see how the sensation of life and the sensation of ego are connected to different potencies as changes occur in the body.

The life of the waking individual is represented by an undifferentiated body-soul, a general life-soul, or a number of different organ-souls controlling vital functions. The chief life-soul is commonly identical with the breath. When during sleep the body sinks into passivity, the intensity of life-soul activity declines to the point where the concept of the life-soul no longer exists. This does not necessarily mean that the life-soul has fled. It still remains in dreams, and although it is barely active it is there. Were it not, as the Ojibway point out, the dreamer would be dead (Schoolcraft, 1860).

The Iroquois say that in dreams the free-soul "leaves its *human* in the care of its *material* spirit," according to Converse. In other words although the free-soul is there, the only soul concept still extant, the life-soul, continues to administer the body. The free-soul of an Algonquin may have been in the realm of the dead for several years, but the man still lives as long as the body-soul remains. However, the continued absence of the free-soul causes the life-soul to waste away, depart, or simply end.

The "life" of the individual is therefore not independent as a specific potency because the free-soul has a part in it. The Bella Coola, for instance, connect the free-soul with the breath and with the life of the individual. The dream-soul, while it combines all the properties of the body-souls, is in fact an entity in itself, especially in the way it demands attention.

The ego-consciousness of the waking individual is represented by an undifferentiated body-soul, a general ego-soul, or a number of different ego-souls controlling the functions of consciousness. And while the life-soul is able to continue its activity in the body, even if at a slower rate, when the person falls asleep, the ego-soul is completely shut off. In effect the functions of the ego-soul are transferred to the free-soul.

In an advanced dual soul relationship, where the free-soul is a potency among potencies, the dream-soul and the dream-ego are not always identical. A free-soul which may be exchanged, for-feited, or lost without any detriment to the subject, or which can be seen in dreams or in the waking state, is not particularly suit-able as an expression for the conscious ego of the individual. Logically, the ego-soul in such circumstances should operate as the dream-ego; but it is not possible to determine whether the In-dians believed that.

Never is soul dualism more pronounced than in its relation-ship to the conscious ego. As the representative of the ego, the ego-soul regards the free-soul as a strange being, as a double-ganger separate from the individual, but it is certainly not uncom-mon for the free-soul, as the representative of the ego in dreams, to regard the body as a strange being.

Despite this tension between the souls, the conscious ego glides imperceptibly back and forth between the ego-soul and the free-soul. As soon as the activity of the ego-soul ceases, the free-soul steps into the breach without the continuity of consciousness being broken and without the transition being perceived by the ego. In some cases among the Blackfoot, Navajo, and Wind River Shoshone, the person "feels" the soul departing from the body.

When the free-soul appears it is generally the bearer of the conscious ego. But where it is a more independent entity, Radin says, the ego experience may glide between the body-subject (the ego-soul?) and the extra-physical subject (the free-soul). In cer-tain circumstances a transitional situation may arise while the per-son is awake so that the ego-sensation is torn between the scarce-ly functioning ego-soul and the free-soul which is present.

The Ojibway, Jenness reports, believe that the ego-soul is oc-casionally chased away leaving the individual with only a body and a free-soul. While this crosses the boundary and becomes an irregular soul dualism, it should be pointed out that in many quar-ters the unity of the two ego-souls is a perceived truth regardless of how it is arrived at. The Quileute, who boast a complicated soul dualism, "express their assurance of the ultimate unity be-hind the said souls in their belief that after death the free-soul is united with the ego-soul" (Frachtenberg, 1920).

Strict dualism may be broken up in two ways: either the speci-fic soul-functions are transferred to other souls or the souls are coordinated with wider unities. In both cases the development takes the direction of soul monism, especially in the first case.

The latter transfer of function produces irregular reciprocal action between the souls. In this form, however, the interplay shows certain modes of action

In principle, irregular reciprocal action is conditioned by the fact that free-soul function has been transferred to the body-souls, and the psychological free-soul and the specific free-soul no longer coincide. Furthermore, the concept of this soul is not always bound to a single soul-entity. The term free-soul, after all, is sometimes used as a technical term for a soul appearing outside the body rather than designating a specific soul-concept. Souls of different origin may temporarily act as free-souls, and then they assume the peculiarities and function which characterize the specific free-soul when it appears outside the body.

Irregular reciprocal action between the souls arising from body-soul expansion is based upon the unique physical conditions of the individual. A survey of the relationships between the specific souls which may appear as free-souls and the occasions when these appearances occur, serves as a guide to the nature of the physical conditions. In the scheme below the functional situations of the free-soul have been combined with various nominal soul aspects. The specific free-soul is presented first as a dream-soul, which is as we know its normal manifestation, and second as a double-ganger.

A. The free-soul in twilight states.
    1. In sleep: the dream-soul.
    2. In shallow trance: the ego-soul, the double-ganger.
    3. In deep trance: the dream-soul or the body-soul.
    4. In coma: the dream-soul or the body-soul.
B. The free-soul in the state of waking consciousness.
    1. In anormal soul-states (insanity, loss of memory and other mental debility): the dream-soul, the ego-soul.
    2. In states relatively normal but conditioned by strong emotions: the dream-soul, in some cases perhaps the ego-soul.
    3. In normal soul states but with physical enfeeblement: a specialized life-soul.

A study of this scheme reveals that physical states regulate the encroachments of the life-soul and the ego-soul upon the function of the free-soul. The life-soul becomes an extra-physical soul if lethargy is so deep that the body seems to be without life (deep trance or coma). If there are several life-souls, one of them may depart without the life of the person being jeopardized but that does not relieve the illness. The ego-soul becomes an extra-physical soul if during the apparent lifelessness of the individual it represents the entire body-soul concept, but above all if the person's mental balance is in any way upset. In one case there is an extension of the functional sphere of the free-soul in which the specific free-soul has no part, because the free-soul of physical enfeeblement is always a life-soul. The ego of shallow trance is seldom extra-physical, but in this case it is always identical with the ego-soul not with the dream-soul. Only when the trance is deepened does the dream-soul appear.

The relationship between the active free-soul and the conscious ego presents an interesting picture. The identity between the free-soul and the ego is only experienced in twilight states. A free-soul that is absent in the waking state is never identical with the ego. Both the specific free-soul and the body-soul acting as a free-soul bear the conscious ego. Free-soul function may, after all, be distinct from the ego and in some cases can be experienced as an object separate from the ego. In other cases the individual simply understands that the free-soul is absent.

The free-soul as an object occurs chiefly during twilight states, while the conclusion that the free-soul is missing applies chiefly to waking states. A shaman makes the diagnosis. From this it would seem that the free-soul was originally the ego of the individual in twilight states, above all during dreams, but that later it also became the symbol for any separated soul. The effect was to extend its functions to consciousness, even as those functions were assigned to souls of another order, such as the body-souls.

There is of course an irregular reciprocal action between souls of differing kinds, and although the cases are rare, occasionally the free-soul encroaches upon the sphere of the life-soul without ousting the latter (the Arikara), or the free-soul may encroach upon the sphere of the ego-soul without the ego-soul being expelled (the Wind River Shoshone). Whether it is possible for the life-soul and the ego-soul to transfer their activities to each other's spheres without ousting each other is a more difficult question, but it seems probable because they frequently function as a particular aspect of a single undifferentiated body-soul concept.

At a later stage of development a soul whose functions have been largely taken over by another soul is absorbed by the latter, producing irregular groups of dual souls. The reciprocal action taking place in such a soul constellation is characterized by diminished tension. In a dual relationship in which the free-soul and the ego-soul have merged, the single consciousness soul survives because it is not disturbed by the transitions between the dream-world and waking life.

Reciprocal action between the souls may gradually, to a greater or lesser extent, be replaced by two or more souls cooperating when they are in the same situation. In a way such cooperation already occurs in regular soul-relationships; the ego-soul and the life-soul sometimes appearing as poles in the same general body-soul conception Then life-soul activity informs both components even though the body-soul is activated successively, not simultaneously, with the ego-soul and the life-soul. Real soul cooperation occurs when two or more souls function in a common activity at the same time.

The coordination of souls can be either horizontal or vertical. Horizontal coordination implies that the souls act as partners with equal rights. During serious illness among the Quileute, both the inner and outer souls (probably the ego-soul and the free-soul) operate outside the patient's body (Frachtenberg). Vertical coordination implies that one of the active souls is dependent upon or subordinated to the other. A less pronounced form of vertical coordination occurs when one soul sustains the other. In a Niska legend we are told how the free-soul can take the life-soul with it (in the shape of a heart) on its journey to the realm of the dead. Its activity helps the free-soul return to the world of the living (Boas, 1895).

In the extreme form of vertical coordination one soul is superior and dominant. That is common when the ego-soul or the free-soul has been transformed into a guardian soul or super-ego. The Bella Coola believe that the ego-soul (the mentality) receives its impulses from the active free-soul acting simultaneously as a guardian spirit (McIlwraith), and the Fox think, according to

Michelson, that the free-soul watches over the life-soul.

Perhaps the most interesting interplay between souls takes place in cases of sickness and death, an interaction which casts considerable light upon the fate of souls after death.

Chapter Sixteen
Soul Loss and Death

Soul-loss is the technical term the Indians used to describe their concept of the nature of illness. The diagnosis is made either by the sick person (who in the twilight state experiences the movements of the soul, in this case the psychological free-soul) or by a shaman with healing powers.

It is important here to distinguish between the concept of soul-loss and the extraphysical wanderings of the free-soul. The dream journey does not include the idea of any soul loss, and this is especially true if the free-soul is experienced as identical with the ego. Only when the dreamer finds that his soul has disappeared or strayed to a place from which it cannot return, such as the realm of the dead, does soul loss occur.

Attempts to arrive at the age of the soul-loss idea in North America by contrasting it with the other dominant notions of disease, and with the notion of objects, animals and spirits intruding into the human body, seem to have failed. In North America the intrusion idea occurs practically everywhere, whereas soul loss is less widely represented, especially on the Plains, an area which has a young culture.

Soul loss occurs frequently among the Eskimo, the Northwest Indians (down to California), the Northern Plateau Indians and the Central Algonquin. Moreover it is the most common theory of illness in the far north and Northwest. Soul loss appears frequently among the West Athapascans, the Shoshone and the Yuman tribes. It also occurs in Northern California but ebbs again in Central and Southern California. In general, intrusion is more common among the Indians of California. Nor does the soul-loss diagnosis occur to any great extent in the Southeast, the Southwest or in Mexico. Only a few definite instances of soul loss can be documented among the Plains Indians. The infrequency with which the notion occurs on the outskirts of the high-culture is probably connected with the development of the single soul.

Attempts to determine the age of the theories of disease are obstructed by the fact that they often occur side by side in the same diagnosis (Rogers, 1944) and indeed, often influence each other. Soul-loss may be caused by intrusion, just as intrusion may be caused by soul-loss. In addition it can be cured using the therapy for intrusion, just as intrusion may be cured with the methods designed to cure soul-loss. Sometimes a person's sufferings are the result of having become the host for a strange spirit while also having been deprived of the (free-)soul.

While both theories are old it is impossible to prove whether they are of equal antiquity, though it seems likely that in ancient times they complemented each other. I intimated earlier in my discussion of the free-soul that concept of soul-loss as a cause of illness probably arose only when consciousness had been disturbed. The intrusion of a foreign object or being was probably assumed as the cause in connection with physical illness not accompanied by a change of consciousness. If this reconstruction is correct, then the causes of illness occurred side by side, and the diagnosis was adapted to the patient's state of consciousness. This does not mean that intrusion, in certain cases, was not capable of changing the character of consciousness. Indeed, in a number of cases insanity has been ascribed to the intrusion of an alien spirit. Probably such possession was well-known in even the earliest prehistoric times. But having one of the body-souls depart after the fashion of the free-soul without the consciousness of the patient being changed, is a more recent phenomenon.

What needs to be understood is the connection between body and soul, and between the souls themselves during the period from the commencement of the illness to the moment of death, when the nature of the illness is soul-loss. Then the soul is believed to leave its owner without immediately jeopardizing life. The Indians often express that in the phrase "the soul goes before death." Sometimes it may be seen departing. The departing soul is a free-soul, but it may also be a body-soul. The Yuma think that during illness both the shadow-soul and a body-soul may leave the body (Forde, 1931). Some Ojibway think it is the ego-soul which is lost (Jenness, 1935). Among the Wind River Shoshone it is, as a rule, the dream-soul and less frequently the life-soul that disappears.

In all of these cases the specific free-soul (the dream-soul) is absent when consciousness is abnormal. That also occurs when one or others (except when the ailment is physical) believes that the soul is absent. In addition it occurs when the general body-soul is absent during the unconsciousness accompanying a nearly lifeless state or when a local body-soul is absent though the patient is suffering only from ordinary illness which causes no change of consciousness. Only in a four-soul speculation, where the identity and contours of the souls have become blurred, can different souls function as the missing entity (or entities) without assuming the peculiarities of each.

The conditions for soul-loss lie in the nature of the free-soul and its relation to the body. It can occur when the soul has become so weak that the shaman must restore its vigor (the Bella Coola, Boas, 1892), or among children, women, and old people who have frail souls which are easily lost, or when the soul is so loosely attached that it may easily fasten in the people one meets or in bushes and thickets. A person who has not yet recovered from illness has not, according to Tanner's reports on the Ojibway, got his soul safely encapsuled in his body and should exercise great care because then the soul is drawn automatically to the realm of the dead.

The direct causes of (free-)soul loss may be classified in the following groups:

1. The soul is driven away by its owner through the transference of the life-breath to another person.

2. The soul leaves on its own initiative. In many cases shocks, fainting fits and other psychic reactions are not the causes but the consequences of soul-loss. Sometimes there are clear motives for the free-soul's behavior. The guardian-soul of the Naskapi, for example, abandons its protégé if the latter does not comply with its requirements.

3. The soul is thrown out in connection with external injury or

physical trials. If the body gets a bump, or if it is manhandled or beaten, the soul is ejected. If a Yuma Indian gets several blows to the head and body "the soul is driven out of the body by the severity of the blow. The soul goes up with the dust caused by the fall and hovers above, undecided whether to return" (Forde). A less dangerous form of soul loss occurs when, after a rapid journey by train, the Missisauga Indian lies down on the ground to await his soul which has not been able to travel at the same speed (Chamberlain, 1888).

4. The soul is driven out by strong emotions. A Quinault who grieves deeply risks losing his soul according to Olsen. But above all, soul-loss may be caused by a psychic shock: the soul rushing from its owner out of fear. The Bella Coola say that the soul on such occasions does not expel itself but is ejected by the contraction of the muscles, according to McIlwraith. This interpretation, however, is not representative of the way the Indians generally regard the occurrence.

5. The soul goes astray on dangerous roads, during sleep, trance, and coma, and is in this way lost to its owner, unless he is a shaman. In trance or coma the individual is regarded as dead or almost dead, and his soul is therefore in or near the realm of death. It is especially dangerous to dream while running a fever which occupies an intermediate position between the ordinary dream and the comatose dream (Frazer, 1886).

6. The soul is stolen. This motif is the one most often associated with soul-loss, and it also constitutes the dominant cause of this pathological situation. Those who commit this crime are either living beings with supernatural capacities and/or supernatural beings. The former, Forde says, are wizards and malevolent shamans who can hide a captured soul so that it cannot be found either among the living or the dead. First and foremost among the supernatural beings are the dead, who are experts Bouteiller says, in matters of soul loss. In most cases these ghosts are identical with deceased relatives who long for the company of the living, but they may also be avenging spirits (murdered persons, murderers and those who have been unjustly buried). The theft may occur at any time and place, but it is generally committed when

the individual is asleep or in the dark. Among the Lummi, certain spirits have a magnetic capacity to attract souls to themselves (Stern).

There is a correspondence between the states of the body and the soul in connection with soul loss. The mere risk of a physical catastrophe immediately directs an Indian's thoughts to the free-soul. "I almost lost my *yega*" is the phrase used by the Coyukon for "I was in great danger" (Jette, 1911). The course of the disease may therefore be followed on two fronts: soul and body. However we should remember that the fate of the body is only a result of the fate of the soul.

After the separation from the body, the free-soul either goes on its own or is conducted to a place whose location will depend upon whether the soul is wandering of its own accord, or whether it has been stolen, and if so, by whom. The destination may lie in the surrounding landscape, traditionally the home of supernatural beings, in the air above or in the realm of the dead. But usually the soul makes for the realm of the dead. In a number of Plateau and Southwest groups, the soul is, at this point, regarded as irrevocably lost, and even if death does not occur immediately, it is inevitable. But as Elmendorf points out, this concept is geographically peripheral to the greater area of distribution where the idea of soul-loss occurs.

Normally soul-loss can be cured, but the sick person's chances of recovering diminish as his soul comes nearer to the realm of the dead. The beliefs vary according to whether the runaway soul is a specific free-soul or a body-soul, and whether the sick person is conscious or not. In brief, the soul is lost if it has been absent for too long, if it has gotten too far on its way to the realm of the dead, if it has crossed the river of death or if it is in the land of the dead.

Some say the soul may remain for some time in the realm of the dead without immediate risk, but that can only happen if it is a soul which has already associated itself with the dead without having cut the tie connecting it with the living; or if it is the soul of a shaman who has come to fetch a stolen soul. But some people believe, according to Deveraux, that not even a shaman can always venture into the realm of the dead. The nearer to this realm the soul gets, the more its owner's health and strength are reduced, though physical and mental reactions are to a considerable extent determined by the nature of the departing soul. The immediate consequences of the soul's departure may be: state unchanged, physical or mental enfeeblement or death.

The first eventuality is fairly common, where the concepts of the double-ganger and the guardian-soul have developed, for it is the free-soul that has departed. Without the diagnosis of the shaman, the patient does not know that he is ill or expected to become ill; nor, in many cases, does he have any notion of the soul's disappearance.

The Duwamish shaman, according to Underhill, can find the soul of a healthy and sound person in the realm of the dead when it has gone there without its owner's knowledge. Wilkes says the Spokan believe that "the spirit within a person may be separated from the body for a short time, without the person being aware of it, or causing death, provided it be quickly restored to him." The shaman learns of the soul's absence in a dream and reports the matter to the patient, who until then has been unaware that his soul has fled. The patient then commissions the shaman to recover the soul.

More commonly the soul's departure is the result of a pathological state, which in the long run may cause death. Then either the free-soul or one of the body-souls is absent. Which soul has been lost depends upon whether the illness is the result of mental disturbance (when the free-soul or the ego-soul has fled), loss of consciousness (when the free-soul or one of the body-souls has left) or is a purely physical disorder (when one of the life-souls has departed).

Several sources say that soul-loss may cause the owner to lose the ability to reason. Others say that loss of consciousness, fainting fits, and epileptic seizures are caused by soul-loss. People with a fever who sleep and dream are believed to have lost their soul. A common consequence of soul-loss is that the individual's physical resources dwindle; he becomes lazy and languid, wastes away, becomes emaciated. A gradual decline means to the Hidatsa that the many souls are leaving the body one after another, according to Matthews. Finally, soul-loss can also occur when the disease is localized to a part of the body.

While loss of the soul may have immediate and serious consequences, it is not always clear what the effect will be, even if the nature of the absent soul is known. Le Jeune writes that when the Montagnais "see that a poor invalid no longer speaks, or that he has fainted, or been seized by a frenzy, they say that the spirit is no longer in the body; and, if the invalid returns to his senses, it is the spirit which has returned."

A third consequence of soul-loss may be that the person dies. This however, is not a typical result, though it is important here to bear in mind that death is not a fixed state among the Indians. First, the loss of the free-soul may, independent of its consequences, be understood as a preliminary death, and according to Kelly, a Chemehuevi, who has lost his soul, is said to be "as good as dead." Second, soul-loss may simply designate death. And third, profound torpor (trance, coma) is regarded as tantamount to death. In certain cases soul-loss causes an immediate actual death, but only if the stolen soul is, to judge from the evidence, a single soul. It is then, meaningless to speak of soul-loss as the cause of disease, for the cause of the disease is commonly the intrusion of some particle, object, or being.

Soul loss does not always have fatal consequences, though only in three categories of soul-loss do dangerous effects fail to appear or have been postponed for an indefinite period. If a person has several souls of a similar kind (body-souls, free-souls), one of them may be lost without serious harm as long as another is procured in its place. If the free-soul is a guardian-spirit type, it may depart without its protégé experiencing any greater injury than the possible forfeit of happiness and safety. The free-soul may leave the old and infirm, and yet they continue to live. An Algonquin claimed to have lived without his free-soul for more than two years, though the loss of the soul is the prelude to dying.

Normally no human being who loses his soul can escape being afflicted with sickness either sooner or later, and if the soul is not returned in time, the person dies. From widely separate parts of North America, people believe that a lost soul must be regained as soon as possible. Osgood's informant among the Tanaina spoke of a person "as dead as soon as the spirit-shadow had disassociated itself from the body, the physical effects of death being delayed until the human mechanism, like a clock, had run down." Frequently the number of days a sick person may have left to live is reckoned from the date the soul took flight. The time may vary from a couple of years to a couple of hours. In the majority of cases the time limit is not fixed. Naturally the length of the period between soul-loss and death (physical death) is connected to the nature of the departing soul.

This raises the question of the internal relationships between the souls at the moment of death. Clearly the Indians view death as a state in which the symptoms of life are either absent or only faintly perceptible. The many cases of apparent death and the numerous narratives in which the dead person returns to life, lie in the confusion of deep coma with physical death. In the following "death" will be used to designate both these states, whereas "definitive death" will designate for physical death where it is necessary to make the difference clear.

"Definitively dead" or "again dead" is the Indian way of referring to someone who has returned to his senses after deep unconsciousness and then once more lost consciousness, but this time without regaining it. From the viewpoint of soul belief, death implies that the activity of the souls in the living individual comes to an end; the free-soul is definitively liberated from its physical bondage and the body-soul ceases to function. From the point of view of the living individual, the departure of all his souls implies that he dies.

In a normal dual soul relationship it is the departure of the life-soul that marks the advent of death, though it should be noted that the loss of the life-soul need not necessarily lead to definitive death as long as the free-soul remains in the body. If, however, the free-soul is not there when the life-soul makes its extraphysical appearance, death takes place either immediately or after a short time. In a few cases the life-soul remains in the body after it has ceased to function. In rare cases, after its activity in the living person has come to an end, the life-soul drives the "living corpse."

The order in which the souls depart bears closer examination. In normal soul-dualism the order depends on whether the cause of the illness is soul-loss or intrusion. In cases of soul-loss the free-soul usually goes first, marking the onset of the disease. It is followed by the life-soul or the body-soul, either of which marks the occurrence of death.

It is, the Coyukon believe, self-evident that if the free-soul is lost then the unprotected life-soul will succumb more easily (Jette, 1911). The soul belief of the Kwakiutl, which in many

ways represents a functioning soul-dualism, affords a good standard example. First the free-soul departs, but the body is still
breathing. Then the breath leaves the body, and the person is dead
(Boas, 1930). The Wind River Shoshone told me that if the free-
soul departs without returning, the life-soul will also eventually
follow suit; and when both souls have gone, the person is dead.

Normally the departure of the body-soul coincides with the
moment at which the free-soul crosses to the realm of the dead. If
the person returns to life, the succession of the souls is reversed:
first the body recovers life and the power to move, and only after
that does it become an instrument for the personality.

In cases of spirit intrusion and object intrusion, the order in
which the souls depart may present several combinations. It is
theoretically possible that when an intrusion is fatal, the free-soul
departs before the life-soul. Generally, however, both dual- souls
leave the body at about the same time. In practice it is the life-
soul which the intruder destroys, making it the first to go, immediately followed by the free-soul.

A Seneca legend tells how after a bear cub was shot the hunter
could see it appear to throw off a burden, while "it continued
straight on its way without stopping" (Curtin & Hewitt, 1918).
The burden is the body, the bear itself. The free-soul, which after
the life-soul has been stopped, hurries on.

Sometimes the free-soul leaves the body after life has departed. Among the Modoc, Curtin says, only when the heart of the
dead person has broken is it abandoned by the free-soul. When
the life-soul abandons the body, death appears. The Shasta believe that the spirit of the disease leaves the body shortly before
the life-soul (Holt, 1946).

A variant of intrusion-disease occurs when one of the souls, as
a rule the free-soul, succumbs. In such cases the person dies almost immediately. The Haida shaman accompanies his fellow
tribesmen on expeditions of war in order to combat and kill the
souls of the enemy so that their bodies may be slain quickly
(Swanton, 1905). The Algonquin shaman so soundly beats the
soul of the person he wants to kill that its owner sickens and dies,
according to the Jesuits. The Seminole wizard, Greenlee says, destroys his enemy by summoning the soul and burning it in a fire.
The victim then becomes feverish and dies. If a sorcerer causes
the soul of a Cherokee to waste away, the individual will succumb

at the same time as the soul (Mooney, 1891). The last example refers to a single soul, but it has been included here to complete the picture of this peculiar death situation.

If soul-dualism is more complicated, the order in which the souls depart will be more irregular. Among the Quileute, where an elementary dualism forms the pattern of an otherwise diversified soul-belief, it is possible to trace the same fixed scheme of departure which applies in normal soul-dualism. The outside shadow (the free-soul) leaves a person as soon as he becomes sick, the inner soul (the ego-soul?) departs a day or two before his death; and the "ghost (the growth-soul) leaves the body at the moment of death. Death can occur only after the departure of either the inner soul or the ghost. The loss of the outer soul does not necessarily involve death," Frachtenberg reports. Since the loss of the free-soul only means sickness while loss of the ego-soul forebodes death, the shaman can fetch the free-soul from the realm of the dead, while he must catch the ego-soul before it has got there. When the ego-soul has reached the realm of the dead, the growth-soul flies and the person is then dead. The ego-soul in this case has played, to a certain extent, the role generally played by the free-soul

Among the Hidatsa the order in which the souls leave is more arbitrary. These Indians believe in a gradual sort of death in which the extremities are apparently dead while consciousness remains, the result of the four souls departing in succession. When dissolution is complete, they say that "all the souls are gone." (Matthews, 1877). Among the Wintu the dark free-soul departs thirty days before death and the light free-soul three days after death (DuBois, 1935). The light free-soul here has taken over the role of the spook-ghost during the tabooed period after death.

Logically, a single soul ought to leave the body when the person dies, but this is far from being true. The single soul is a late-occurring concept, and its adherence to the circumstances of the body is sometimes feeble. Sickness caused by soul-loss may force the single soul to depart long before death. It is much more natural for the soul, according to the Zuni, to depart only in connection with unconsciousness at death which is why the Zuni have the same word for unconsciousness and physical death (Bunzel, 1932). In cases of intrusion the soul departs at the moment of death. The Lemhi believe that only some moments after the departure of the single soul does the body become lifeless (Lowie, 1909).

The history of the different souls is not always concluded with physical death. The dead person, the spook-ghost, and so forth, are often seen as a continuation of the existence of an individual soul.

Chapter Seventeen
The Soul After Death

The North American Indians have developed a rich flora of legend concerning fate after death. It is both exciting and fascinating and offers a wealth of subtle variation. The question here, however, is what happens to the soul after death, especially since the soul, or a particular soul, is not necessarily the same as the person who has died.

When considered more narrowly, there are three different problems. First, are the soul and the deceased identical? Second, if such an identity does exist, which soul carries on the life and consciousness of the individual? And third, is it possible to deduce a connection between the different souls and the forms which the deceased may assume?

The deceased should first be understood, like the free-soul of the living individual, as the total person, or as Feuerbach says, the deceased is the memory-image of an earlier existing person. At death the person assumes a new form of existence. No soul-idea is needed to mediate this transition, for it is the person who lives this new existence. The transition of soul to ghost may be theoretical, but the concepts of soul and ghost are distinct from each other, though they arise through the same psychic processes. In some cases the dead person is called simply "the deceased," though in many cases, other terms are used to refer to the deceased and the soul (or the souls). In this connection the soul (one of the souls) usually remains in the deceased. However sometimes, there is no hint of whether any soul serves as the link between the living and the dead person.

In general the concept of the deceased and the concept of the free-soul were originally separate entities, even though they resemble each because they have the same psychological origin. Sometimes no connection occurs because either the soul has died, or the person has been transformed into a totem or guardian spirit. In the latter case the soul has no place.

Comments by Indians from different parts of America show that the soul's identification with the deceased is not evident. They say that the *person* survives. Opinion about the roles played by the souls in the transition to a new existence is divided, confused and contradictory. Rainey, writing about the Point Hope Eskimo, says there is no clear concept of the forms taken by the body-soul and the free-soul after death, and that they have discussions among themselves as to which soul is the life-form of the deceased. The Wind River Shoshone hold several views about which soul survives, but they have given little thought to the problem. They simply say it is the human being, the individual who survives.

A Paviotso told Kelly that "when a person sees a ghost, he sees the individual himself, not his spirit or soul." Navajo beliefs on this point are vague, and they shift from soul to soul when asked which soul represents the human being after death. One Navajo said that at death "man, the symbol, but not the body" goes to the underworld (Wyman, Hill & Orsani, 1942).

When Voth asked the Hopi, who believe in a single soul, *hikvsi,* "whether it is this *hikvsi* or the deceased person that continues to live in the realm of the dead, the average Hopi seemed confused by the question. They know a body decays, and they believe that the part which escapes from the body through the mouth at death is the part that lives on in the future world. But beyond that the Hopi are vague and vary considerably in traditions among clans and villages."

In most quarters, however, the identity between the soul (of the free-soul type) and the deceased occurs when two such similar concepts succeed each other and confront each other for any length of time. Linguistic information shows that for the concepts of the soul and the deceased people use the same word.

The soul that offers the best contact with the deceased is the free-soul. Psychologically, the deceased is nothing more than a free-soul that has freed itself from all physical bonds. Some characteristics are common to each concept. Both the free-soul and the idea of the deceased have their origin in the memories of living persons, usually the relatives or acquaintances of those who have died. Both concepts give expression to the human being as a whole, though transferred to a spiritual plane. Both concepts may, in their active form, represent human consciousness, or ego, though not including the free-soul which moves in the direction of the guardian spirit

These resemblances do not imply the absence of differences. The deceased may be a demoniacal, power-charged being, a form which the free-soul seldom assumes. Or the deceased, when it has not succeeded in banishing its physical prototype, the psychophysical, living individual, is sometimes endowed with a substantiality which the free-soul lacks. And finally, the deceased is more diffuse than the free-soul of the living person, once memories fade. Among the Western Dene the free-soul is often described as "a reflection of the individual personality," whereas the spirit of the deceased is "the impalpable, dematerialized remnants of one's individuality" (Morice, 1911).

The resemblance between the ghost and the free-soul more or less facilitates the transition to the world of the dead. This transition is either automatic, unhindered, or else indirect, meaning it goes through a series of intermediate stages. A direct transition without perceptible change in the status of the active entity, an unhindered, natural glide from free-soul to death being is also possible. A free-soul that during a fainting fit or state of unconsciousness (apparent death) has reached the realm of the dead is as much a potential inhabitant as the ghost. It automatically becomes a ghost when the body-soul has fled and physical death is a fact. But in those cases in which death occurs without the free-soul having had time to depart, the gliding occurs. In such an event, the recently deceased person is seen as a fragile substance and the concept of the person has been formed according to the demands of the free-soul.

The indirect transition of the free-soul to the sphere of death implies a successive adaptation between the free-soul and the ghost. The process goes forward in stages during the soul's journey to the realm of the dead. The transition begins with the soul marking its aloofness from death by remaining for a period in the body, at the grave, or in the vicinity of its former home. But gradually the soul looses its moorings to the corpse, takes its exit through the mouth or the fontanelle and begins its journey, surmounting obstacles (especially among the Central Algonquin) along the way. The obstacles are intended to reduce the remaining vital qualities of the deceased.

The deader a person is, the easier and more rapid the journey, according to Drucker. Among several Shoshone groups the soul transforms *itself* into a ghost, instead of becoming one automatically. DuBois says that among the Wintu a similar transformation occurs when the free-soul prefers to become a wandering spook-ghost instead of an inhabitant of the realm of death. This implies that the more substantial the deceased, the more the free-soul must be changed.

In such cases, the free-soul appears as the natural, adaptable entity, able to continue the life of the individual *post mortem.* Every psychological probability supports the assumption that in most cases of continuity between free-soul and ghost, the free-soul is the instigator. However this does mean that the way has been paved for the opposite possibility by religious and philosophical speculation.

The surviving soul is most often the specific free-soul, the soul which after the death of the body merges into a concept which contains the post-mortal ego. In about half of all cases it is the free-soul which is the surviving soul, but that does not mean that in half of all cases the body-soul fulfills the same function. Several soul-entities may assume this role, and in a large number of cases an undefined personality entity takes the place of the soul as the surviving factor.

Frequently enough the body-soul or one of the body-souls is the surviving soul, though this is not the original function of the body-soul. In a thoroughgoing dual soul-belief, the body-soul may survive death, but it does not represent the personality. Not even the breath sent out by the deity represents the ego after death. The chief reason why the body-soul occurs as the bearer of existence in the next life is that over and above its normal functions in the body, it has become an extra-physical soul, and as such has taken over the qualities of the free-soul. The body-soul's advance to surviving soul has undoubtedly been caused by an increased distancing of the free-soul from its owner. Psychologically, the deceased is a continuation of the free-soul, but from an ideological viewpoint the surviving entity is a body-soul.

In some cases the surviving principle of consciousness is an ego-soul or a body-soul with a predominantly ego-soul aspect. This is the case among the Ojibway on Parry Island (Jenness, 1935) and probably among the Choctaw (Swanton, 1931). Finally, the ego-soul often occurs as the surviving soul when combined with the free-soul to form one soul concept as it does for the Eastern Dakota (Lynd, 1888) and the Oglala (Walker, 1917), and in some measure among the Creek (Hewitt & Swanton, 1939).

The ego-soul appears as the personality after death because in certain cases of nervous disorder and mental illness, it constitutes the lost soul-entity. In such cases among the Ojibway and Wind River Shoshone, it is probably the pure ego-soul that is the lost potency, and the ego-soul combined with the free-soul that is the lost potency among the Oglala.

It is probable that the ego-soul occurring as the surviving soul among some other peoples is connected with the fact that the free-soul acting as guardian soul, has arrived at a remove from the individual and cannot carry on existence. More frequently the life-soul or an undifferentiated body-soul is the surviving soul. It occurs clearly in this capacity among the Northwest Athapascans, the Central Algonquin, the Yuman, possibly also among some of the Coast Salish, and less clearly in one Shoshone tribe and among the Southern Athapascans. A survey shows that the uniformity within certain geographically adjacent groups must have an historical background, whether it is a matter of a common heritage or diffusion.

The decisive causes for the functioning of the ego-soul as surviving soul also apply to several of the Yuman peoples (the Cocopa, Yuma, and the Maricopa). There the life-soul appears to be the surviving soul, since it also disappears in connection with serious illness. This means that the soul which is temporarily lost during an illness accompanied by loss of consciousness is the soul which continues the individual's existence after definitive death (Gifford, 1931).

Among other groups the distancing of the free-soul from its owner has resulted in the life-soul representing the surviving individual, and that is the case among the Coyukon, Bella Coola, Fox and (possibly) the Eastern Mono. When among the Wind River Shoshone religious speculation has tried to bridge the gulf between the souls of the living person and the spirit of the deceased, the life-soul has been understood as the connecting entity. The free-soul develops into a guardian spirit and is removed from its original function. A third cause of the representation of the personality after death by the life-soul may be that the material structure of the deceased coincides with the breath.

Finally, in some cases the deceased is constituted by all the souls he has had during his life time. A typical example occurs among the Tubatulabal (Voegelin, 1938). An equally typical instance of the fusion of all the souls, but in a more elastic form, occurs among the Quileute (Frachtenberg, 1920). Matthews' notes on Hidatsa soul-belief show how the deceased, from an ideological viewpoint, becomes the bearer of the components in a shamanistically constructed soul-pluralism.

The third and last of the problems I suggested earlier, refers to the extent to which there is any correspondence between the souls of the living person and the forms of existence taken by the deceased. The concept includes forms of existence and manifestation (Arbman). Of particular note are the deceased as a spirit in the realm of the dead, as a grave-ghost or wandering spook-ghost, as theriomorphic being, and as reincarnated in a new individual (Straubinger, 1937). It is natural for religious speculation to find links between the numerous souls during the lifetime of the individual and the forms of the deceased. A number of investigators have suggested that these links existed from the outset. In other words the forms of death-belief have been projected upon soul-belief, or the forms of soul-belief have been projected upon death-belief.

But only in certain cases has religious speculation been so active that artificial soul-concepts have been created to correspond to the forms in which the deceased may appear or that one of these forms has been adapted as a soul. It is still less common for the forms in which the deceased may be manifested to emanate from the forms of soul-belief. The varying conceptions of the deceased have their origin in quite other factors than the conceptions of the plural souls in the living individual. However, it is probable that where speculation has closed the distance between these concepts, it has been the forms of soul-belief and not death-belief that have established the norm. By being connected to soul-conceptions, concepts of the deceased have become fixed. The forms in which the dead person appears all began as manifestations of the same being. Through the connection to soul-belief, they have become several different persons.

But which of these manifestations carries on the conscious ego of the living individual? An analysis of the North American concepts connected with the dead has shown that the deceased in the realm of the dead is always believed to continue the existence and the consciousness of the dead person (even if the latter is in a changed form). That means that the same person can figure in two realms of the dead, though not at the same time.

The Indians believe that the ghost at the grave or at other places near the living is the deceased returning to the living. If the connection between soul and ghost is emphasized, the latter appears only as a remote echo of the departed individual and not as his real ego or his personality (the Iroquois, Converse, 1908, and Navajo, Wyman, Hill & Osanai). The same notion applies to the other forms of the deceased in relation to the ghost.

Earlier investigators have tried to fix the connection between the souls of the living person and the different forms of existence assumed by the dead. To James it is evident that the deceased in the realm of the dead is an isolated concept, separate from the soul substance of the living, which transmigrates, remains in the body, or goes to the supreme God. Schmidt is of the opinion that in animistic matrilineal religion in North America the breath goes to the sky-god and the shadow-soul to the underworld. Walk says that the image-soul goes to the realm of the dead while the body-soul succumbs with the body.

However the matter is more complicated than these writers make out. But proceeding on the assumption that there are one or several souls and that the forms which the deceased assumes are always more than one, it is possible to divide the combinations into two main groups.

A. Only one of the souls survives and continues its existence in all the forms which the deceased assumes. (1.) *Soul-dualism.* The soul concepts of the Carrier and Yuma provide typical examples. Among the Carrier the free-soul of the deceased goes to heaven, while the life-soul is extinguished (Morice, 1889). Among the Yuma the free-soul is extinguished while the body-soul, divided into several potencies, transmigrates to animals or goes to the realm of the dead (Forde, 1931). The normal belief was that the free-soul went on living, while the life-soul disappeared. Many people offer great detail about the fate of the free-soul after death, while not mentioning the fate of the opposed body-soul. Others explain that this soul (as a rule the life-soul) dies with the body, travels out into space, or disappears. The disappearance may imply that the breath of life returns to the deity from which it came. Walker writes that among the Oglala the life-soul, "the ghost," after death "returns whence it came and is no more." But Walker also says that "the ghost returns to the stars...the ghost goes to where Skan got it...the ghost is like smoke and it goes upward until it arrives at the stars." In any case the life-soul is effaced. (2.) *Four-soul pluralism.* The example here comes from the Mohave who say that after death real free-soul appears as either a ghost or being in the realm of the dead, while the two power-souls and the "soul which forebodes death" succumb when the corpse is burned. (3.) *Monism.* The single soul of the Nomlaki may after death occur as a grave-ghost, wandering spook or celestial being, according to Goldschmidt. Here it seems logical to suspect that a previous dual soul-belief had distributed the post-mortal forms of existence among different souls. However, this is probably out of the question, since the dualistic Wintu, who are closely akin to the Nomlaki, allow the free-soul to appear after death both as a being in the land of the dead and as an earth-bound revenant.

B. Several souls survive and continue their existence in various manifestations of the deceased. This is generally a matter of souls in a dualistic soul-constellation. In these cases only two of the dual souls survive, the free-soul and one of the body-souls. One of these souls, the free-soul, is destined for the realm of the dead. The contrary soul becomes a grave or spook-ghost (which is the general rule), then is reincarnated in a new person, transmigrates to animals, or goes on to the realm of the dead.

A fundamental opposition after death exists between the soul which goes to the realm of the dead and the soul which becomes either a grave-ghost or a wandering ghost. Normally the spirit which goes to the realm of the dead is a specific free-soul and represents the conscious ego of the individual, whereas "the ghost" derives from a body-soul and only loosely represents the deceased individual. The soul-forms and the forms in which the deceased is manifested offer the following combinations. 1. *The free-soul becomes a spirit, the life-soul a ghost.* Examples occur among the Algonquin and the Ojibway. In fact all the relevant instances of which I am certain, belong to the eastern areas: the Delaware, Huron, Iroquois, and Yuchi. The instances which seem less certain are found more to the west: the Mandan, Coeur d'Alene, and Navajo. 2. *The ego-soul becomes a spirit, the free-soul a ghost*. The Ojibway on Parry Island and the Choctaw, and possibly also the Plains Cree, furnish us with examples. The distribution seems much the same as the previous group. 3. *The life-soul becomes a spirit, the free-soul a ghost*. The Fox provide the typical example, though similar instances come from the Menomini and Sauk (among whom the free-soul also appears to be an ego-soul), the Maricopa, the Walapai, and perhaps the Tanaina and Cowichan as well. The tendency toward a westerly distribution is striking. Theoretically there is a fourth possible combination in which the free-soul becomes a spirit and the ego-soul a ghost, but I have found no instance of that.

While I have localized the above groupings and given them definite geographic locations, the instances are not sufficiently numerous and unequivocal to establish a concrete map or to assume an absolute historical sequence. The following sketch of the course of development is hypothetical. When a dual soul form is coupled with the post-mortal forms of existence, the free-soul becomes the surviving soul while the body-soul disappears, dies, or loses its actuality. Secondarily, the life-soul is connected with the "ghost," the revenant, especially in eastern North America. In other parts of the continent the free-soul is the ghost, while the ego-soul or the life-soul becomes the spirit of the deceased; the two body-souls here having changed places with the free-soul.

If after death one of the dual souls is reincarnated in a new person or transmigrates to an animal, it is important to remember that the same soul may also end up as a spirit in the realm of the dead or as a grave-ghost or spook-ghost. Among the Huron, for example, the free-soul goes to the realm of the dead or transmigrates to the dove, while the life-soul becomes a grave-ghost or is reincarnated in a new being. According to the direction taken, the free-soul of the deceased will appear as a dove on earth or as a being in the realm of the dead. Only among the Eskimo of Baffin Land, the Haida, and the Kikimai Papago, is rebirth in a person or animal the life-soul's only alternative, though this may be the result of scanty information. As a rule it is the life-soul (the body-soul) that is reincarnated or transmigrates, though occasionally the free-soul is mentioned.

A remarkable division of the souls after death occurs among the Bella Coola. The free-soul and the life-soul (or the main part of the life-soul?) combine as a single entity and travel to heaven, while the shadow, the body, and a part of the life-soul journey to the underworld (McIlwraith). The life-soul also disintegrates but in such a way that "its constituent parts also undergo transformation. The one situated in the feet remains with the corpse and disintegrates; the soul located in the legs enters a wolf and nothing more is known of its fate. No one knows what happens to the soul situated in the body. The part in the throat, including the voice, enters an owl." It is probable that this confusing picture of man's post-mortal fate is the result of overlaps in tradition. Drucker's statement that among the Bella Coola only the shadow becomes a ghost is close to what Teit heard from several Plateau Salish. There the ghost is the soul's (the free-soul's) shadow.

A discussion of the fate of the different souls, once their manifestations have stabilized after death, is beyond the scope of this investigation, though it is important to note that such fates unfold according to social and ethical principles. The forms of existence taken by the deceased change shape or succumb. The changes may take place rather soon after death. This is true among the Ojibway on Parry Island who are able to decide the fates of the various souls after death according to the age and occupation of the deceased and the manner in which the person died. The ego-soul of the wicked sorcerer succumbs on its way to the realm of the dead, but his shadow-soul, the ghost or wraith, goes on. The unburied and those who die too early do not reach the realm of the dead, but their ego-soul, like the shadow-soul, becomes a ghost on earth (Jenness, 1935).

This enquiry has shown that the free-soul and the life-soul are often mentioned as surviving soul-entities, while the ego-soul rarely occurs in this connection. A survey of the fates incurred by individual souls produced the following results.

Over the whole continent the free-soul is commonly destined for the realm of the dead, except among the Central Algonquin, the Yuman tribes and a few marginal groups, the Coyukon, the Cowichan, and the Choctaw. Among these peoples it often appears instead as an earth-bound ghost. Among the Yuma, and possibly among the Walapai as well, it is destroyed. In a couple of cases the free-soul is reincarnated or it transmigrates. In a few cases its fate has been forgotten. Among the Wind River Shoshone the free-soul returns to the Creator.

The ego-soul is forgotten. Some say it goes to the realm of the dead (the Ojibway, the Muskhogean, and the Sioux). Jenness says that among the Carrier "the mind probably persisted after death, though whether it then became identified with the shadow (-soul), or what happened to it, the natives held to be quite uncertain." It is rare for the ego-soul to become a spook-ghost, and there is never any talk of its being destroyed.

The life-soul is seldom forgotten. Frequently it is destroyed or disappears or turns into air, merging with the wind or even with the Supreme Deity as it is generally identical with the breath. In many cases the life-soul is reincarnated or it transmigrates. Among the Central Algonquin, the Yuman tribes and a number of groups in the northwest (the Athapascans, the Coast Salish) it is the life-soul that goes to the realm of the dead. Finally, the life-soul occurs in many cases as either a grave-ghost or a wandering ghost.

The typical post-mortal role of the free-soul as a being in the realm of the dead has been discussed in detail earlier in this chapter. What remains is a consideration of the earth-bound ghost form of the life-soul and the undifferentiated body-soul when they survive beyond death.

The identification of the life-soul with the spook-ghost is a consequence of the fact that the free-soul had already been combined with the other main post-mortal figure, the deceased, in the realm of the dead. The life-soul then automatically becomes a ghost. That wandering ghost, especially when it is not bound to the corpse and yet still incarnates the life-soul, probably belongs here. Of course the free-soul is sometimes a spook-ghost. And even when, as it is among the Fox, it is sometimes connected with the dead body, this relationship is nonetheless more characteristic of the life-soul.

The life-soul's post-mortal dependence upon the body is, like its extinction on the death or decay of the body, a consequence of its intimate attachment to the body during the lifetime of the individual. If, as it does among the Coeur d'Alene or the Mandan, the life-soul continues to stay near the grave, or if it "remains with or near the body" (Lynd), this reflects its lifetime attachment to the body.

The life-soul can, after death, even continue its existence in the corpse. Some Seminole say that it does not leave the dead body until long after death (Greenlee, 1944). Sometimes it remains for a longer period in its disintegrating body, as is reported by the Algonquin, the Ojibway, the Huron and the Yuchi. Among several tribes, especially in the Southwest, the life-soul retains its old function as the force behind movement and vital action. It occurs here as the propelling force in the revenant so that even after death the life-soul tries to assert its accustomed functions.

Abbreviations

AA—American Anthropologist. Washington, New York, Lancaster, Penn., Menasha, Wisc.

AAOJ—Antiquarian and Oriental Journal. Chicago.

AAPF—Annales de l'Assoc. de la Propagation de la Foi. Paris.

AAR—Annual Archaeological Report. Toronto, Can..

AJS—American Journal of Sociology. Chicago, Ill.

AMJ—American Museum Journal. New York, N.Y.

AMNHHS—American Museum of Natural History, Handbook. New York, N.Y.

ANA—Anthropology in North America, by Franz Boas et al. Neew York, N.Y. 1915.

APAM—Anthropological Papers of the Am. Museum of Natural History. New York, N.Y.

AR—Anthropological Records. Berkeley, Calif.

ARBAE—Annual Reports of the Bureau of American Ethnology. Washington, D.C.

ARSI—Annual Reports of the Board of Regents of the Smithsonian Institution. Washington, D.C.

ARW—Archiv fur Religionswissenschaft. Leipzig, Ger.

ASSF—Acta Societatis Scientiarum Fennicae. Helsingfors, Den.

BAAS—Reports of the Meetings of the British Association for the Advancement of Science. London, U.K.

BAMNH—Bulletins of the American Museum of Natural History. New York, N.Y.

BBAE—Bulletins of the Bureau of American Ethnology. Wash.

BCDM—Bulletins (and Annual Reports) of the Canada Department of Mines, National Museum of Canada. Ottawa, Can.

BCIS—Bulletins of the Cranbrook Institute of Science. Bloomfield Hills, Mich.

BMJ—British Medical Journal. London, U.K..

BPMCM —Bulletins of the Public Museum of the City of Milwaukee. Milwaukee, Wisc.

BVV—Beitrage zur Volks-und Volkerkunde. Weimar, Ger.

CE—The Catholic Encyclopedia. New York, N.Y.

CED—Culture Element Distributions. Berkeley, Calif.

CIHR—Actes du Congres International d'histoire des religions. 5th Congress in Lund, Swe.

CIWP—Carnegie Inst of Washington, Publications. Washington, D.C.

CMA—Contributions from the Museum of the American Indian, Heye Foundation. New York, N.Y.

CMHS—Collections of the Minnesota. Historical Society. St. Paul, Minn.

CNAE—Contributions to North American Ethnology, U. S. Geographical and Geological Survey of the Rocky Mountain Region. Washington, D.C..

CUAS—Catholic University of America, Anthropological Series. Washington, D.C.

CUCA—Columbia University. Contributions to Anthropology. New York, N.Y.

DLZ—Deutsche Literaturzeitung.

EAK—Essays in Anthropology Presented to A. L. Kroeber. Berkeley, Calif. 1936.

ERE—Encyclopedia of Religion and Ethics. Edinburgh, Scotland

FFC—FF Communications. Helsingfors, Den.

FL—Folk-Lore. London, U.K.

FMAS—Field Museum of Natural History, Anthropological Series. Chicago, Ill.

FMDAL—Field Museum of Natural History, Dept. of Anthropology Leaflets. Chicago, Ill.

GSA—General Series in Anthropology. Menasha, Wisc.

HTR—Harvard Theological Review. Cambridge, Mass.

IA—Ibero-Americana. Berkeley, Calif.

IAE—Internationales Archiv fur Ethnographie. Leiden, Neth.

ICA—Proceedings of the International Congress of Americanists. Paris, France.

IN—Indian Notes, Museum of the American Indian, Heye Foundation. New York, N.Y.

INM—Indian Notes and Monographs, Museum of the American Indian, Heye Foundation. New York, N.Y.

ISA—Institute of Social Anthropology, Smithsonian Institution, Publications. Washington, D.C.

JAFL—Journal of American Folk-Lore. Boston, Mass., New York, N.Y.

JAI—Journal of the (Royal) Anthropological Institute of Great Britain and Ireland. London, U.K.

JASP—Journal of Abnormal and Social Psychology.

JGP—Journal of General Psychology.

JR—Travels and Explorations of the Jesuit Missionaries in New France 1610-1791, ed. by Reuben Gold Thwaites. Vols. I—LXXIII. Cleveland, Ill. 1896—1901.

JSAP—Journal de la Société des Americanistes. Paris.

JWAS—Journal of the Washington Academy of Sciences. Washington, D.C.

LAAL—Library of Aboriginal American Literature. Philadelphia, Penn.

LTK—Lexikon fur Theologie und Kirche. 2nd ed. Freiburg im Breisgau.

MAAA—Memoirs of the American Anthropological Association. Lancaster, Penn., Menasha, Wisc.

MAES—Monographs of the American Ethnological Society. New York, N. Y.

MAFLS—Memoirs of the American Folk-Lore Society. Boston, Mass.

MAGW—Mitteilungen der Anthropologischen Gesellschaft. Wien, Ger.

MAMNH—Memoirs of the American Museum of Natural History. New York, N Y.

MCDM—Memoirs of the Canada Department of Mines, Geological Survey.

MG—Meddelelser om Gronland. Copenhagen.

MIJAL—Memoirs of the International Journal of American Linguistics. Baltimore, Md.

MJ—Museum Journal, University of Pennsylvania. Philadelphia, Penn.

MMVH—Mitteilungen aus dem Museum fur Volkerkunde in Hamburg. Hamburg, Ger.

MO—Le Monde Oriental. Uppsala, Swe.

NYSMB—New York State Museum Bulletin. Albany, N.Y.

OAHQ—Ohio Archaeological and Historical Quart. Columbus, Ohio.

OCMA—Occasional Contributions J from the Museum of Anthropology of the University of Michigan. Ann Arbor, Mich.

PAAS—Proceedings of the American. Antiquarian Society. Worcester, Mass.

PAES- Publications of the American. Ethnological Society. New York, N.Y.

PAPS—Proceedings of the Americn. Philosophical Society. Philadelphia, Penn.

PCI—Proceedings of the Canadian Institute. Toronto, Can.

PCS—Publications of the Champlain Society. Toronto, Can..

PHAPF—Publications of the F. W. Hodge Anniversary Publication Fund, Southwest Museum. Los Angeles, Calif.

PM—Primitive Man. Washington, D.C.

PMP—Peabody Museum Papers. Cambridge, Mass.

PPFA—Papers of the Robert S. Peabody Foundation for Archaeology. Andover, Mass.

PPHC—Publications of the Pennsylvania. Hist. Commission. Harrisburg, Penn.

PSM—Popular Science Monthly. New York, N.Y.

RCAE—Report of the Canadian Arctic Expedition. Ottawa, Can.

RFTE—Report of the Fifth Thule Expedition. Copenhagen, Den.

RGG—Die Religion in Geschichte und Gegenwart. 2nd ed. Tubingen, Ger.

RH—Revue de l'histoire des religions. Paris, France.

RLC—*Race, Language, and Culture*, Franz Boas. New York, N. Y. 1940.

ROB—Religion och Bibel. Nathan Soderblom-sallskapets arsbok. Uppsala, Swe.

RPM—Reports of the Peabody Museum of American Archaeology and Ethnology, Harvard University. Cambridge, Mass.

RUSNM—Reports of the United States National Museum. Washington, D.C.

SCK—Smithsonian Contributions to Knowledge. Washington, D.C..

SMC—Smithsonian Miscellaneous Collections. Washington, D.C.

SP—Sherman Pamphlets. Riverside, Calif.

SWJ—Southwestern Journal of Anthropology. Albuquerque, N.M.

TAES—Transactions of the American Ethnological Society. New York, N.Y.

TAPS—Transactions of the American. Philosophical Society. Philaelphia, Penn.

UCP—University. of California. Publications in American Archaeology and Ethnology. Berkeley, Calif.

UNMB—University. of New Mexico Bulletin, Anthropological Series. Albuquerque, N.M.

UNMPA—University. of New Mexico Publications in Anthropology. Albuquerque, N.M.

UPMAP—University. of Pennsylvania Museum Anthropological Publications. Philadelphia, Penn.

UWPA—University. of Washington Publications in Anthropology. Seattle, Wash.

VKAW—Verhandelingen der Koninklijke Akademie van Wetenschappen, Afdeeling Letterkunde. Amsterdam, Neth.

YAS—Yale Anthropological Studies. New Haven, Conn.

YUPA—Yale University. Publications in Anthropology. New Haven, Conn.

ZE—Zeieschrift fur Ethnologie. Berlin, Ger.

BIBLIOGRAPHY

Adam, Leonhard 1923. *Nordwest-amerikamsche Indianerkunst.* Orbis Pictis17. Berlin. 1949. *Primitive Art.* Pelican Books.

Aginsky, B. W. 1943. *Central Sierra.* AR 8:4 (CED XXIV)

Alexander, H. B. 1916. "North American Mythology." *The Mythology of All Races,* Vol. X, Boston. 1920. Soul Primitive. ERE 11

Allison, S. S. 1892. "Account of the Similkameen Indians of British Columbia." JAI 21.

Andrae, Tor. 1934. *Det osyoligas varld.* Stockholm.

Andree, Richard. 1889. *Neue Folge,* Leipzig.

deAngulo, Jaime. 1926. "The Background of the Religious Feeling in a Primitive Tribe." AA 28:2. 1928. *La Psychologie religieus des Achumawi.* Anthropos 23. Wien.

Ankermann, Bernhard. 1918. "Totenkult und Seeleng laube bei afrikanischen Volkern." ZE 50. 1920 *Die Religion der Naturvolker.* (Chantepie de la Saussaye, Lehrbuch der Religionsgeshichte, 4th ed., I). Tubingen.

Arbman, Ernst.1927. "Untersuchungen zur primitive Seelenvors-tellung mit besonderer Rucksicht auf Indien." MO 20, 1926. Seele und Mana. ARW 29:3-4. 1939. "Mythic and Religious Thought" in: *Dragma,* Martino P. Nilsson...dedicatum. Lund.

Baervald, R. (No date) *Okkultismus, Spiritismus, und unterbewusste Seelenzustande.* New York.

Bahnson, Kristian. 1882. *Gravskikke hos Amerikanske Folk. Aarbog for Nordisk Oldkyndighed og Historie.* Copenhagen.

Bancroft, H. H. 1875-76. *The Native Races of the Pacific States of North America.* I—V London & New York.

Barbeau, C. M. 1915. "Huron and Wyandot Mythology." MCDM 80. 1950. "Totem Poles." I-II. BCDM ll9.

Barrett, H. G. 1937. "Oregon Coast." AR I:3 (CED VII). 1938. "The Coast Salish of Canada." AA 40:1. 1939. "Gulf of Georgia Salish." AR 1:5 (CED IX).

Barnouw, Victor. 1950. "Acculturation and Personality among the Wisconsin Chippewa." MAAA 72.

Barrett, S. A. 1917. "Pomo Bear Doctors." UCP 12: 11.

Bartels, M. 1893. *Die Medicin der Naturvolker.* Leipzig.

Bartram, W. l853. "Observations on the Creek and Cherokee Indians." TAES 3.

Beaglehole, Ernest and Pearl. 1935. "Hopi of the Second Mesa." MAAA 44.

Bears, Ralph L. 1932. "The Comparative Ethnology of Northern Mexico before I750." IA 2. 1943 a. "Northern Mexico and the Southwest." Tercera "Reunion de Mesa Redonda Castillo de Chapultepec." 1943 b. "The Aboriginal Culture of the Cahita Indians." IA I9. 1946. Cheran: "A Sierra Tarascan Village." ISA 2.

Beckwith, Paul. 1889. "Notes on Customs of the Dakotahs." ARSI 1886:1.

Bendann, E. 1930. *Death Customs.* London.

Benedict, Ruth Fulton. 1923. "The Concept of the Guardian Spirit in North America." MAAA 29. 1926. "Serrano Tales." JAFL 39. 1928. "Psychological Types in the Cultures of the Southwest." ICA 23. 1931. "Tales of the Cochiti Indians." BBAE 98. 1932. "Configurations of Culture in North America." AA 34:1. 1934. "Anthropology and the Abnormal." JGP 10. 1946. *Patterns of Culture.* London.

Bertholet, Alfred. 1930. "Dynamismus und Personalismus in der Seelenauffassung." CIHR 5. 1931. "Tod und Totenreich, Religionsgeschichtlich." RGG 5.

Birket-Smith, Kaj. 1924. "Ethnography of the Egedesminde District." MG 66. 1928.

"Five Hundred Eskimo Words. A Comparative Vocabulary from Greenland and Central Eskimo Dialects." RFTE 3:3. 1929. "The Caribou Eskimos. Material and Social Life and Their Cultural Position." RFTE 5: 1-2. 1930. "Contributions to Chipewyan Ethnology." RFTE 6:3. 1943. *Kulturens vagar*. I—II. Stockholm.

Birket-Smith, Kaj & deLaguna, F. 1938. *The Eyak Indians of the Copper River Delta, Alaska. Det Kgl. Danske Videnskabernes Selskab*, Copenhagen.

Blair, Emma Helen. 1911-12. *The Indian Tribes of the Upper Mississippi Valley and Region of the Great Lakes.* Cleveland, Ohio.

Bloomfield, Louis. 1928. "Menomini Texts." PAES 12.

Boas, Franz. 1888. "The Central Eskimo." ARBAE 6. 1890. "First General Report on the Indians of British Columbia. 1891 "Dissemination of Tales Among the Natives of North America." JAFL 4. 1891. "Second General Report on the Indians of British Columbia." BAAS 60. 1892. "Third Report on the Indians of British Columbia." BAAS 61. 1893. "The Doctrine of Souls and of Disease among the Chinook Indians." JAFL 6. 1894 "Chinook Texts." BBAE 20. 1894. "The Indian Tribes of the Lower Fraser River." BAAS 64. 1895. "Fifth Report on the Indians of British Columbia." BAAS 6S. 1895. *Indianische Sagen von der Nord-pacifischen Kuste Amerikas.* Berlin. 1896. "Sixth Report on the Indians of British Columbia." BAAS 66. 1897."Northern Elements in the Mythology of the Navaho." AA 10:11. 1897. "The Social Organization and the Secret Societies of the Kwakiutl Indians." RUSNM 1895. 1898. "The Mythology of the Bella Coola Indians." MAMNH 2. 1898. "Traditions of the Tillamook Indians." JAFL 11. 1900. "Religious Beliefs of the Central Eskimo." PSM 57 7. 1901. "Kathlamet Texts." BBAE 26. 19011-07. "The Eskimo of Baffin Land and Hudson Bay." BAMNH I5. 1906. "The Salish Tribes of the Interior of British Columbia." AAR I905. 1910. "Religion." BBAE 30:2. 1910. "Soul." BBAE 30:2. 1910 "Kwakiutl Tales." CUCA 2. 1912. "Tsimshian Texts." New Series. PAES 3. 1916. "Tsimshian Mythology." ARBAE 31. 1921. "Ethnology of the Kwakiotl." I-II. ARBAE 3S 1923. "Notes on the Tillamook". UCP 20. 1927. "Primitive Art." Instituttet for sammenlignende kulturforskning. Ser. B: 8. Oslo. 1930. "The Religion of the Kwaklutl Indians." CUCA IO: 1-2. 1932. "Bella Bella Tales." MAFLS 2 1932. "Current Beliefs of the Kwakiutl Indians." JAFL 45. 1935. "Kwakiutl Culture as Reflected in Mythology." MAFLS 28. 1938. *The Mind of Primitive Man.* New York. 1940. "Religious Terminology of the Kwakiutl". RLC. 1940. "The Idea of the Future Life among Primitive Tribes." RLC.

Boas, F., & Hunt, G. 1902. "Kwaklutl Texts." MAMNH. 5: 1-2. 1906. "Kwakiutl Texts. Second Series." MAMNH 14:1.

Bogoras, Waldemar 1902. "The Folklore of Northeastern Asia, as compared with that of Northwestern America.." AA 4:4. 1925. "Ideas of Space and Time in the Conception of Primitive Religion." AA 27:2.

Bourke, John G. 1889. "Notes on the Cosmogony and Theogony of the Mojave Indians of the Rio Colorado, Arizona.." JAFL 2. 1891. "Notes upon the Religion of the Apache Indians." FL 2:4.

Bouteiller, Marcelle 1950. *Chamanisme et Guerison magique.* Paris.

Boyle, David 1900. "On the Paganism of the Civilised Iroquois of Ontario." JAI 30.

Bracket, Col. Albert G. 1880. "The Shoshonis, or Snake Indians, Their Religion, Superstitions, and Manners." ARSI 1879.

Briem, Efraim 1933. *Gudstrooch gudsupplevelse.* Malmo. 1948. På trons troskel. Stockholm.

Brinton, Dankl G. 1868. *The Myths of the New World.* New York. 1885. "The Lenape and Their Legends." LAAL 5. 1893. "A Vocabulary of the Nanticoke Dialect." PAPS 31. 1894. *Nagualism. A Study in Native American Folk-lore and History.* Philadelphia. Reprint from PAPS 33. 1897. *Religions of Primitive Peoples.* New York & London.

Bros, A. 1936. *L'Ethnologie Religieuse.* Paris.

Bunzel, Ruth L. 1928. "The Emergence (San Felipe)." JAFL 41. 1932. a. "Introduction to Zuni Ceremonialism." ARBAE 47. b. "Zuni Katcinas." ARBAE 47. 1933. "Zuni Texts." PAES 15.

Buschan, Georg 1922. *Illustrierte Volkerkunde.* I. 3rd ed. Stuttgart.

Bushnell, David I. Jr. 1909. "The Choctaw of Bayou Lacomb," St. Tammany Parish, Louisa. BBAE 48. 1927. "Burials of the Algonquian, Siouan, and Caddoan Tribes West of the Mississippi. BBAE 83. 1934. "Tribal Migrations East of the Mississippi." SMC 89: 12.

Carpenter, I. E. 1913. *Comparative Religion.* New York.

Carver, Jonathan 1784. *Voyage dans les parties interieures de l'Amerique septentrionale.* Yverdon.

Catlin, George 1841. *Letters and Notes on the Manners, Customs, and Condition of the North American Indians.* I-II. London.

Chamberlain, A. F. 1888. "Notes on the History, Customs, and Beliefs of the Mississagua Indians." JAFL I. 1893. "Report on the Kootenay Indians of South-Eastern British Columbia." BAAS 62. 1906. "Terms for the Body, Its Parts, Organs, etc., in the Language of the Kootenay Indians of Southeastern British Columbia." Boas Anniversary Volume, New York. 1913. Haida. ERE 6.

Chapman, Rev. John W. 1921. "Tinneh Animism." AA 23: 3.

Charles, Lucile Hoerr 1951. "Drama in First-Naming Ceremonies." JAFL 64.

Charlevoix, P. de 1744. "Histoire de la Nouvelle France," Tome III: Journal d'un voyage fait par ordre du roi dans l'Amerique septentrionale. Paris.

Chief Buffalo Child Long Lance 1928. Long Lance. New York.

Clements, Forrest E. 1932. "Primitive Concepts of Disease." UCP 32.

Codere, Helen 1950. Fighting with Property. A Study of Kwakiutl Potlatching and Warfare 1792-1930." MAES I8.

Cody, B. P. 1940. "Pomo Bear Impersonators." Masterkey 14.

Coleman, Sister Bernard 1937. "The Religion of the Ojibwa of Northern Minnesota." PM 10:3-4.

Collier, John 1948. *Indians of the Americas.* Mentor Books. New York.

Collinder, Bjorn 1949. *The Lapps.* New York.

Collins, June McCormick 1952 a. "An Interpretation of Skagit Intragroup Conflict during Acculturation." AA 54:3. b. "The Mythological Basis for Attitudes toward Animals among Salish-Speaking Indians." JAFL 65.

Conard, E. Laetitia Moon 1900. "Les idees des indiens algonquins relatives a la vie d'outre-tombe." RHR 42.

Connelley, William E. 1899. "Notes on the Folk-Lore of the Wyandots." JAFL 12.

Converse, Harriet Maxwell 1908. "Myths and Legends of the New York State Iroquois." NYSMB 125.

Coolidge, Dane & Mary Roberts 1930. *The Navajo Indians.* Boston & New York.

Cooper, John M. 1933. "The Cree Witiko Psychosis." PM 6:1. 1933. "The Northern Algonquian Supreme Being." PM 6:3-4. 1944. "The Shaking Tent Rite among Plains and Forest Algonquians." PM 27:3-4. 1946. "The Culture of the Northeastern Indian Hunters: A Reconstructive Interpretation." In: Johnson 1946.

Cranz, D. 1765. *Historie von Gronland*, I. Barby.

Crawley, A. E. 1909. *The Idea of the Soul*. London. 1911. "Doubles." ERE 4.

Curtin, Jeremiah. 1898. *Creation Myths of Primitive America*. Boston. 1912. *Myths of the Modocs*. Boston.

Curtin, J., & Hewitt, J. N. B. 1918." Seneca Fiction, Legends, and Myths." I—II. ARBAE 32.

Curtis, Edward S. 1907-13. *The North American Indian*. I—IX. Cambridge, Mass.

Curtis, Natalie. 1907. *The Indians' Book*. New York & London.

Cushing, Frank Hamilton.1892. "A Zuni Folk-Tale of the Underworld." JAFL 5. 1896. "Outlines of Zuni Creation Myths." BBAE 13.

Dali, W. H. 1870. *Alaska and Its Resources*. Boston.

Dangel, Richard. 1929. "Tirawa, der Hochste Gott der Pawnee." ARW 27.

Davis, Edward H. 1919. "The Dieguefio Ceremony of the Death Images". CMAI 5:2. 1921. "Early Cremation Ceremonies of the Luisefio and Dieguefio Indians of Southern California.." INM 7:3.

Dawson, G. M. 1880. "Report on the Haida Indians of the Queen Charlotte Islands." Geological Survey of Canada, Report of Progress for 1878-1879. Montreal.

Delacroix, H. 1922. *La Religion et la foi*. Paris.

Deloria, Ella. 1944. *Speaking of Indians*. New York.

Demetracopoulou, D. 1935. "Wintu Songs." Anthropos 30. Wien.

Denig, Edwin Thompson. 1930. "Indian Tribes of the Upper Missouri." ARBAE 46.

Densmore, Frances 1910. "Chippewa Music." BBAE 45. 1918. "Teton Sioux Music." BBAE 61. 1929. "Chippewa Customs." BBAE 86. 1948. "Notes on the Indians' Belief in the Friendliness of Nature." SWJ 4:1.

De Smet, Father P. J. 1905. "Life, Letters and Travels of Father Pierre-Jean De Smet," S. J., 1801-73 I-IV. Editors: H. M. Chittendon & A. T. Richardson. New York.

van Deursen, A.. 1931. *Der Heilbringer*. Groningen.

Devereux, George 1937. "Mohave Soul Concepts." AA 39:3.

Dieterich, Albrecht. 1913. *Mutter Erde*. 2nd ed. Berlin.

Dixon, Roland B. 1899. "The Color-Symbolism of the Cardinal Points." JAFL 12. 1905. "The Northern Maidu." BAMNH 17:3. 1907. "The Shasta." BMNH 17:S. 1910 "Shasta Myths." JAFL 23. 1910 "The Chimariko Indians and Language." UCP 5: 5.

Dorsey, George A. 1903. "The Arapaho Sun Dance." FMAS 4. 1905. "The Cheyenne," I. FMAS 9:1. 1906 "Legend of the Teton Sioux Medicine Pipe." JAFL 19. 1906 "The Pawnee Mythology." CIWP 59

Dorsey, G. A., & Kroeber, A. L. 1903. Traditions of the Arapaho. FMAS 5.

Dorsey, G. A., & Murie, J. R.. 1940. "Notes on Skidi Pawnee Society." FMAS 27:2.

Dorsey, James Owen. 1884. "Omaha Sociology." ARBAE 3. 1889 "Indians of Siletz Reservation." AA, Old Series, 2:1. 1889 "Omaha Folk-Lore Notes." JAFL 2. 1889 c. "Teton Folk-Lore." AA, Old Series, 2:2. 1893. "Indian Doctrine of Souls." JAFL 6. 1894. A Study of Siouan Cults. ARBAE 11.

Driver, Harold E. 1936. "Wappo Ethnography." UCP 36:3. 1937. "Southern Sierra Nevada." AR 1:2 (CED VI). 1939. "Northwest California." AR 1:6 (CED X).

Drucker, Philip. 1937 a. "Southern California." AR 1:1 (CED V).1937 b. "The Tolowa and Their Southwest Oregon Kin." UCP 36:4. 1939. "Contributions to Alsea

Ethnography." UCP 35 7. 1940. "Kwakiutl Dancing Societies." AR 2:6. 1941. "Yuman-Piman." AR 6:3 (CED XVII). 1950. "Northwest Coast." AR 9: 3 (CED XXVI). 1951. The Northern and Central Nootkan Tribes. BBAE 144.

DuBois, Constance Goddard. 1901. "The Mythology of the Dieguefios." JAFL I4. 1904. "Mythology of the Mission Indians." JAFL I7. 1906. Mythology of the Mission Indians. JAFL I9. 1908. "The Religion of the Luiseno Indians of Southern California." UCP 8:3.

DuBois, Cora.1935. "Wintu Ethnography UCP 36: I.1938. "The Feather Cult of the Middle Columbia." GSA 7.

Dumarest, Father Noel. 1919. "Notes on Cochiti, New Mexico." MAAA 6:3.

Durkheim, Emil. 1912. Le*s Formes elementaires de la vie religieuse*. Paris.

Earle, E., & Kennard, E. A. 1938. *Hopi Kachinas*. New York.

Eastman, Charles Alexander (Ohiyesa).1911. *The Soul of the Indian*. Boston. & New York.

Eastman, Mary. 1849. *Dahcotah; or, Life and Legends of the Sioux around Fort Snelling*. New York.

Edsman, Carl-Martin. 1947. "Dod, forintelse och evigt liv. ROB 6.

Eells, Myron. 1889. "The Twana, Chemakum, and Klallam Indians." ARSI 1887:1.

Ehnmark, Errand. 1948. "Some Remarks on the Idea of Immortality in Greek Religion." Eranos 46: 1-2. I950. *Religionshistoriens grans*. Lund.

Eliade, Mircea. 1951. *Le Chamanisme et les techniques archaiques de l'extase*. Paris.

Elmendorf, William W. 1952. "Soul Loss Illness in Western N. A." In: Tax 1952.

Emmons, G. T. 1911. "The Tahltan Indians." UPMAP 4:1.

Erixon, Sigurd. 1951. "Ethnologie régionale ou folklore." Laos I. Stockholm.

Essene, Frank. 1942. "Round Valley." AR 8:I (CED XXI).

Farrand, Livingston. 1900. "Traditions of the Chilcotin Indians." MAMNH 4:I. 1902. "Traditions of the Quinault Indians". MAMNH 4:3.

Featherman, A. 1888. *Social History of the Races of Mankind, III*. London.

Fewkes, J. Walter. 1895. "The Tusayan Ritual." ARSI 1895:1. 1896. "The Prehistoric Culture of Tusayan." AA, Old Series, 9:5. 1897. "Tusayan Katcinas." ARBAE 15. 1901. "An Interpretation of Katcina Worship." JAFL 14.

Fisher, Margaret. 1946. "The Mythology of the Northern and Northeastern Algonkians in Reference to Algonkian Mythology as a Whole." In, Johnson 1946.

Flannery, Regina. 1939. "An Analysis of Coastal Algonquian Culture." CUAS 7.

Fletcher, Alice C. 1884. "The Shadow or Ghost Lodge: A Ceremony of the Ogallala Sioux." RPM 16 - 17. 1891. "The Indian Messiah." JAFL 4. 1897. "A Study from the Omaha Tribe: the Import of the Totem." ARSI 1897. 1904. "The Hako: A Pawnee Ceremony." ARBAE 22:2. 1910. "Wakonda." BBAE 30:2.

Fletcher, A. C. & La Flesche, F. 1911. "The Omaha Tribe." ARBAE 27.

Forbes, William H. 1894. "Traditions of Sioux Indians." CMHS 6:3.

Forde, C. Darryll. 1931. "Ethnography of the Yuma Indians." UCP 28:4.

Forsberg, Nils. 1943. "Une Forme elementaire d'organisation ceremoniale." Contribution a l'etude de la morphologic du culte. Uppsala.

Fortune, R. F. 1932. "Omaha Secret Societies." CUCA 14.

Foster, George M. 1944. a. "A Summary of Yuki Culture." AR 5:3. 1944. b. "Nagualism in Mexico and Guatemala." Acta Americana 2:1-2.

Frachtenberg, L. J. 1920. "Eschatology of the Quileute Indians." AA 22:4.

Frazer, Sir James George. 1886. "On Certain Burial Customs as Illustrative of the Primitive Theory of the Soul." JAI 15. 1910. *Totemism and Exogamy*. I-IV. London. 1919. "The Magic Art and the Evolution of Kings." *The Golden Bough*, I:2. London. 1920. "The Scapegoat." *The Golden Bough*, VI. London. 1923. "Balder the Beautiful." *The Golden Bough*, VII:2. London. 1925. "Spirits of the Corn and of the Wild". *The Golden Bough*, V: I-2. London. 1927. "Taboo and the Perils of the Soul." *The Golden Bough*, II. London. 1933-36. *The Fear of the Dead in Primitive Religion*. I-III. London. 1949. *The Golden Bough*: Abridged Edition. London.

Freeland, L. S. 1923. "Pomo Doctors and Poisoners." UCP 20.

Freud, Sigmund. 1950. *Totem and Taboo*. London.

Friederici, Georg. 1906. *Skalpieren und ahnliche Kriegsgebrauche in Amerika*. Braunschweig.

Frobenius, L. 1928. "Die Weltanschauung der Naturvolker." BVV 6.

Gadelius, B. 1912-13. *Tro och ofvertro i gangna tider*. I-II. Stockholm.

Garfield, Viola E. & Forrest, Linn A. 1948. *The Wolf and the Raven*. Seattle.

Gatschet, A. S. 1888. "Human Bones." JAFL I. 1891. "The Karankawa Indians, the Coast People of Texas." PMP I:2. 1899. "Various Ethnographic Notes: the Deities of the Early New England Indians." JAFL 12

Gayton, A. H. 1935. "The Orpheus Myth in North America." JAFL 48. 1948. "Yokuts and Western Mono Ethnography." I-II. AR10: 1-2.

van Gennep, A. 1909. *Les Rites de passage*. Paris.

Gifford, E. W. 1918. "Clans and Moieties in Southern California." UCP 14:2. 1926. "Clear Lake Pomo Society." UCP I8:2. 1931. "The Kamia of Imperial Valley." BBAE 97. 1932 a. "The Northfork Mono." UCP 31:2. 1932 b. "The Southeastern Yavapai." UCP 29:3. 1933 a. "Northeastern and Western Yavapai Myths." JAFL 46. 1933 b. "The Cocopa." UCP 3I:5. 1936. "Northeastern and Western Yavapai." UCP 34:4. 1939. "The Coast Yuki." Anthropos 34: I -3. Wien. 1940. "Apache-Pueblo." AR 4:1 (CED XII).

Gifford, E. W. & Kroeber, A. L. 1937. "Pomo." UCP 37 4 (CED IV).

Gifford, E. W. & Lowie, R. H. 1928. "Notes on the Akwa'ala Indians of Lower California." UCP 23:7.

Gilbert, William H. 1943. "The Eastern Cherokees." BBAE 133.

Gjessing, Gutorm. 1944. "Circumpolar Stone Age." Acta Arctica, Fasc. II. Copenhagen. 1948. *Guden med det éne øye*. Viking, 1948. Oslo.

Goddard, Pliny Earle. 1903. "Life and Culture of the Hupa." UCP I:1. 1909. "Kato Texts." UCP 5:3. 1911. "Jicarilla Apache Texts." APAM 8. 1915. "The Present Condition of Our Knowledge of North American Languages." In: ANA. 1931. "Indians of the Southwest." AMNHHS 2 1945. "Indians of the Northwest Coast." AMNHHS 10.

Goldenweiser, A. A. 1946. *Anthropology: An Introduction to Primitive Culture*. N. Y.

Goldfrank, Esther Schiff. 1927. "The Social and Ceremonial Organization of Cochiti." MAAA 33.

Goldman, Irving. 1940. "The Alkatcho Carrier of British Columbia." In: Linton 1940.

Goldschmidt, Walter. 1951 I. "Nomlaki Ethnography." UCP 42:4.

Goodwin, Grenville. 1938. "White Mountain Apache Religion." AA 40:1.

Gower, Charlotte D. 1927. "The Northern and Southern Affiliations of Antillean Culture." MAAA 35.

Greenlee, Robert F. 1944. "Medicine and Curing Practices of the Modern Florida Seminoles." AA 46:3.

Gregg, Josiah. 1844. *Commerce of the Prairies*. I-II. New York.

Grinnell, George Bird. 1892. *Blackfoot Lodge Tales*. New York. 1910. "Coup and Scalp Among the Plains Indians." AA 12:2. 1912. *Pawnee Hero Stories and Folk Tales with Notes*. New York. 1923. *The Cheyenne Indians. Their History and Ways of Life*. 1-2. New Haven.

Guinard, Rev. Joseph E. 1930. "Witiko Among the Tete-de-Boule." PM 3:3-4.

Gunther, Erna. 1927. "Klallam Ethnography." UWPA 1:5. 1928. "A Further Analysis of the First Salmon Ceremony." UWPA 2:5.

Haeberlin, H. K. 1916. "The Idea of Fertilization in the Culture of the Pueblo Indians." MAAA 3:1. 1918. "A Shamanistic Performance of the Coast Salish." AA 20:3.

Haeberlin, H. K. & Gunther, E. 1930. "The Indians of Puget Sound." UWPA 4:1.

Haebler, Konrad. 1899. "Die Religion des mittleren Amerika." Munster in Westfalen.

Haeckel, Josef. 1937. "Totemismus und Zweiklassensystem bei den Sioux-Indianern." Anthropos 32 3, 4. Wien.

Hagar, Stansbury. 1908. "Ancestor-Worship and Cult of the Dead." ERE 1.

Haile, Father Berard. 1942. "Navaho Upward-Reaching Way and Emergence Place." AA 44.

Hale, H. 1846. "Ethnology and Philology." *Narrative of the United States Exploring Expedition, under Command of Charles Wilkes*. Vol. VI. Philadelphia.

Hallowell, A. Irving. 1926. "Bear Ceremonialism in the Northern Hemisphere." AA Z28:1. 1940. "The Spirits of the Dead in Saulteaux Life and Thought." JAI 70:1. 1946. "Some Psychological Characteristics of the Northeastern Indians." In: Johnson 1946.

Handbook of American Indians North of Mexico. 1907-1910. Ed. by Frederick Webb Hodge. I-II. BBAE 30: 1-2.

Handhook of South American Indians. 1945-1950. Ed. by J. H. Steward. I-VI. BBAE 143.

Harmon, D. W. 1903. *An Account of the Indians Living West of the Rocky Mountains*. New York.

Harrington, John Peabody. 1908. "A Yuma Account of Origins." JAFL 21. 1928. "Picuris Children's Stories, with Texts and Songs." ARBAE 43. 1934. "A New Original Version of Boscana's Historical Account of the San Juan Capistrano Indians of Southern California." SMC 92:4. 1942. "Central California Coast." AR 7:I (CED XIX).

Harrington, M. R. 1910. "Some Customs of the Delaware Indians." MJ 1:3. 1913. "A Preliminary Sketch of Lenape Culture." AA 15:2. 192I. "Religion and Ceremonies of the Lenape." INM, Ser. 2, No. 19.

Harris, Jack S. 1940. "The White Knife Shoshoni of Nevada." In: Linton 1940.

Harrison, Rev. C. 1892. "Religion and Family among the Haidas, Queen Charlotte Islands." JAI 21.

Hartland, Edwin Sidney. 1894—96 *The Legend of Perseus. A Study of Tradition in Story, Custom, and Belief.* I-III. (Grimm Library 2-4). London.

Hartman, C. W. 1895. *Indianer i nordvestra Mexiko. Ymer.* Stockholm.

Harva, Uno. 1927. "Finno-Ugric, Siberian Mythology." *The Mythology of All Races*. Vol. IV. 1938. "Die Religiosen Vorstellungen der Altaischen Volker." FFC I25.

Hatcher, M. A. 1927. "Descriptions of the Tejas or Asinai Indians." Southwestern Historical Quarterly 30.

Hatt, Gudmund. 1949. "Asiatic Influences in American Folklore." Det Kgl. Danske Videnskabernes Selskab, Historisk-Filologiske Meddelelser, Vol. 31: 6.

Hawkes, E. W. 1916. "The Labrador Eskimo." MCDM 91.

Hayden, F. V. 1862." Contributions to the Ethnography and Philology of the Indian Tribes of the Missouri Valley." TAPS 12:2, Article 3.

Heckewelder. J. 1821. *Nachricht von der Geschichte, den Sitten und Gebrauchen der Indianischen Volkerschaften, welche ehemals Pennsylvanien und die benachbarten Stasten bewohnten.* Gottingen.

Heizer, R. F. & Whipple, M. A. 1951. *The California Indians. A Source Book.* Berkeley & Los Angeles.

Hewitt, J. N. B. 1895. "The Iroquoian Concept of the Soul." JAFL 8. 1902. "Orenda and a Definition of Religion." AA 4:1. 1903. "Iroquoian Cosmology." ARBAE 21. 1910. a. "Orenda." BBAE 30:2. 1910. b. "Oyaron." BBAE 30:2.1910. C. Totem. BBAE 30:2.

Hewitt, J. N. B. & Sruanton, J. R. 1939. "Notes on the Creek Indians". BBAE I23.

Hilger, Sister M. Inez.1951. "Chippewa Child Life and Its Cultural Background." BBAE 146.

Hill, W. W. 1943. "Navaho Humor." GSA 10.

Hill, W. W. & Dorothy. 1945. "Navaho Coyote Tales and Their Position in the Southern Athabaskan Group." JAFL 58.

Hill-Tout, Charles. 1899. "Haida Stories and Beliefs." BAAS 68. 1900. "Notes on the Skqo'mic of British Columbia, a Branch of the Great Salish Stock of North America." BAAS 70. 1904. "Report on the Ethnology of the Siciatl of British Columbia, a Coast Division of the Salish Stock." JAI 34. 1905. "Report on the Ethnology of the StlatumH of British Columbia." JAI 35. 1907 a. *British North America: The Far West, the Home of the Salish and Dene.* London. 1907 b. "Report on the Ethnology of the South-Eastern Tribes of Vancouver Island." JAI 37.

Hoffman, W. J. 1891. "The Mide'wiwin or 'Grand Medicine Society' of the Ojibwa." ARBAE 7.

Holm, G. 1888. "Ethnologisk Skizze af Angmagsalikerne." MG 10. 1914. "Ethnological Sketch of the Angmagsalik Eskimo." MG 39.

Holmberg, Henrik J. 1855 "Ethnographische Skizzen uber die Volker des Russischen Amerika." Helsingfors. (Also in ASSF, Vol. 4).

Holmberg-Harva, *see* **Harva.**

Holt, Catharine. 1946. "Shasta Ethnography." AR 3:4.

Honigmann, John J. 1945. "Northern and Southern Athapaskan Eschatology." AA 47:3. 1946. "Ethnography and Acculturation of the Fort Nelson Slave." YUPA 33. 1949. "Culture and Ethos of Kaska Society." YUPA 40.

Hooper, Lucile. 1920. "The Cahuilla Indians." UCP 16:6.

Hrdlicka, A. 1907. "Cannibalism." BBAE 30:1.

Hudson, J.W. 1902. "An Indian Myth of the San Joaquin Basin." JAFL 15.

Hulbert, A. B., & Schwarze, W. N. *(editors)* 1910. "David Zeisberger's History of Northern American Indians." OAHQ 19:1-2.

Hulthrantz, Åke. 1947. "Naturfolk och kulturfolk." In: *Varldens lander och folk*, ed. by S. Dahl. Stockholm. 1949. "Kulturbildningen hos Wyomings Shoshoni-indianer." Ymer 1949:2. 1951. "The Concept of the Soul held by the Wind River Shoshone." Ethnos 1-2. Ms. Wind River Shoshone Field Notes.

Hunter, J. D. 1826. "Minnesteckningar rorande en fangenskap bland Indianerna."

Arch. f. Resebeskr., II. Mariefred.

Jackson. Rev. Sheldon. 1879. "Alaska and Its Inhabitants." AAOJ 2: 2.

James, Edwin. 1823. *Account of an Expedition from Pittsburgh to the Rocky Mountains, performed in the years 1819 and 1820.* I—II. Philadelphia.

James, E. O. 1921. "Tutelary Gods and Spirits." ERE 12. 1927. "The Concept of the Soul in North America." FL 38. 1948. *The Beginnings of Religion.* Hutchinson's University Library 8, London.

Jenness, Diamond. 1922. "The Life of the Copper Eskimos". RCAE 12. 1932. "The Indians of Canada." BCDM 65. 1933. "The American Aborigines. Their Origin and Antiquity." Papers, edited by D. J. Toronto. 1935. "The Ojibwa Indians of Parry Island. Their Social and Religious Life." BCDM 78. 1937. "The Sekani Indians of British Columbia." BCDM 84. 1938. "The Sarcee Indians of Alberta." BCDM 90. 1943. "The Carrier Indians of the Bulkley River." BBAE 133.

Jette, Rev. Julius. 1907. "On the Medicine-Men of the Ten'a." JAI 37. 1911. "On the Superstitions of the Ten'a Indians (middle part of the Yukon Valley, Alaska)." Anthropos 6, Wien.

Joffe, Natalie F. 1940. "The Fox of Iowa." In: Linton 1940.

Johnson, Frederick. 1943. "Notes on Micmac Shamanism." PM 16:3 - 4. 1946. "Man in Northeastern North America," edited by F. J. PPFA 3.

Johnson, Jean B. 1950. "The Opata: An Inland Tribe of Sonora." UNMPA 6.

Jones, Peter. 1861. *History of the Ojebway Indians.* London.

Jones, William. 1900. "The Heart of the Brave." Harvard Monthly 30. 1905. "The Algonkin Manitou." JAFL I8. 1906. "Central Algonkin." AAR 1905. 1907 a. "Fox Texts." PAES 1. 1907 b. "Mortuary Observances and the Adoption Rites of the Algonkin Foxes of Iowa." ICA 15:1. 1911. "Notes on the Fox Indians." JAFL 24. 1913. "Kickapoo Ethnological Notes." AA 15:2. 1916. "Ojibwa Tales from the North Shore of Lake Superior." JAFL 29. 1939. "Ethnography of the Fox Indians" (edited by M. W. Fisher). BBAE 125.

Juel, Eric. 1945. "Notes on Seal-Hunting Ceremonialism in the Arctics." Ethnos 1945:2-3.

Jung, C. G. 1932. *Seelenprobleme der Gegenwart.* Leipzig und Stuttgart.

Kane, Paul. 1925. *Wanderings of an Artist among the Indians of North America.* Toronto.

Karsten, Rafael. 1928. *Inledning till religionsvetenskapen.* Helsingfors.

Keating, William H. 1825. *Narrative of an Expedition to the Source of St. Peter's River.* I—II. London.

Kelly, Isabel T. 1932. "Ethnography of the Surprise Valley Paiute." UCP 31:3. 1936. "Chemehuevi Shamanism." EAK. 1939. "Southern Paiute Shamanism." AR 2:4.

Kennard, E. A. 1937. "Hopi Reactions to Death." AA 39:3.

Kidder, A. V. 1936. "Speculations on New World Prehistory." EAK.

Kinietz, W. Vernon. 1940. "The Indians of the Western Great Lakes." 1618-1760. OCMA 10. 1947. "Chippewa Village. The Story of Katikitegon." BCIS 25.

Kluckhohn, Clyde. 1942. "Myths and Rituals: A General Theory." HTR 35:1. 1944. "Navaho Witchcraft." PMP 22: 2.

Kluckhohn, C. & Leighton, D. 1947. *The Navaho.* Cambridge, Mass.

Kohl, J. G. 1859. *Kitschi-Gami oder Erzahlungen vom Obern See.* I—II. Bremen.

Korner, Theo. 1937. "Zur Frage der Differenzierung der psychologischen und etymologischen Grundlage der sogenannten 'Seelen'-Begriffe im Austronesischen." ZE 69:1-3.

Krause, Aurel. I885. *Die Tlinkit-Indianer.* Jena.

Krause, Fritz. 1921. "Die Kultur der kalifornischen Indianer." Institut fur Volkerkunde, I. Reihe, 4. Leipzig.

Krickeberg, W. 1922. "Amerika." In: Buschan 1922.

Kroeber, Alfred. 1899. "The Eskimo of Smith Sound." BAMNH 12. 1900. "Cheyenne Tales." JAFL 13. 1902. "Preliminary Sketch of the Mohave Indians." AA 4:2. 1902-07. "The Arapaho." I-V. BAMNH 18:1 -4. 1906. "Two Myths of the Mission Indians of California." JAFL 19. 1907 a. "Indian Myths of South Central California." UCP 4:4. 1907 b. "The Religion of the Indians of California." UCP 4:6. 1908 a. "A Mission Record of the California Indians." UCP 8:1. 1908 b. "Ethnology of the Gros Ventre." APAM 1:4. 1910. "California." ERE 3. 1923. "The History of Native Culture in California." UCP 20. 1925. "Handbook of the Indians of California." BBAE 78. 1929. "The Valley Nisenan." UCP 24:4 .1932 a. "The Patwin and Their Neighbors." UCP 29:4. 1932 b. "Yuki Myths." Anthropos 27. Wien. 1935. 'Walapai Ethnography," edited by A. L. K. MAAA 42. 1939. "Cultural and Natural Areas of Native North America." UCP 38. 1940. "Stimulus Diffusion." AA 42:1. 1943. "Franz Boas." MAAA 61 1946. "History and Evolution." SWJ 2:1. 1948 a. *Anthropology.* 2nd ed. New York. 1948 b. "Seven Mohave Myths." AR 11:1

Kroeher, A. L, & Gifford, E. W. 1949. "World Renewal: A Cult System of Native Northwest California." AR 13:1.

Lafitau, J. F. 1724. *Moeurs des sauvages ameriquains, comparees aux moeurs des premiers temps.* I-II. Paris

La Flesche, Francis. 1889. "Death and Funeral Customs among the Omahas." JAFL 2. 1930. "The Osage Tribe: Rite of the Wa-Xo-Be." ARBAE 49. 1939. "War Ceremony and Peace Ceremony of the Osage Indians." BBAE 101.

Lagercrantz, S. 1940. "Bildangst der Schwarzen." ARW 37:2.

Lantis, Margaret. 1950. "The Religion of the Eskimos." In: *Forgotten Religions,* V. Ferm, ed. New York.

Larock, V. 1932. *Essai sur la Valeur sacree et la Valeur sociale des noms de personne dans les Societes inferieures.* Paris.

Leach, Maria, (ed.) 1949-50. *Standard Dictionary of Folklore, Mythology and Legend.* I-II. New York.

Le Clercq, Father Chrestien. 1910. "New Relation of Gaspesia. With the Customs and Religion of the Gaspesian Indians." PCS 5.

van der Leeuw, G. 1930. "Phanomenologie der Seele." CIHR 5.

Le Page Du Pratz, Antoine S. 1758. *Histoire de la Louisiane.* I-III. Paris..

Lesser, Alexander. 1952. "Evolution in Social Anthropology." SWJ 8:2.

(Le Sueur). 1872. "Le Sueur, the Explorer of the Minnesota River." CMHS 1.

Levy-Bruhl, L. 1922. *Les Fonctions mentales dans les societes inferieures.* 5th ed. Paris. 1925. *La Mentalité primitive.* Paris. 1927. *L'Ame primitive.* Paris. 1936. *La Mythologie primitive.* Paris.

Lhermitte, Jean. 1951. "Visual Hallucination of the Self." BMJ 3.3.1951.

Linck, Olaf. 1926. *En sommar bland siouxindianer.* Helsingfors.

Lincoln, Jackson Steward. 1935. *The Dream in Primitive Culture.* London.

Lindquist, G. E. E. 1944. *The Indian in American Life.* New York.

Linne, Sigvald. 1929. *Darien in the Past*. Goteborg.

Linton, Ralph. 1922. "The Sacrifice to the Morning Star by the Skidi Pawnee." FMDAL 6. 1926. "The Origin of the Skidi Pawnee Sacrifice to the Morning Star." AA 28:4. 1940. *Acculturation in Seven American Indian Tribes*, ed. by R. L. New York & London. 1945. *The Cultural Background of Personality*. New York.

Llewellyn, K. N. & Hoebel, E. A. 1941. *The Cheyenne Way*. Norman.

Loeb, E. M. 1923. "The Blood Sacrifice Complex". MAAA 30. 1926. "Pomo Folkways." UCP 19:2 1932. "The Western Kuksu Cult." UCP 33:1. 1933. "The Eastern Kuksu Cult." UCP 33:2.

Loewenthal, J. W. J. 1913. *Die Religion der Ostalgonkin*. Berlin.

Lonborg, Sven. 1910. "Doden och uppstandelsen." Ymer 1910:2. Stockholm.

Lopatin, Ivan A. 1945. *Social Life and Religion of the Indians in Kitimat, British Columbia*. Los Angeles.

Loskiel, Georg Heinrich. 1789. *Geschichte der Mission der evangelischen Brudcr... in Nordamerika*. Barby.

Lowie, Robert H. 1909 a. "The Norehern Shoshone APAM 2:2. 1909 b. "The Assiniboine." APAM 4:1. 1917. "Ojibwa." ERE 9. 1922 "The Religion of the Crow Indians." APAM 25: 2. 1923. "The Cultural Connection of Californian and Plateau Shoshonean Tribes." UCP 20. 1924. "Notes on Shoshonean Ethnography." APAM 20:3. 1925 a. "On the Historical Connection Between Certain Old World and New World Beliefs." ICA 21:2. 1925 b. *Primitive Religion*. 1st ed. London. 1930. "A Crow Text, with Grammatical Notes." UCP 29: 2. 1934. *An Introduction to Cultural Anthropology*. New York. 1935 *The Crow Indians*. New York. 1937 *The History of Ethnological Theory*. London. 1948. *Primitive Religion*. 2nd ed. New York. 1951. "Beitrage zur Volkerkunde Nordamerikas." MMVH 23.

Lubbock, Sir John. 1882. *Origin of Civilization*. London.

Lumholtz, Carl. 1900. "Symbolism of the Huichol Indians." MAMNH 3:1. 1905 *Unknown Mexico*. I-II. New York. 1904 *Bland Mexikos indianer*. I-II. Stockholm. 1912. *New Trails in Mexico*. London.

Lyman, William D. 1904. "Myths and Superstitions of thc Oregon Indians." PAAS 16:2.

Lynd, James W. 1889. "The Religion of the Dakotas." CMHS 2.

MacCauley, Clay. 1887. "Seminole Indians of Florida." ARBAE 5.

MacCulloch, J. A. 1910. "Cannibalism." LR 1:3.

Macfie, Harry. 1944. *Lagereldar langesen*. Stockholm.

Maillard, A. S. 1758. *An Account of the Customs and Manners of the Mickakis and Maricheets*. London.

Mallery, Garrick. 1886. "Pictographs of the North American Indians—A Preliminary Paper." ARBAE 4. 1894. "Picture-Writing of the American Indians." ARBAE 10.

Mandelbaum, David G. 1940. "The Plains Cree." APAM 37:2.

Marett, R. R. 1909. *The Threshold of Religion*. London.

Mason, J. Alden. 1946. "Notes on the Indians of the Great Slave Lake Area." YUPA 34.

Matthews, Washington. 1877. "Ethnography and Philology of thc Hidatsa Indians." United States Geological and Geographical Survey, Misc. Publ., No. 7. 1887. "The Mountain Chant: A Navajo Ceremony." ARBAE 5. 1897. "Navaho Legends." MAFLS 5.

Mauss, Marcel. 1947. *Manuel d'Ethnographie*. Paris. 1950. "Une Categorie de l'esprit humain: la notion de personne, celle de 'moi'." In: Mauss, *Sociologie et Anthropologie*. Paris.

McClean. J. 1849. *Notes of a Twenty-Five Years' Service in the Hudson's Bay Territory*. I-II. London.

McClintock, Walter. 1910 *The Old North Trail or Life, Legends and Religion of the Blackfeet Indians*. London. 1923. *Old Indian Trails*. London, Bombay, Sidney.

McGee, W. J. 1897. "The Siouan Indians. A Preliminary Sketch." ARBAE 15.

McIlwraith, T. F. 1948. *The Bella Coola Indians*. I-II. Toronto.

McKenney, T. L. 1827. *Sketches of a Tour of the Lakes*. Baltimore.

McLean, John. 1892. *The Indians of Canada: Their Manners and Customs*. London.

Meigs, Peveril III. 1939. "The Kiliwa Indians of Lower California." IA 15.

Mensching, Gustav. 1949. *Vergleichende Religionswissenschaft*. Heidelberg

Michelson, Truman. 1925. "Notes on Fox Mortuary Customs and Beliefs." ARBAE 40. 1927. "Contributions to Fox Ethnology." BBAE 85. 1930. "Contributions to Fox Ethnology II." BBAE 95. 1932. "Notes on the Fox Wapanowiweni." BBAE 105.

Miller, N. 1927. Some Aspects of the Name in Culture-History. AJS 32.

Mishkin, Bernard. 1940. "Rank and Warfare among the Plains Indians." MAES 3.

Mooney, James. 1891. "The Sacred Formulas of the Cherokees." ARBAE 7. 1896. "The Ghost-Dance Religion and the Sioux Outbreak of 1890." ARBAE 14:2. 1900 "Myths of the Cherokee." ARBAE 19:1.

Mooney, J. & Olbrechts, Frans M. 1932. "The Swimmer Manuscript: Cherokee Sacred Formulas and Medicinal Prescriptions." BBAE 99.

Morgan, Lewis H. 1904. *League of the Ho-de-no-sau-nee or Iroquois*. Ed. by Herbere M. Lloyd. I-II. New York.

Morgan, William 1932. "Navaho Dreams." AA 34:3. 1936. "Human-Wolves among the Navaho." YUPA 11.

Morice, A. G. 1889. "The Western Denes—Their Manners and Customs." PCI, Series 3, No. 7. 1897. *Au pays de l'ours noir. Chez les sauvages de la Colombie Britannique*. Paris. 1906. "The Canadian Denes." AAR 1905. 1910 a. "Carrier Indians." ERE 3. 1910 b. "Hare Indians." CE 7. 1911. "Denes." ERE 4.

Murdock, George Pete. 1941. "Ethnographic Bibliography of N. America." YAS 1.

Nansen, Fridtjof. 1891. "Eskimoliv." Christiania, Nor.

Natches, Gilbert. 1923. "Northern Paiute Verbs." UCP 20.

Neill, E. D. 1872. "Dakota Land and Dakota Life." CMHS 1.

Nelson, E. W. 1899. "The Eskimo about Bering Strait." ARBAE 18:1.

Niblack, Albert P. 1890. "The Coast Indians of Southern Alaska and Northern British Columbia." RUSNM 1888.

Nieuwenhuis, A. W. 1917. "Die Wurzeln des Animismus." IAE 24: Supplement. 1924 "The Differences between the Conception of Soul (Animus) and of Spirit (Spiritus) among the American Indians." ICA 21

Nilsson, Martin P. 1930. "Existiert ein primitiver Seelenbegriff?" CIHR 5. 1934. *Primitiv religion*. 3rd ed. Uppsala, Swe.

Nomland, Gladys Ayer 1935. "Sinkyone Notes." UCP 36: 2. 1938. "Bear River Ethnography." AR 2: 2.

Nuttall, Zelia. 1897. "Ancient Mexican Superstitions." JAFL 10.

Oakes, Maud. 1951 *The Two Crosses of Todos Saneos: Survivals of Mayan Religious*

Ritual. Bollingen Series 27. New York.

Ohlmarks, Åke. 1939. *Studien zum Problem des Schamanismus.* Lund.

Olson, Ronald L. 1933. "Clan and Moiety in Native America." UCP 33:4. 1936. 'The Quinault Indians." UWPA 6:1. 1940. "The Social Organization of the Haisla of British Columbia." AR 2:5.

Opler, Marvin K. 1940. "The Southern Ute of Colorado." In: Linton 1940.

Opler, Morris Edward. 1936 "A Summary of Jicarilla Apache Culture." AA 38: 2. 1941. *An Apache Life-Way. The Economic, Social, and Religious Institutions of the Chiricahua Indians.* Chicago. 1945. "The Lipan Apache Death Complex and Its Extensions." SWJ 1:1. 1947. "Mythology and Folk Belief in the Maintenance of Jicarilla Apache Tribal Endogamy." JAFL 60.

Osgood, Cornelius. 1932. "The Ethnography of the Great Bear Lake Indians." BCDM 70. 1936. "Contributions to the Ethnography of the Kutchin." YUPA 14. "1937. The Ethnography of the Tanaina." YUPA I6. 1940. "Ingalik Material Culture." YUPA 22. 1951 "Culture: Its Empirical and Non-Empirical Character." SWJ 7:2.

Otto, Rudolf. 1927. *Das Heilige.* 16th ed. Gotha.

Park, Willard Z. 1934." Pavioeso Shamanism." AA 36:1. 1938. "Shamanism in Western North America." Northwestern University Studies in the Social Sciences, 2. Evanston & Chicago.

Parker, A. C. 1913. "The Code of Handsome Lake, the Seneca Prophet." NYSMB 163.

Parsons, Elsie Clews. 1916. "A few Zuni Death Beliefs and Practices." AA 18: 2. 1917. "Notes on Zuni." I-II. MAAA 4: 3-4. 1918. "Notes on Acoma and Laguna." AA 20:2. 1920. "Notes on Ceremonialism at Laguna." APAM 19:4. 1921. "Hopi Mothers and Children." Man 21. 1921—22. "A Narrative of the Tenta of Anvik, Alaska." Anthropos 16-17. Wien. 1924 a. "The Religion of the Pueblo Indians." ICA 21: 1. 1924 b. "The Scalp Ceremonial of Zuni. MAAA 31. 1925. "A Pueblo Indian Journal I920-1921". MAAA 32. 1926. "Tevra Tales." MAFLS 19. 1929. "The Social Organization of the Tewa of New Mexico." MAAA 36. 1932. "Isleta, New Mexico." ARBAE 47. 1936 a. *Mitla: Town of the Souls*. Chicago. 1936 b. "Taos Pueblo." GSA 2. 1939. *Pueblo Indian Religion.* I—II. Chicago. 1941. "Notes on the Caddo." MAAA 57.

Pascher, Josef. 1929. "Der Seelenbegriff im Animismus Edward Burnett Tylors." *Abhandlungen zur Philosophie und Psychologie der Religion*, 23. Wurzburg.

Paulus , Diaconus. 1878. "Pauli Historia Langobardorum." Ed.: G. Waitz. *Scripeores Rerum Germanicarum.* Hannoverae 1878.

Perry, W. J. 1927. *The Children of the Sun. A Study in the Early History of Civilization.* 2nd ed. London.

Petitot, R. P. E. 1875. "Les Dene-Dindjies." ICA 1:2.

Pettitt, George A. 1946. "Primitive Education in North America." UCP 43:1. 1950. "The Quileute of La Push 1775-1945. *AR* 14:1.

Pond, Rev. Gideon H. 1889. "Dakota Superstitions." CMHS 2:3.

Pond, Rev. Samuel William. 1908. "The Dakotas or Sioux in Minnesota as they were in 1834." CMHS 12.

Powell, J. W. 1881. "Sketch of the Mythology of the North American Indians." ARBAE 1. 1891. "Indian Linguistic Families of America North of Mexico." ARBAE 7.

Powers, Stephen. 1877. "Tribes of California." CNAE 3.

Pratt, James B. 1945. *The Religious Consciousness. A Psychological Study.* New York.

Preuss, K. T. 1904. "Religionen der Naturvolker." ARW 7. 1908. *Ethnographische*

Ergebnisse einer Reise in die mexikanische Sierra Madre. 1912. *Die Nayaritexpedition, I:Die Religion der Coraindianer in Texten nebst Worterbuch.* Leipzig. 1923. *Die geistige Kultur der Naturvolker. Aus Natur und Geisteswelt,* 452. Leipzig. 1923. "Religionen der Naturvolker." ARW 22. 1929. "Indianer, Religionsgeschichtlich." RGG 3.

Prince, J. Dyneley. 1908. "Algonquins, Eastern." ERE 1.

Radcliffe-Brown, A. R. 1952. *Structure and Function in Primitive Society.* London.

Radin, Paul. 1909. "Winnebago Tales." JAFL 22. 1915. "Religion of the North American Indians." ANA. 1920. "The Autobiography of a Winnebago Indian." UCP 16:7. 1923. "The Winnebago Tribe." ARBAE 37. 1924. *Monotheism Among Primitive Peoples.* London. 1926. "Literary Aspects of Winnebago Mythology." JAFL 39. 1927. *Primitive Man as Philosopher.* New York & London. 1936. "Ojibwa and Ottawa Puberty Dreams." EAK. 1937. *Primitive Religion. Its Nature and Origin.* New York. 1944. *The Story of the American Indian.* New York. 1945. *The Road of Life and Death.* New York. 1948. "Winnebago Hero Cycles: A Study in Aboriginal Literature." MIJAL 1. 1951. "Die Religiose Erfahrung der Naturvolker." *Albae Vigiliae* 11. Zürich.

Rainey, Froelich G. 1947. "The Whale Hunters of Tigara." APAM 41:2.

Raknes, Ola. 1927. *Motet med det Heilage.* Oslo.

Rand, Silas T. 1888. *Dictionary of the Language of the Micmac Indians.* Halifax. 1894. *Legends of the Micmacs.* New York.

Rasmuseen, Knud. 1905. *Nye Mennesker.* Copenhagen. 1908. *The People of the Polar North.* London. 1921. *Myter og Sagn fra Gronland. I. Ostgronlaendere.* Copenhagen. 1925. *Myter og Sagn fra Gronland. III. Kap York-distriktet og Nordgronland.* Copenhagen. 1929. "Intellectual Culture of the Iglulik Eskimos." RFTE 7:1. 1930. "Observations on the Intellectual Culture of the Caribou Eskimos." RFTE 7:2. 1931. "The Netsilik Eskimos: Social Life and Spiritual Culture." RFTE 8:1.

Ray, Verne F. 1932. "The Sanpoil and Nespelem." UWPA 5. 1938. "Lower Chinook Ethnographic Notes." UWPA 7:2. 1939. "Cultural Relations in the Plateau of North America." PHAPF 3. 1942. "Plateau." AR 8:2 (CED XXII).

Read, Carveth 1925. *Man and His Superstitions.* Cambridge.

Reichard, Gladys A. 1928. "Social Life of the Navajo Indians." CUCA 7. 1944. "Prayer: The Compulsive Word." MAES 7. 1947. "An Analysis of Coeur d'Alene Indian Myths." MAFLS 41. 1950. "Navaho Religion: A Study of Symbolism." I-II. Bollingen Series 18. New York.

Reid, A. P. 1874. "Religious Beliefs of the Ojibois or Sauteux Indians." JAI 3

Reuterskiold, Edgar. 1908. *Till fragan om uppkomsten af sakramentala maltider med sarskild hansyn till eotemismen.* Uppsala.

Richardson. J. 1851. *Arctic Searching Expedition.* I-II. London.

Riggs, S. R. 1869. *Tah-koo Wah-kan'.* Boston 1883. "Mythology of the Dakotas." AAOJ 5. 1890. "A Dakota-English Dictionary." CNAE 7. 1893. "Dakota Grammar, Texts, and Ethnography." CNAE 9.

Rink, H. 1875. *Tales and Traditions of the Eskimo.* London.

Rivers, W. H. R. 1926. *Psychology and Ethnology.* London.

Rohinson, H. W. 1925. "Hebrew Psychology." In: *The People and the Book. Essays on the Old Testament,* by H. W. R. Oxford.

Rogers, Spencer L. 1944."Disease Concepts in North America." AA 46: 4.

Roheim, Geza. 1952. "Culture Hero and Trickster in North American Mythology." In: *Tax 1952.*

Russell, Frank. 1898. "Myths of the Jicarilla Apaches." JAFL 11. 1908. "The Pima Indians." ARBAE 26.

Sagard-Theodat, Gabriel. 1632. *Le Grand voyage du pays des Hurons*. Paris.

Sahagun, Fray Bernardino de. 1880. *Histoire generale des choses de la Nouvelle-Espagne*. Trad. par D. Jourdanet & Remi Simeon. Paris.

Saindon, Rev. J. E. 1933. "Mental Disorders among the James Bay Cree." PM 6:1.

Saint Clair, H. H., & Frachtenberg, L. J. 1909. "Traditions of the Coos Indians of Oregon." JAFL 22.

Sapir, Edward. 1907. "Religious Ideas of the Takelma Indians of Southwestern Oregon." JAFL 20.1909. "Wishram Texts." PAES 2. 1915. "The Na-dene Languages, a Preliminary Report." AA 17:4. 1916. "Time Pe.rspective in Aboriginal American Culture, a Study in Method." MCDM 90. 1921. "Vancouver Island Indians." ERE 12. 1929. "Central and North American Languages. *Encyclopaedia Britannica*, 14th ed. London & New York. 1949. "The Meaning of Religion." In: *Selected Writings of Edward Sapir*, ed. by D. G. Mandelbaum, Berkeley & Los Angeles.

Sapir, E., & Spier, L. 1943. "Notes on the Culture of the Yana." AR 3:3.

Schmidt, Father Wilhelm. 1926. *Der Ursprung der Gottesidee*. Quoted volumes: I (1926), II (1929), V(1934), VI (1935). Munster in Westfalen.1930. *Handbuch der vergleichenden Religionsgeschichte. Ursprung und Werden der Religion*. Munster in Westfalen. 1933. *High Gods in North America*. Oxford.

Schmidt, Karl Hermann. 1923. "Die okkulten Phanomene im Lichte der Wissenschaft." Sammlung Goschen 872. Berlin & Leipzig.

Schnepp, Gerald J. 1932. "The Concept of Mana". PM 5:4.

Schoolcraft, Henry R. 1851-1857. *Historical and Statistical Information Respecting the History, Condition and Prospects of the Indian Tribes of the United States*. I—VI. Philadelphia.

Schurtz, H. 1895. "Das Augenornament und verwandte Probleme." Kgl. Sachsische Gesellschaft der Wissenschaften, Philologisch-historische Classe. Abhandlungen 15: 2. Leipzig.

Segerstedt, Torgny. 1910. "Sjalavandringslarans ursprung." MO 4..

Seligson, Miriam. 1951. *The Meaning of* nefesh meth *in the Old Testament*. Helsinki.

Senter, D. & Hawley, F. 1937. "Hopi and Navajo Child Burials." AA 39: 1.

Shimkin, D. B. 1947. "Wind River Shoshone Literary Forms: An Introduction." JWAS 37:10.

Simmons, Leo W. 1945. *The Role of the Aged in Primitive Society*. New Haven.

Sjoberg, Andree F. 1951. "The Bidai Indians of Southeastern Texas." SWJ 7:4.

Skinner, Alanson. 1913. "Social Life and Ceremonial Bundles of the Menomini Indians." APAM 13:1. 1914. "Notes on the Plains Cree" AA 16:1. 1919 a. "A Sketch of Eastern Dakota Ethnology." AA 21:2. 1919 b. "Notes on the Sun Dance of the Sisseton Dakota." APAM 16:4. 1920 a. "Medicine Ceremony of the Menomini, Iowa, and Wahpeton Dakota, etc." INM 4. 1920 b. "Siouans." ERE 11. 1921. "Material Culture of the Menomini." INM. 1923. "Observations on the Ethnology of the Sauk Indians." BPMCM 5:1. 1924. "The Mascoutens or Prairie Potawatomi Indians." Part I. BPMCM 6:1. 1925 a. "Songs of the Menomini Medicine Ceremony." AA 27:2. 1925 b. "Traditions of the Iowa Indians." JAFL 38.

Skinner, A. & Satterlee, J. V. 1915. "Folklore of the Menomini Indians." APAM 13:3.

Smith, D. A. & Spier, L. 1927. "The Dot and Circle Design in Northwestern America."

JSAP 19.

Smith, E. A. 1883. "Myths of the Iroquois." ARBAE 2.

Smith, Marian W. 1940. "The Puiallup-Nisqually." CUCA 32.

Soderblom, Nathan. 1914. *Gudstrons uppkomst*. Stockholm. 1926. *Das Werden des Gottesglaubens. Untersuchungen uber die Anfange der Religion*. Leipzig.

Soustelle, Jaques. 1940. *La Pensee cosmologique des anciens Mexicains*. Paris.

Sparkman, Philip Stedman. 1908. "The Culture of the Luiseno Indians." UCP 8:4.

Speck, F. G. 1907. "The Creek Indians of Taskigi Town." MAAA 2:2. 1909 a. "Ethnology of the Yuchi Indians." UPMAP 1:1. 1909 b. "Notes on the Mohegan and Niantic Indians." APAM 3. 1919. "Penobscot Shamanism." MAA-A 6:4. 1924. "Spiritual Beliefs Among Labrador Indians." ICA 21:1. 1928 a. "Native Tribes and Dialects of Connecticut." ARBAE 43. 1928 b. "Wawenock Myth Texts from Maine." ARBAE 43. 1935 a. *Naskapi. The Savage Hunters of the Labrador Peninsula*. Norman. 1935 b. "Penobscot Tales and Religious Beliefs." JAFL 48. 1931. "A Study of the Delaware Indian Big House Ceremony." PPHC 2. 1939. "Catawba Religious Beliefs, Mortuary Customs, and Dances." PM 12:2. 1949, *Midwinter Rites of the Cayuga Long House*. Philadelphia.

Spence, Lewis. 1910 a. "Chinooks." ERE 3. 1910 b. "Choctaws." ERE 3. 1914. *Myths and Legends of the North American Indians*. Boston.

Spencer. J. 1910. "Capturing the Soul." JAFL 23.

Spier, Leslie. 1921. "The Sun Dance of the Plains Indians: Its Development and Diffusion." APAM 16:7. 1923. "Southern Diegueno Customs." UCP 20. 1927 a. "The Association Test." AA 29:2. 1927 b. "The Ghost Dance Among the Klamath." UWPA 2:2. 1928. "Havasupai Ethnography." APAM 29:3. 1930. "Klamath Ethnography." UCP 30. 1933. *Yuman Tribes of the Gila River*. Chicago. 1935. "The Prophet Dance of the Northwest and Its Derivatives: the Source of the Ghost Dance." GSA 1. 1936. "Cultural Relations of the Gila River and Lower Colorado Tribes." YUPA 3. 1938. "The Sinkaietk or Southern Okanagon of Washington," edited by L. S. GSA 6. 1946. "Comparative Vocabularies and Parallel Texts in Two Yuman Languages of Arizona." UNMPA 2.

Spier, L. & Sapir, E. 1930. "Wishram Ethnography." UWPA 3:3.

Spinden, Herbert Joseph. 1908. "The Nez Perce Indians." MAAA 2:3. 1940. "Sun Worship." ARSI 1939.

Spott, R. & Kroeber, A. L. 1942. "Yurok Narratives." UCP 35:9.

Sproat, G. M. 1868. *Scenes and Studies of Savage Life*. London.

Stefansson, V. 1913. *My Life with the Eskimo*. New York & London. 1914. "The Stefansson-Anderson Arctic Expedition of the American Museum: Preliminary Ethnological Report." APAM 14:1.

Steinmetz, R. S. 1896. "Endokannibalismus." MAGW 26.

Stephen, A. M. 1936. "Hopi Journal," ed. by E. C. Parsons. I—II. CUCA 23.

Stern, Bernard, J. 1934. "The Lummi Indians of Northwest Washington." CUCA 17.

Stevenson, Matilda Coxe.1894. "The Sia." ARBAE 11. 1904. "The Zuni Indians. Their Mythology, Esoteric Fraternities, and Ceremonies." ARBAE 23.

Steward, Julian H. 1933. "Ethnography of the Owens Valley Paiute." UCP 33:3. 1934. "Two Paiute Autobiographies." UCP 33. 1936. "The Economic and Social Basis of Primitive Bands." EAK. 1937. "Petroglyphs of the United States." ARSI 1936. 1940." Native Cultures in the Intermontane (Great Basin) Area." SMC 100. 1941. "Nevada

Shoshone." AR 4:2 (CED XIII). 1943. "Northern and Gosiute Shoshoni." AR 8:3 (CED XXIII). 1947. "American Culture History in the Light of South America." SWJ 3:2.

Stewart, K. M. 1946. "Spirit Possession in Native America." SWJ 2:3.

Stewart, O. C. 1941. "Northern Palute." AR 4:3 (CED XIV). 1942. "Ute-Southern Palute." AR 6:4 (CED XVIII).

Stirling, Matthew W. 1942. "Origin Myth of Acoma and Other Records." BBAE 13S.

Straubinger, H. 1937. "Seele." LTK 9.

Strom, Folke. 1947. "Den doendes makt och Odin i tradet." Goteborgs hogskolas arsskrift, 53. 1947:1. Goteborg.

Strong, William Duncan. 1929. "Cross-Cousin Marriage and the Culture of the Northeastern Algonquian." AA 31:2. 1938. "The Indian Tribes of the Chicago Region." FMDAL 24.

Swadesh, Morris. 1949. "The Linguistic Approach to Salish Prehistory." In: *Indians of the Urban Northwest*, Ed. by M. W. Smith, CUCA 36. 1951 "Diffusional Cumulation and Archaic Residue as Historical Explanations." SWJ 7:1.

Swan, James G. 1870. "The Indians of Cape Flattery." SCK 220.

Swanton, John R. 1905 a. "Haida Texts and Myths." BBAE 29. 1905 b. "The Haida of Queen Charlotte Islands." MAMNH 8:1. 1908. "Social Condition, Beliefs, and Linguistic Relationship of the Tlingit Indians." ARBAE 26. 1909. "Tlingit Myths and Texts." BBAE 39. 1910. "Names and Naming." BBAE 30:2. 1911. "Indian Tribes of the Lower Mississippi and Adjacent Coast of the Gulf of Mexico." BBAE 43. 1928 a. "Aboriginal Culture of the Southeast." ARBAE 42. 1928 b. "Religious Beliefs and Medical Practices of the Creek Indians." ARBAE 42. 1928 c. "Social and Religious Beliefs and Usages of the Chickasaw Indians." ARBAE 44. 1931. "Source Material for the Social and Ceremonial Life of the Choctaw Indians." BBAE 103. 1942. "Source Material on the History and Ethnology of the Caddo Indians." BBAE 132. 1946. "The Indians of the Southeastern United States." BBAE 137.

von Sydow, C. W. 1941. *Gammal och ny traditionsforskning. Folkkultur.* Lund. 1948. *Selected Papers on Folklore.* Copenhagen.

Taliqvist, Knut. 1948. *Manen i myt och dikt, folktro och kult.* Helsingfors.

Tanner, John. 1830. *Narrative of the Captivity and Adventures of John Tanner during Thirty Years' Residence among the Indians in the Interior of North America.* Ed. by E. James. New York & London.

Tanner, V. 1944. *Outlines of the Geography, Life and Customs of Newfoundland-Labrador. Acea Geographica 8.* Helsingfors.

Tax, Sol. 1952. *Indian Tribes of Aboriginal America*, Ed. by S. T. (Selected Papers of the XXIXth International Congress of Americanists). Chicago.

Tegnaeus, Harry. 1952. "Blood-Brothers. An Ethno-Sociological Study of the Institutions of Blood Brotherhood with Special Reference to Africa." SEMP 10.

Teit, James. 1900. "The Thompson Indians of British Columbia." MAMNH 2. 1906. "The Lillooet Indians." MAMNH 4:5. 1909. "The Shuswap." MAMNH 4:7. 1930. "The Salishan Tribes of the Western Plateaus." ARBAE 45

Thalbitzer, William. 1930 a. "Eskimo Conception of Soul." CIHR 5. 1930 b. "Les Magiciens esquimaux, leurs conceptions du monde, de l'ame et de la vie." JSAP 22.

Thomas, Cyrus. 1887. Burial Mounds of the Northern Sections of the United States. ARBAE 5.

Thomas, N. W. 1908. "Animals." ERE 1.

Thompson, David. 1916. *David Thompson's Narrative of His Explorations in Western America*. Ed. by J. B. Tyrrell. PCS 12.

Thompson, Stith. 1929. *Tales of the North American Indians*. Cambridge, Mass. 1932-36. "Motif-Index of Folk-Literature." I-VI FFC 106 - 109, 116, 117. 1946. *The Folktale*. New York.

Titrev, Mischa 1937. "A Hopi Salt Expedition." AA 39:2. 1944. "Old Oraibi. A Study of the Hopi Indians of Third Mesa." PMP 22:1.

Trowbrilge, C. C. 1938. "Meearmeear Traditions." OCMA 7. 1939. "Shawnese Traditions." OCMA 9.

Trumbull, H. 1903. "Natick Dictionary." BBAE 25.

Turner, Lucien M. 1894. Ethnology of the Ungava Distict, Hudson Bay Territory. ARBAE 11.

Turney-High, Harry Holbert. 1937. "The Flathead Indians of Montana." MAAA 48. 1941. "Ethnography of the Kutenai." MAAA 56.

Turquetil, Mgr. Arsene. 1926 "Notes sur les Esquimaux de Baie Hudson." Anthropos 21. Wien. 1929 "The Religion of the Central Eskimo." PM 2:3-4.

Tylor, Edward B. 1871. *Primitive Culture: Researches into the Development of Mythology, Philosophy, Religion, Art, and Custom*. I-II. London. 1929. *Primitive Culture, etc.* I-II. 6th ed. London.

Uhlenbeck, C. C. & van Gulik, R. H. 1930. "An English-Blackfoot Vocabulary." VKAW 29:4. 1934. "A Blackfoot-English Vocabulary." VKAW 33: 2.

Underhill, Ruth M. 1945. "Indians of the Pacific Norehwest." SP 5. 1946 a. "Papago Indian Religion." CUCA 33. 1946 b. "Workaday Life of the Pueblos." SP 4. 1948. "Ceremonial Patterns in the Greater Southwest." MAES 13.

Vaillant, George C. 1947. *Aztecs of Mexico*. Garden City, New York.

Villa Rojas, Alfonso. 1947 "Kinship and Nagualism in a Tzeltal Community, Southeaseern Mexico." AA 49: 4.

Voegelin, C. F. 1936. "The Shawnee Female Deity." YUPA 10.

Voegelin, E. W. 1938. "Tubatulabal Ethnography." AR 2:1. 1942. "Northeast California." AR 7: 2 (CED XX).

Vogt, Hans. 1940. *The Kalispel Language*. Oslo.

Volhard, E. 1939. *Kannibalismus*. Stuttgart.

Volney, C. F. C. 1803. *Tableau du climae et du sol des Etats-Unis d'Amerique*. I—II. Paris.

Voth, Henry R. 1901. "The Oraibi Powamu Ceremony." FMAS 3:2. 1903. "The Oraibi Summer Snake Ceremony." FMAS 3:4. 1905. "The Traditions of the Hopi." FMAS 9. 1912 "Notes on Modern Burial Customs of the Hopi of Arizona." FMAS 11:2.

Wachtmeister, Arvid. 1925. *Primitiv sjalavandringsero*. Stockholm.

Wagley, Charles. 1949. "The Social and Religious Life of a Guatemalan Village." MAAA 71.

Walk, Leopold. 1938. "Tod:II. Religionsgeschichtlich." LTK 10.

Walker, J. R. 1917. "The Sun Dance and Other Ceremonies of the Oglala Division of the Teton Dakota." APAM I6:2.

Wallace, W. J. 1947. "The Dream in Mohave Life." JAFL 60.

Wallis, Wilson D. 1919. "The Sun Dance of the Canadian Dakota." APAM 16:4. 1923. "Beliefs and Tales of the Canadian Dakota." JAFL 36. 1945. "Inference of Relative Age of Culture Traits from Magnitude of Distribution." SWJ 1:1. 1947. "The Canadian

Dakota." APAM 41:1.

Warneck, J. 1909. *Die Religion der Baeak. Religiose Urkunden der Volker*, 4:1. Leipzig.

Washington, F. B. 1906. "Customs of the Indians of Western Tehama County." JAFL 19.

Waterman, T. T. 1930. "The Paraphernalia of the Duwamish 'Spirit-Canoe' Ceremony." IN 7:2.

Wegrocki, Henry J. 1939. "A Critique of Cultural and Statistical Concepts of Abnormality." JASP 34.

White, Leslie A. 1932 a. "The Acoma Indians." ARBAE 47. 1932 b. "The Pueblo of San Felipe." MAAA 38. 1942. "The Pueblo of Santa Ana, New Mexico." MAAA 60.

Whitman, William. 1937. "The Oto." CUCA 28.

Widen, Albin. 1937. "Om gudsbegreppet hos lenape." Ethnos 1937:4

Widengren, Geo. 1945. *Religionens varld.* Uppsala.

Wied, Prinz Maximilian zu 1839-1941. *Reise in das Innere Nord-Amerika in den Jahren 1832 bis 1834.* I—II. Coblenz.

Wilkes, Charles. I845. *Narrative of the United States Exploring Expedition.* I-V. Philadelphia.

Will, G. F. & Spinden, H. J. 1906. "The Mandans." PMP 3:4.

Williams, Roger. 1827. *A Key into the Language of America.* Collections of the Rhode Island Historical Society, 1. Providence.

Wilson, Eddie W. 1950. "The Owl and the American Indian". JAFL 63.

Winchell, N. H. 1911. *The Aborigines of Minnesota.* St. Paul.

Wissler, Clark. 1911 "The Social Life of the Blackfoot Indians." APAM 7-1. 1912. "Ceremonial Bundles of the Blackfoot Indians." APAM 7:2. 1926. *The Relation of Nature to Man in Aboriginal America.* New York. 1940. *Indians of the United States.* New York. 1946. *Masks.* New York.

Wissler, C. & Spinden, H. J. 1916. "The Pawnee Human Sacrifice to the Morningstar." AMJ 16.

Wolf, Morris. 1919. *Iroquois Religion and Its Relation to Their Morals.* New York.

Wundt, Wilhelm. 1910 *Volkerpsychologie IV: I (Mythus und Religlon).* Leipzig.

Wyman, L. C., Hill, W. W., & Osanai, Iva. 1942. "Navajo Eschatology." UNMB 4:1. 1881. "A Further Contribution to the Study of the Mortuary Customs of the North American Indians." ARBAE 1.

Zeisberger, see Hulbert & Schwarze.

Zelenin, Dm. 1936. "Die animistische Philosophie des sibirischen Schamanismus." Ethnos 1936: 4.